"First-Year Teacher" Eight Years Later

An Inquiry into Teacher Development

ROBERT V. BULLOUGH, JR.
KERRIE BAUGHMAN

Foreword by DAVID C. BERLINER

TEACHERS COLLEGE PRESS

Teachers College, Columbia University
New York and London

Published by Teachers College Press, 1234 Amsterdam Avenue, New York, NY 10027

Library of Congress Cataloging-in-Publication Data

Bullough, Robert V., 1949–
  "First-year teacher" eight years later : an inquiry into teacher
  development / Robert V. Bullough, Jr., Kerrie Baughman.
      p.   cm.
  "An update of First year teacher" — Pref.
  Includes bibliographical references (p.   ) and index.
  ISBN 0-8077-3651-1. — ISBN 0-8077-3650-3 (pbk.)
    1. Baughman, Kerrie. 2. First year teachers — United States —
  Longitudinal studies.   3. Teachers — United States — Longitudinal
  studies.   4. Teachers — In-service training — United States —
  Longitudinal studies.   I. Baughman, Kerrie.   II. Bullough, Robert
  V., 1949–   First-year teacher.   III. Title.
  LB2844.1.N4B85   1997
  372.1102 — dc21   97-14053

ISBN 0-8077-3650-3 (paper)
ISBN 0-8077-3651-1 (cloth)

Printed on acid-free paper
Manufactured in the United States of America

04 03 02 01 00 99 98 97   8 7 6 5 4 3 2 1

Contents

Foreword

This book is a treasure for three reasons. First, it is the only work I know of that describes the growth and development of a single teacher over many years. This 10-year longitudinal study of teacher development has no equals. Second, it is co-authored by the researcher and the teacher who worked collaboratively over those years; studies of teacher development, in their own voices, have not existed until now. Third, this joint study relies upon narrative as the basis for inquiry into the study of beliefs about one's self, one's life, and one's work. It is rigorous research that we encounter here, though the data are in story form and the scholarship of both the researcher and the subject of the research is in the analyses of the stories told. Methodologically, this book has no equivalents. Moreover, it exudes verisimilitude, providing the reader with a sense of the real thoughts of a teacher seeking to be successful as an instructor and as a caregiver.

But methodological uniqueness and verisimilitude are the only things that make this an important book. It is filled with insights that both provoke the reader and then linger on, as the reader contemplates the life of a teacher and the aspirations of our nation. Let me give a few examples.

One insight gleaned from this and other scholarships is that the educational reform programs created by legislators and others are doomed to failure unless they are sensitive to the personal lives and working conditions of teachers. Without adequate concern for these elements the myriad contemporary attempts at school improvement will disappoint. Teachers need to work in environments that foster and reward the hard work, commitment, and creativity that characterized Kerrie, the teacher in this study, for most of her career. The noble need to serve, which motivates Kerrie and so many other teachers, must not be thwarted.

The poignant descriptions of Kerrie's problems in dealing with children of poverty, or those who are blind, have Down's syndrome, or are menacing, raise issues that educators and the public must soon address. I was struck by how hard it must be for teachers like Kerrie, who possess strong personal and professional needs to do good things for others, to end up believing that they are not accomplishing that at all. This seemed even more demoralizing because Kerrie interpreted the problems she encountered as *her* problems. As Bob Bullough, the researcher, notes, she seems not to have understood the systemic, structural, and communal nature of those problems. Kerrie's story reveals that we, collectively, have created too many schools where it is hard to teach. Then we compound this problem by either blaming teachers for their inept ways, or we allow the Kerries of the world to think it is their personal problem. This is not fair. Kerrie was the type of teacher we all want for our children, someone called to teach, to serve, who worked hard to be proficient at what she does. And yet we have created school environments for Kerrie and others that push them out of the profession. Kerrie no longer teaches. Obviously, unless schools are places for teachers to thrive, they will not be places for children to thrive. I believe that most of those who suggest school improvements do not consider the importance of this lesson.

I am convinced that Kerrie possessed the agency to develop her teaching skills well. But the impetus to think longer and harder about her teaching also came from her participation in this study. The weekly meetings, in which she was asked questions by Bob, served as a catalyst for her reflection on teaching as she acquired her skills. This exercise allowed her "to peel teaching like an onion." But university teacher educators and school district personnel directors usually abandon their first-year teachers, leaving them to sink or swim. So another insight of this collaboration is that if people or institutions ever wish to display a bit of humanity and can find a little bit of money, then the novice year of teaching can be improved enormously. In Kerrie's journey, there are many suggestions for alternatives to the trial-by-fire that consitutes the first year of many a first-year teacher.

Kerrie's story also reminded me that what is taught in teacher education programs is actually learned by the students. In fact, we learn that ideas about professionalism — ideas shaped in teacher education courses — profoundly affect the ways that teachers come to judge their own and their colleagues' behavior. We are all reminded, therefore, of the seriousness with which a teacher education curriculum must be designed and implemented. Images of what it means to be a professional greatly influence and direct the lives of teachers.

Still another insight from this collaboration is that theories of teacher development seem to have reasonably good descriptive power — but they are inevitably wrong in describing the individual. This occurs because each genuine individual is markedly more complex than are the simplifications that are needed to build a theory about artificial groups of individuals. Moreover, we also see how Kerrie's story is bounded. It is situated in our "postmodern" times and in her places of employment. These facets of life have enormous impact on the functioning of human teachers. We learn through Kerrie and Bob how the context in which Kerrie works turns out to be immensely powerful in shaping her perceptions of her impact and usefulness. Thus, since educational contexts vary so much, general theories about teacher behavior will always be lacking.

The power of context showed up when Kerrie changed schools — changing as well the norms for teacher behavior, and the kinds of students and parents with whom she usually interacted. She suffered a loss of expertise, which undermined her self-confidence. This part of the story serves to remind us all about the narrowness of our acquired skills, situated as they are in the contexts in which they were learned. Perhaps the clear evidence of this in Kerrie's journey might help to curb the tendency of educational policy makers to treat teachers and schools as if they are interchangeable. They are not. Each has its own histories and its own adaptations, and therefore, each is unique. Kerrie and Bob eloquently bring this out as they describe Kerrie's struggle to master new environments.

The reader comes to understand that Kerrie's journey is really two stories. One story is of her mastery of a complex craft, including classroom routines, management, discipline, and curriculum; the development of her finely honed moral sensitivity; the implementation of her mothering skills in her classrooms coupled with her ability to "love the kids along"; her pride in her growth of expertise; her achievement of the level of professionalism she set out to attain. But the second story sits side-by-side with the first. It is of collegiality rarely offered; of rejection from children who do not know how to love back; of shared governance gone amok, burdening teachers with a never-ending series of tasks to accomplish until they nearly burst; of social class warfare among the students in the classroom and the school; of the irresponsibility of a system that requires teaching children with special needs by teachers without special training; of the wearing down of teachers due to the never-ending demands that are made on these good people, who are ethically committed to serve a system with absolutely no end of needs. Kerrie's journey, then, is about the development of an admirable and successful teacher, and also about how that teacher was worn out. The story of Kerrie is about someone who sought a chance to serve her community through teaching, but eventually found that she simply held a job.

"First-Year Teacher" Eight Years Later gives us all a chance to look at the wonders of the growth and development of professionalism and pedagogical expertise in a caring-to-the-core teacher, and a chance to see how it all can be undone. Lessons that could improve education are easily derived from the tales and their analyses, if we only choose to learn from Kerrie and Bob's extraordinary journey.

— *David C. Berliner*

Acknowledgments

We wish to thank Sherry Southerland and Julie Gess-Newsome for helpful feedback on Chapter 5. Cliff Mayes made useful suggestions for reworking Chapters 1 and 2. Don Kauchak read the entire manuscript and his honest criticism was crucial to our efforts to reorient it more toward teachers. We are deeply indebted to him. Finally, we are grateful to Dave Berliner for writing the foreword, for his ongoing support of this project, and especially for the important place his scholarship has played in shaping the conversation about teacher development.

Parts of Chapters 2 and 3 were initially published in *Curriculum Inquiry*, 26(2). Part of Chapter 6 first appeared in *Teaching & Teacher Education*, 11(5), and an early version of Chapter 7 was published in *The Journal of Teacher Education*, 46(2). Each is used here with the publisher's permission.

Preface

Democracy, as John Dewey long ago observed, is an experiment in education (1916). Virtually every problem from the silly to the significant — economic, political, social, moral, personal — finds its way to the school's threshold, and not surprisingly, disappointment often follows close behind. As other social institutions have been divested of their educational responsibilities or are failing to meet those obligations, expectations of public schools and of teachers continue to rise, even as it is increasingly clear that schools, as we have long known them, were never designed to do what is now being asked of them (Bullough, 1988). Not surprisingly, in their ambition, enthusiasm, naïveté, and perhaps desperation, would-be school reformers rarely can deliver what they promise because what is promised is beyond their means to deliver (Pogrow, 1996; Sarason, 1990).

Following the release of *A Nation at Risk*, the talk of the past 15 years has been of reforming, then restructuring, and now reculturing schools. Sadly, efforts at school *reform* have been disappointing. *Restructuring* has been more about rhetoric than reality (Taylor & Bogotch, 1994). The jury is still out on *reculturing* (Sarason, 1996). One lesson learned is that institutional change is less radical and revolutionary than evolutionary, arising out of institutional and personal history rather than breaking from it. Nothing sticks — no change of any kind — that does not grow out of institutional roots. A second lesson is that for a change to stick it must find a place in teachers' thinking, in their belief systems, and in their habitual ways of acting and interacting within the classroom or grow out of their thinking. A third lesson is that efforts to improve education must be continuous.

The message is clear and direct: the most hopeful approach to creating better education is to shift school improvement metaphors and to think about school improvement as not only reculturing but simultaneously as *teacher development* (Sykes, 1996). Better schools for children will result only when schools are better places for teachers to learn about teaching and are more supportive of their efforts to improve their practice and enrich their lives:

. . . for our schools to do better than they do we have to give up the belief
that it is possible to create the conditions for productive learning when those
conditions do not exist for educational personnel. (Sarason, 1990, p. 145)

It is within this context of heightened interest in school improvement that
Kerrie Baughman taught. It is in recognition of this message that we
undertook this study of teaching and teacher development.

"First-Year Teacher" Eight Years Later is an update of *First-Year
Teacher* (Bullough, 1989) and, we hope, much more. We write first to
practicing teachers: this is a teacher's story. The problems Kerrie faced are
quite common ones, although her understanding of them and her solutions
might be unique in various ways. Nevertheless, we believe her experience
speaks to a good many of the challenges all teachers face. By reading
Kerrie's story and attending to the research literature we have called on to
illuminate her story and the questions we have posed at the end of each
chapter, we seek to encourage teachers to consider or reconsider their own
development and teaching experience in helpful ways, with an eye toward
more thoughtfully directing that development and more fully participating in efforts to create contexts more hospitable to teacher learning. We
intend to challenge beliefs and stimulate questioning. In addition, we have
sought to portray some of the complexity of teacher learning in ways useful
for informing the wider conversation about development, including its
aims and means. Like other teachers we have participated in in-service
programs of various kinds and of doubtful value, most often "one-shot
deals" involving inspirational speakers and sometimes the educational
equivalent of video infomercials. Such programs are driven by an impoverished and remarkably simplistic view of teacher development and accomplish little, if anything, except to increase feelings of guilt and inade-
quacy momentarily. They do not produce growth (Sprinthall, Reiman,
and Thies-Sprinthall, 1996). Thus we also write to in-service leaders and
others concerned with teacher development in hopes of influencing how
they think about development and the means for encouraging teacher
learning. These are our audiences and aims.

1

Setting the Stage

This is a teacher's story. It is also a story of a ten-year-long joint inquiry into teaching and teacher development. We began working together when Kerrie enrolled in the secondary education certification program at the University of Utah. Initially, our relationship was one of teacher education student to professor, but gradually this changed. The nature of our relationship and how it has evolved speaks to what Ross Mooney (1957) called the "inner drama" of educational research. The researcher is "inside" the research, shaping its assumptions and outcomes; and the research is "inside" the researcher, changing the ways in which the world is understood and encountered. We cannot, as Mooney argued, "split" ourselves from our data (p. 186). A few scenes from that drama and a bit of our story follow. They will serve as a context for material in subsequent chapters.

As a teacher education student in 1985 and 1986, Kerrie was assigned to a cohort of two dozen secondary education students. The program ran for three quarters. The first-term students enrolled in a secondary curriculum course, along with other professional courses, which was taught Tuesday and Thursday mornings. School placements were made early in the program so that field experience paralleled coursework. In the second term, they took a secondary methods course, which included teaching a short course, a two- or three-week unit, in the classrooms where they would student teach in the spring term. Along with student teaching in the spring, students were enrolled in a two-hour problem solving seminar. Bob served as instructor and coordinated field experiences and supervised student teachers along with a teaching associate. It is in this context that we first got to know one another.

Bob. Kerrie's cohort had a profound effect on my thinking about teaching and teacher education. The members bonded quickly, and friendships formed that still endure. It was an intellectually active and energetic group that openly confronted issues while it offered support for each person's quest to become a teacher. Kerrie quickly made friends with some of the other women in the group and together they always sat right of center in the U-shaped arrangement of desks. They were an active group, one I could always count on for interesting comments and challenging questions. Supporting one another and meeting socially outside of class, they became increasingly powerful as the year progressed. Occasionally class members pushed my thinking in unanticipated directions. Passive they weren't. I liked the challenge and appreciated their remarkable degree of openness. Students felt able to confront one another and me.

Kerrie was 28 years old then and the mother of two young children. She is 40 now. Her return to college involved considerable family sacrifice, and she was determined to make the most of the opportunity. Unlike many of her colleagues, she knew even as a child that she wanted to teach and was especially eager to find a job upon completing the program. Early in the spring, while student teaching and well before her other classmates, she was actively seeking employment and was first in the cohort to land a job. I still remember the day I asked her to make the announcement — "I have a job" — which was received with disbelief and amazement by some of her colleagues. A few had yet to complete the placement file needed in order for them to make applications.

When the year ended, Kerrie was employed at Rocky Mountain Junior High School. I was proud of her accomplishments and of her classmates; all who'd wanted jobs had gotten them.

For me it was a disturbing year. I felt uneasy, uncertain. Much had gone very well, and the evaluations of my teaching were high, but I was disappointed with my instruction, although I was not fully certain why. I did not see myself as a teacher educator then. My thoughts were elsewhere. In the late 1970s and early 1980s I had been deeply engaged in a study of the writings of Karl Marx and Jurgen Habermas, among others. This study resulted in the publication of *Human Interests in the Curriculum: Teaching and Learning in a Technological Society* (Bullough, Goldstein, & Holt, 1984), a neo-Marxian critique of a variety of educational innovations. I taught introductory foundations courses, which I enjoyed, while teaching undergraduate curriculum and instruction courses, which I found frustrating. My emphasis on critique was separate from my work in the cohort. I was not a teacher educator. I did not want to be a teacher educator.

Ironically, in 1983 I was elected chair of secondary education and became intimately involved in teacher education program development, even though I had relatively limited experience and lacked essential knowledge of the field and its history. Through the dean's efforts, the department early became involved with the Holmes Group (1986), which brought with it numerous opportunities for me to think further about teacher education and to ponder my place within it.

Just before I was elected chair, the program was reorganized around cohorts of students. My first cohort was a rocky experience, but spending a year with a group of students inevitably forced me to attend to developmental issues. I noticed, for example, that some teacher education students seemed able to ignore what I taught, while others grasped it easily, as though what I had to say confirmed beliefs but failed to challenge them. A graduate student helped me begin to see this issue more clearly (Crow, 1987), and it has since come to define much of my work in teacher education.

Enter Kerrie's cohort — again. My previous uneasiness at the conclusion of the cohort had many sources. I was uncertain whether anything I taught actually stuck. I had my doubts. I wondered if the heavily foundational curriculum was appropriate for beginning teachers. I wondered whether it was developmentally responsive to my students. Were there ways for them to encounter content that would likely increase its impact? Were there curricular gaps, topics I should have addressed but did not? There were also structural issues that puzzled me: for example, were the field experiences worthwhile, and if so, what was worthwhile about them? Kerrie had been placed with a football coach who knew a lot more about football than he did about history and teaching. What could she possibly have learned from him? These are just a few of the questions I struggled to answer but couldn't, since I lacked useful data and had only limited experience. I had hunches, but that was all.

After the school year ended, while I was on the way with my family to vacation at a friend's cabin in West Yellowstone, I decided that the only way to settle my uncertainty was to study my work, beginning by conducting a case study of one student who'd just completed the cohort. Kerrie was an obvious choice. She had a job, and I knew she'd speak her mind. I also knew she'd have the self-confidence needed to allow me to observe her teaching over an extended period of time. And I thought she'd do well. I wasn't interested in conducting a study of failure. What I couldn't have imagined then was that the study would run for so long and evolve as it did.

Despite the cautious tone she could hear in my voice, Kerrie greeted my initial phone call enthusiastically. To my relief and surprise, she said, without hesitating even momentarily, sure, she'd be involved. I hastily put together a proposal and presented it to her, and we began our inquiry. Parts of the first interview we conducted are included in chapter 2. Following traditional case study methodology (Yin, 1989), I observed Kerrie teaching weekly, usually for a couple of hours, for the first year and a half of her teaching. Interviews followed observations. I generated protocols by analyzing my observations, and each interview was transcribed and analyzed following constant comparative methods (Glasser and Strauss, 1967). Themes were identified, and I began reading widely in the teacher education literature, seeking to make sense of what I was seeing and of how Kerrie was evolving as a teacher. At the time, Ryan's stages of teacher development (1986) made the most sense of what I was seeing and helped me begin to answer the question good case studies must answer, "What is the story here?"

As the study proceeded week by week, my understanding of teaching and teacher education and development grew, sometimes rapidly. But so did my list of unanswered questions. I began to see foundational issues in teacher education more clearly, particularly those related to how school context both enabled and limited teacher thought and action, and how teachers actively shaped their work contexts. I came to understand better how socialization always involves contradiction, contestation, and compromise. With good humor and remarkable forbearance, Kerrie endured my seemingly unending questions without ever asking for a judgment or direct feedback on the quality of her teaching. Early on we agreed that my role was to observe, not to assess her performance, yet occasionally I slipped out of that role, as I wrote in *First-Year Teacher: A Case Study* (1989).

> From time to time in my interviews with Kerrie, I shared insights that seemed important to share. . . . When Kerrie asked questions, I responded, although throughout our time together she understood that my role was emphatically not to tell her what to do. Indeed, she was quite clear about this: had I attempted to function in a teacher's role, she would have withdrawn from the project. In addition, beginning about March of the first year, I shared and we discussed my written interpretations of events. . . . This was done not only to confirm the accuracy of my understanding, which is fundamental, but also to provide her with an opportunity to critique my work and to use it as a source of feedback, if she wished. (pp. 137–138)

Only later did I understand the powerful, albeit indirect, influence I had on Kerrie's professional development. The questions that formed the initial basis of our ongoing discussion of teaching had a surprising and unanticipated impact. As Kerrie stated then:

> The questions you asked me make me really think. Sometimes I think about them all week long. It really has that effect. It has made a change weekly. We've talked about these things on a weekly basis. . . . Every time I talk to you . . . it's just a catalyst, because it makes me think about what I'm doing. It's not necessarily you, it's me thinking more about me. (pp. 138–139)

As I look back on that first year of teaching, I am amazed at how the students came so quickly to think of me as a classroom fixture, something taken for granted and not very interesting. They paid remarkably little attention to me. Kerrie seemed not to notice me, either. I felt comfortable in this role, although there were times, particularly after school, as I waited for her to finish with students so we could chat, when I felt out of place, a grand imposition and potential irritant. I was acutely aware that I was taking up Kerrie's time, which she could have spent with her family or working on her curriculum, for instance. Often I wondered what Kerrie got out of our time together, if anything.

First-Year Teacher signaled a watershed for me professionally. Formerly, I had sought to distance myself from teacher education, but this changed. I not only began to think of myself as a teacher educator, but to find teacher education issues progressively more engaging. My practice changed rapidly. I reconceptualized each of my courses to reflect my growing understanding of teaching and teacher development. I need to be especially clear here: I did not assume Kerrie's experience was broadly generalizable, but I was convinced that many of the problems she faced were shared by other beginning teachers. I began to build research into each course so that I could more or less systematically study what was transpiring and why, and begin to test different instructional approaches that held promise for increasing the value and impact of the program on student learning. Metaphor analysis, an idea that initially came from Kerrie's reliance on images of teaching as mothering (see chapter 5), classroom ethnographies, shadow studies, textbook analysis, the writing of personal teaching texts (Bullough, 1993), and case records of students' experiences in teacher education — all found a place in my classes (see Bullough & Gitlin, 1995). I studied other beginning teachers' first years of teaching, which helped me put Kerrie's experience into perspective while it deepened my understanding of teacher development (Bullough, Knowles, & Crow, 1992).

In 1991, Kerrie and I renewed our study of teaching after a three-year hiatus. This time, the publications that resulted reflected our changing relationship. Kerrie was coauthor. Much had changed in Kerrie's classroom at Rocky Mountain Junior High School, and understanding why things were so different afforded us an opportunity to explore teacher development in new and unanticipated ways. She had, for example, tossed out her curriculum, and, inspired by the writing of Nancie Atwell (1987), had developed her own version of Reading and Writing Workshop. I was excited about returning to Kerrie's classroom but also slightly apprehensive. What kind of teacher would she be? Still, I delighted in the opportunity to observe her teach once again. This time we added to our data sources by having several classes videotaped, and then we engaged in think-aloud sessions during which I sought to understand the reasons for some of her curriculum and instruction decisions. This change in our way of working together was stimulated in part by a review of *First-Year Teacher* which had suggested that greater attention to teacher thinking would have added a useful dimension to the study. I agreed.

We picked up our study again after Kerrie left Rocky Mountain Junior High School and assumed a teaching position at Clarke Intermediate School near her home. As before, data came from weekly observations running over a year and three months, interviews, and two dozen video-taped classes. Additional data were gathered to address new questions, as will be indicated in the chapters that follow. Altogether, I estimate I have observed Kerrie teach weekly over a total of nearly four years. We have accumulated a few thousand pages of typed transcripts and several dozen sets of observation notes, some running several pages long. This is the data set for *"First-Year Teacher" Eight Years Later*.

For me, Kerrie has been a good teacher. When I think back to our first interview, I realize that through her I have come to see teaching in ways I could not have imagined. Some issues arose and some insights came only because of the depth and length of our study. Kerrie's switching schools opened up a remarkable set of issues of importance to teacher development that only a longitudinal study could have revealed. Over the course of the years, a friendship grew that opened up aspects of Kerrie's life and thinking and also offered the opportunity for us to develop new insights. Trust develops slowly and is a precondition for quality teacher case studies. I was fortunate. Kerrie gave her trust, but still it deepened over time.

Our inquiry has changed me. This change has not been merely intel-lectual. I know and understand more about teaching and teacher develop-ment, and I also *feel* more. I have found that when I observe other classes, I am intuitively sharper; as a result of our study, I have a better nose for what is going right or wrong in a classroom and I have greater empathy for the difficulty of teaching and relating to young people. I am a bit less likely to rush to judgment than before, and I am certainly more forgiving of mistakes. This is a result of Kerrie's allowing me to come to see the classroom, to a degree, through her eyes, and to recognize my own biases and blindness. These are no small gifts, and for them I am profoundly grateful. Like other teachers, effective teacher educators and in-service coordinators must be able to see the world through the eyes of those they teach. Without seeing clearly, we develop programs that are certain to have minimal educational value.

When I left graduate school in 1976, I never imagined that participating in research could be the key to my professional development. Then, the purpose of research was generally understood to be to influence—to "cause," or, more gently, to "invite"—changes in others, to alter practice, and never a thought was given to what is now commonly understood, partly as a result of the influence of action research the past decade or so, that conducting research can be liberative and transformative, and is itself a form of teacher education (Elliot, 1991). Certainly social science research seeks to illuminate human experience in various ways that will add to the quality of that experience, but it also has remarkable potential for altering the way researchers encounter and make sense of the world, and this may be one of its most lasting values. C. Wright Mills understood that life and intellectual work are of a piece. He wrote, "You must learn to use your life experience in your intellectual work: continually to examine and interpret it. In this sense craftsmanship is the center of yourself and you are personally involved in every intellectual product upon which you may work" (1959, p. 196). This brings us full circle to the inner drama of educational research.

Kerrie. Bob's teaching had a profound effect on my thinking about teaching and teacher education. A tall, bearded man with round glasses who sometimes waited too long for a haircut, Bob often stood in the corner of the room leaning on a piano that no one ever played. Listing the day's agenda on the board in his almost indecipherable script, he led us in inquiry, as ready to learn as the rest of us. Feeling that I had been called to teaching, I was sure of myself, inexplicably knowing that I would be good as a teacher. What I wanted to learn from the cohort were the little things that would help me pull the classroom together, and make it run smoothly. Despite the fact that he tortured us with quizzes, I liked Bob and the series of cohort classes, knowing that each day's sessions would be well worth attending because the subject matter was timely and would soon be put to use in my own classroom. Bob linked the philosophical aspects of teaching with the concrete.

While Bob may have questioned his instruction, the class very much enjoyed it, unaware that he was uncertain of himself. In fact, I much preferred his teaching to that of other instructors. Bob's efforts shaped me greatly, and in positive ways. The cohort served as a security blanket, a place to find an answer to every question imaginable, from content to discipline. Toward the end of the year, it allowed me to see where I stood as I compared my relatively successful student teaching experience to the tears and trials of others.

A lot that was taught stayed with me. Regardless of the teacher, every student chooses what is of importance, depending on her individual understanding and needs, her schema. All of us found plenty to pay attention to. For example, we discussed teacher professionalism and what a true professional might look like. This topic came up again during my student teaching in a meeting with Bob and my cooperating teacher and stayed with me through the years as I came in contact with other teachers, comparing them and myself to that professional teacher touchstone. One quality we sought was the ability to guard against burnout, the fate of too many great teachers. We discussed at length what we could do to avoid burnout, and although we came up with many techniques, I was most impacted just by the knowledge that it was a potential problem, one whose encroachment I needed to watch for and guard against. This one day's topic influenced many of the career decisions I later made. I took classes, changed schools, and got my gifted and talented program endorsement.

Field experiences were very beneficial. I spent a day shadowing a tenth-grade student from one of the classes I would be student teaching. I happened to choose a boy who was in resource classes, the lowest level courses offered in both math and reading. This gave me some insight into what I could expect in the classroom (and why) when I taught my short course and in student teaching. During my short course and then again during student teaching, I was able to observe how the teacher whose classes I taught handled some troublesome students. These were boys who had dug themselves into a hole with him but were offered a fresh start by me. When their term ended and I was tabulating the grades, my cooperating teacher, the football coach, insisted on failing them because of past poor performance despite their improvement while I was teaching. I learned a good lesson in fairness and retribution, one which has stayed with me to this day.

While the thought of doing my student teaching under the supervision of a football coach–history teacher caused many of the students in the cohort to roll their eyes, I saw it as an opportunity. Shortly after I began teaching, "Coach" took off for the gym and weight room, leaving me in charge of my own classroom. I saw him only three times after that, twice during rather momentous events—once when he came to see how I was coping in the dark during a power outage, and once when he came to announce that the space shuttle *Challenger* had just exploded. Being alone in the classroom meant I was really in charge. I didn't have the experience of feeling intimidated by having a cooperating teacher constantly watching over my shoulder. But I also missed out because I received little feedback, relying solely on observations by Bob and his teaching associate. Indeed, I got my most practical piece of advice that quarter from my mother (a second-grade teacher), when she told me to handle "mouthy" teenage girls on an individual basis out in the hallway, where they wouldn't have an audience to perform for. She was right.

Graduating from the university at the end of spring quarter, I was excited to get a job and then be offered the chance to continue my education by working with Bob. I found him somewhat intimidating, but I liked him and knew he was fair. My part of our study was easy — or so it seemed. I taught school (ignoring his presence in my classroom) and then answered his questions about my teaching. He cooperated by being unobtrusive. Almost weekly I was quizzed by my colleagues about Bob's role in my life. My explanation, that he was interested in my development as a teacher, brought raised eyebrows and skeptical looks. For them, it was difficult to imagine a professor sitting and observing in a classroom week after week. I had agreed to the study, and it truly required very little of me. Not one to worry or second guess once I've made a decision, I just went about my job of teaching. Little did we know how great an impact our work together would have on our thinking.

As the weeks went by and Bob asked questions, I often wondered why he asked what he did. Almost every question went beyond simple clarification, and I came to feel that a session with him was time well spent. At the end of an hour interview, Bob would stop, even if it looked like he still had questions on his page or we seemed to be in the middle of something. If it was an important topic, I would know it because it would come up again the next week. Bob always acted as though he truly wanted to know what I thought or what my reasoning was. He never acted as though he was testing me to see if I knew the right answer.

Our long association has been very valuable. Over the past decade, Bob and I have been able to peel my teaching like an onion: we dealt with each layer as we came to it. This takes time and trust. For example, a teacher's personal life profoundly affects teaching, but it took time for me to talk about my life. I got pregnant, got married, and had my first child while I was in high school, and still graduated with my class. I have always been open about this subject, but it's not necessarily one that comes up in an interview with a professor. It took us awhile to get around to discussing this part of my life and its ramifications on my teaching; it is more toward the center of the onion. Without a lot of time spent together talking about teaching, without the need to discuss why I left my parents' home, it's unlikely the subject would have come up between us, even though it's an important part of my story.

While Bob has a great sense of humor, he takes teaching seriously. He never seemed judgmental of me in my classroom, and he was open about his frustration with many things he saw going on in schools and with education in general. Today, after our years of work together, his attitude toward schools seems less harsh than it once was; he seems nearer the trenches.

Bob came to see the classroom from my teacher's perspective, and I, in turn, was able to see the goings-on in the classroom from his researcher's perspective. Just as spending time in my classroom made him a more tolerant and understanding teacher educator, as he has stated, it also made me a better teacher — one full of questions about why things, both large and small, are done in schools the way they are and why I did what I did and how I could be more successful. Bob's initial inquiry into my teaching stimulated my own inquiry, and that has changed us both.

AN ADDITIONAL WORD ABOUT METHODOLOGY

Collaborative research, including joint studies of teaching involving teachers and university-based teacher educators, has recently become a hot topic. Studies of this kind present unique methodological problems that are not easily ignored (Cole & Knowles, 1993). Among the most difficult problems, we confronted the following three: determining how to interpret the data so that both our points of view would be adequately represented; establishing the validity of our interpretations; and discovering an effective way for presenting our understanding of the data.

The interpretations presented here have evolved, and they reflect a joint understanding of the issues discussed. We came to this inquiry with differing strengths, and we have tried to be sensitive to these differences, which have enabled us to see data more richly than would otherwise have been possible. Rarely have we had substantial disagreements about an interpretation, but when there have been differences, we have talked them through, paying careful attention to the data before us and to one another's views. Once our relationship evolved, first from that of researcher to student, then later, to subject, and eventually to the more open and collaborative relationship we now enjoy, this process simultaneously became easier and more complicated. In some ways, we have built up a common set of understandings that might prevent us from seeing clearly. Delving into the broader research literature (see Strauss & Corbin, 1990) as well as seeking alternative interpretations of events have been two helpful means of avoiding becoming too comfortable with our ways of seeing and making sense of teaching.

Motives, as Erikson (1975) reminds us, are often elusive. Teachers and teacher educators often do not know fully why they do what they do. Thus interview and even observational data ought not to be taken at face value. Data never speak for themselves but require probing, discussion, and exploration. Interpretations require testing, and honest effort needs to be made at exploring alternative explanations. The entire process was one of creating and testing meaning conversationally. Thus what we present here is a joint construction that represents the truth of things as we have seen it.

We have included a good deal of data to support our conclusions and to illustrate the points made. We have included what we hope is a sufficient amount to sustain our claims for having made valid, compelling interpretations. Validity and credibility are further enhanced by inclusion of a good deal of information about ourselves and our relationship as it has evolved. We trust that we have provided sufficient evidence of various kinds, gathered through "prolonged engagement," to establish that our findings are credible (see Lincoln & Guba, 1985, p. 301), and that we have established what Polkinghorne (1988) calls "verisimilitude, or results that have the appearance of truth or reality" (p. 176). Finally, we have included a large amount of contextual information needed to establish "transferability" (Lincoln & Guba, 1985, p. 316). For case study research of this kind, both verisimilitude and transferability are crucial. By establishing reader confidence in the study and by enabling distancing and comparing of experiences and contexts, one's own with those described, good case studies, besides being memorable, illuminate both experience and context; they help readers see anew what may otherwise be taken for granted in the flow of one's life.

How to present our interpretations has proved a troublesome problem which we do not believe we have adequately solved. Generally, we offer a shared voice. Occasionally, we write separately. And because much of the data comes from interviews, Kerrie speaks for herself. Yet we are aware that interviews are social constructions, and that by virtue of the questions asked and the nature of our relationship, Bob is subtly present in Kerrie's remarks (see Maxwell, 1992). It was Bob's responsibility to work through the entire manuscript to produce a consistent style. However, where Kerrie wrote as an individual, as in the section preceding this one, few, if any, changes were made.

Finally, we should mention that all proper names except ours are fictitious. We have sought especially to mask the identity of students.

THE SCHOOLS: ROCKY MOUNTAIN JUNIOR HIGH AND CLARKE INTERMEDIATE

Kerrie taught at Rocky Mountain Junior High School for six years before changing districts and moving to Thomas Edward Clarke Intermediate School. The two schools and their communities differed dramatically, and that had a profound effect on Kerrie's teaching. Before a change in boundaries that dramatically changed the student population, Kerrie's own children had attended Clarke.

During her first years at Rocky Mountain, Kerrie taught two groups of seventh-grade students reading, social studies, and English in a core. Later, social studies was removed from her teaching load and she taught English and reading to the same students in two-class-period (two-hour) blocks. Given this arrangement, Kerrie was able to integrate content. At Clarke she was hired to teach social studies — including geography — and English. During her first year there, she traveled from room to room, but during her second year she was assigned a large, bright room with an attached private office that overlooked a lush ravine: "Wait until it snows! It's gorgeous, it is gorgeous!" This stood in stark contrast to the drab, windowless space, part of a "pod," a cluster of three doorless rooms separated by carpeted floor-to-ceiling dividers, she had occupied at Rocky Mountain.

Rocky Mountain Junior High, when Kerrie taught there, was a suburban and generally middle-class, working-class school teeming with a student population of 970, in grades seven through nine. The faculty was young and rather transient. The surrounding neighborhood was composed of relatively new and modest but well-kept homes. There were few minority students. In contrast, Clarke was an older urban school with a stable, mature faculty that drew students from a large cross section of neighborhoods characterizing the city. The school drew from among the wealthiest areas of the city as well as from among the poorest. Nearly a third of the 800 students attending Clarke qualified for free or reduced lunch, and the student body was ethnically and racially very diverse. Half were bused to school. It was not a "community school." Clarke students did not mingle easily: "They don't mix; that's a big problem." Early in the year Kerrie described Clarke students as more "street smart" and "sexual" than the students at Rocky Mountain, and there was much more gang activity.

There are other distinguishing characteristics: unlike Rocky Mountain, Clarke had a philosophy that the principal and some staff members, Kerrie included, took very seriously. As the principal stated in an interview:

> When I came here, I told [the faculty] that I was very supportive of the middle school [philosophy] and I would continue that direction. . . . [We've got to break] that old traditional [school] culture down, and it's a difficult thing to do. . . .

One manifestation of this commitment was that the principal set up an integrated core program — math, English, and social studies — for all seventh graders. She did this because she thought the school needed "a strong transition program for sixth graders moving into seventh grade. We felt that teaming—and maybe it was more of a strong feeling on my part—that we need to put a complete team of teachers together in the seventh grade. . . . " In her second year at Clarke, Kerrie was put on one of the teams to teach social studies, which drew on her experience of designing integrated programs at Rocky Mountain. It was the responsibility of these teams to develop two integrated units during the year as a move toward more complete teaming and content integration later. At Rocky Mountain there was more shadow than substance to teaming, and there was no shared educational philosophy of any sort.

Yet another difference that flowed from the middle school philosophy and added to the diversity of the regular classroom population was that the principal and many of the teachers at Clarke were committed to mainstreaming students—to inclusion. Unfortunately, as we shall note in Chapter 7, this commitment did not necessarily bring with it either a reduction in class size or additional instructional support for teachers who worked with mainstreamed students, both issues of importance to teacher development.

At Rocky Mountain Junior High School, the core program was tracked (Oakes, 1985). During her first years of teaching there, Kerrie taught the average- and low-ability classes but eventually began teaching the "Advanced Core," which she enjoyed. Students were well behaved and "generally" academically engaged. Clarke had its own version of an advanced core, but it was smaller, more exclusive, and tied to the desire of some parents to have a gifted and talented program—the Accelerated Academic Program (AAP)—in the school. These parents were influential and well organized. In contrast to the Advanced Core at Rocky Mountain Junior, AAP teachers enjoyed nearly total freedom to design an integrated curriculum as they saw fit. At the end of her first year of teaching at Clarke, an AAP teacher left and the principal solicited applications to replace her. Kerrie was chosen, an indication of her growing reputation as a good teacher with the principal and faculty. This meant that she would be teaching in another four-person team, this one composed of two highly respected long-term veterans of the program and another new AAP teacher, and she would be heavily involved in curriculum development.

Thus, in her second year at Clarke, Kerrie taught three periods of seventh-grade social studies in the morning and planned a small part of the curriculum as one of a team of four teachers. The last two periods of the day she taught social studies in AAP. To fill out her six-period load, she taught a regular eighth-grade English class. Kerrie had never taught eighth graders before. By any measure this was a heavy teaching load.

The burden was increased by Kerrie's selection as social studies department chair, a position she sought because it brought a little additional
income and because she wanted to feel more connected to the school
faculty: "I felt, if I want to get to know these people and get to where I
used to be at my old school, then I need to get involved." By virtue of
serving as department chair, she also sat on two important school committees, the Community Council and the School Improvement Council.

OVERVIEW

Eight chapters follow. Chapter 2 explores the wider social location of
teacher development in relationship to the influence of postmodernism on
teaching and the formation of teacher identity. Drawing on three different
tellings of Kerrie's story of becoming a teacher, Chapter 3 illustrates how
teacher stories evolve and change over time and introduces narrative reasoning as a means for encouraging teacher development. These three versions of Kerrie's story were written before her first year of teaching and
during her fifth and eighth years. Chapter 4 compares Kerrie's story to the
"public theory" embedded in life-cycle research, with the result that both
her story and public theory are enriched. The place of public theory in
teacher development is often discounted as irrelevant. In this chapter we
seek to show how public and private theory, those often unarticulated
theories embedded in teacher beliefs, can be brought into conversation.
Chapter 5 explores the evolution of some of Kerrie's beliefs (as captured
in the metaphor "Teacher is mother") about teaching over time and in
relationship to the research literature on how beliefs change. The focus on
metaphors, we suggest, is a means for making implicit beliefs explicit and
therefore subject to change. Chapter 6 focuses on the development of
teaching expertise in relationship to the context of teaching and creating
contexts, "second-order environments," that support teacher learning.
Teaching diverse populations and inclusion are increasingly powerful contextual factors influencing teacher development and are explored in chapter 7. Chapter 8 addresses conceptions of teacher professionalism and proposes an alternative view arising from the data. Teacher professionalism,
we argue, ought not be taken uncritically as an ideal. Finally, we bring
Kerrie's journey to an end in Chapter 9 and consider her decision to leave
teaching in relation to teacher stress, burnout, and development.

2

The Social Location and Aims
of Teacher Development

Being a teacher is not as simple as it once was. Contradiction and confusion abound, and the quality of teachers' lives is dramatically and often negatively affected. Kerrie was no exception. In this chapter we situate teaching and the social and institutional role of teachers within the wider cultural context of late capitalism, a period often characterized as postmodern. It is a time of increasing cultural tensions, tensions much in evidence within schools:

> On the one hand is an increasingly postindustrial, postmodern world, characterized by accelerating change, intense compression of time and space, cultural diversity, technological complexity, national insecurity and scientific uncertainty. Against this stands a modernistic, monolithic school system that continues to pursue deeply anachronistic purposes within opaque and inflexible structures. (Hargreaves, 1994, p. 3)

Teachers are left to mediate this conflict between worlds. Nothing seems certain, including the teacher's role, which continues to expand even as the teacher's institutional authority contracts.

The clashing of these worlds is profoundly important to teacher development. As we will see in subsequent chapters, the teaching role Kerrie occupied shifted over time and became increasingly difficult to manage as expectations and demands proliferated. Much of the expansion came because of increasingly insistent and, Kerrie thought, generally legitimate claims of increasingly diverse populations of students and their parents. Role boundaries were fluid, and institutional ways of responding to claims for service were sometimes elusive, confused, misguided, and even oppressive to teachers. Like other teachers embracing a service ethic, Kerrie sought to respond to all demands she recognized as legitimate, even as the institutional standards for determining legitimacy became more vague and less dependable. As a result, like many other teachers, Kerrie found herself frustrated as by necessity she engaged in activities she thought should be outside the proper role of teachers.

During times of great uncertainty, one of the more traditional responsibilities of teachers becomes especially insistent, yet increasingly difficult to meet: as caretakers of the young, teachers are morally committed to do their utmost to help orient young people toward the good and to help them find their way as citizens and as producers and consumers of social goods. This responsibility, which sets teaching apart from all other occupations, must be kept at the forefront of any discussion about teacher development. Teacher development efforts must go well beyond training, where outcomes and conditions are known in advance. Such efforts should consider carefully who the individual teachers are and how they are oriented, and how they make the world meaningful so that they can better assist the young to make their own way safely, productively — perhaps even passionately — through uncertainty toward a principled and consistent orientation toward the good, one that will build and strengthen "the public realm" (Arendt, 1958, p. 207).

The sections in this chapter that follow may prove a bit too philosophical for some readers. One reviewer expressed this opinion in sharp and unforgiving terms. We rewrote the chapter in response to his helpful criticisms but decided to keep it here. We believe it is important for teachers and others interested in teacher development to step back and think about the wider sociocultural context within which they work. This context profoundly effects teachers and the directions in which they develop.

POSTMODERNISM

A postmodern social order is one that engages in a "thoroughgoing detraditionalization" (Giddens, 1994, p. 84). It is a society "without criteria . . . without a priori guidelines" (Murphy, 1989, p. 15). In such a society nothing is allowed to be taken for granted; traditions are "forced into open view" (Giddens, 1994, p. 6). Thus postmodernism is less a dramatic shift in human understanding than the continuation of trends that began chipping away at certainty long ago. Globalization has played a central role, as have science and its offspring, modernism, in speeding up the slide into a cultural and philosophical relativism that, some argue, has turned into an avalanche of nihilism. In this slide, authority has shifted from "tradition, social mores, religious beliefs, or other sources of ultimate grounding to the individual" (Bowers, 1987, p. 22). Philosophy has rationalized the changes, and in the process, moved them along. The postmodern challenge has been to the metanarratives, the grand traditions, ideas, or central myths that have been used in the modern world for generations to fix meaning and identity, anchor truth claims, establish authority, and bind communities together (Murphy, 1989). Manifest Destiny, progress, racial superiority, Marx's laws of history, the Protestant work ethic, and various religious tales and traditions have served this function and stand as prime examples of metanarratives.

Education has had and still has its own narratives. Supporting and sustaining metanarratives, these have served to make teaching meaningful and to establish and maintain role boundaries (see Cherryholmes, 1988). In the early part of this century, for example, teachers were at the front lines of efforts to Americanize immigrants, which presumably was done in the name of civilization and for the good of the country and of children. Teachers scrubbed the "great unwashed" who flooded ashore before and after World War I. Presumably a "melting pot" was forming, an image popularized by Israel Zangwill's play by that name (1909), but the reality was quite different; the aim was less a matter of cultural melding than of remaking the immigrant child into a good, clean, middle-class citizen (Carlson, 1975). The melting pot myth shattered under the pressures of changing economics and shifting demographics. Over the past couple of decades, spurred onward by the rhetoric of cultural pluralism, a "diversity myth" has formed which is now being exported worldwide and is the source of much mischief and misunderstanding (Schwarz, 1995). Yet celebrating diversity is no substitute for the hard and contentious work involved in learning to get along and to take concerted action. As the celebration continues, barriers between groups and peoples grow higher, and as a result, the teacher's role has gotten infinitely more complicated and challenging. Gaining access to power, groups insist not only that they be allowed to maintain their languages and cultural identities and that educators respect them, but that they enhance them as well. Times have changed. For compelling reasons, Americanization no longer serves as a narrative upon which to tie one's professional identity, but for some teachers the ideology of multiculturalism does. Old schooling purposes have crumbled, new ones multiply beyond measure, and there seems to be precious little agreement about the future of American public education and its teachers. In such contexts, teachers may feel adrift and increasingly dissatisfied with their work (Bacharach & Bamberger, 1990), and nothing could be more damaging to their students. For Kerrie, work became increasingly stressful and progressively less satisfying.

Signs of Postmodernism

Under the pressures of postmodernity, moral and intellectual certainties are collapsing. Some greet the collapse joyously, while others gaze ahead ominously, warning of an impending doom made certain by our cultural amnesia. Almost imperceptibly, the boundaries of acceptable behavior have slipped outward; definitions of what is normal have expanded, and the social consequences are widely seen as troubling — an explosion in teenage pregnancies, widespread drug usage, open displays of sexuality, and indifference to homelessness, child poverty, and child neglect. This behavior manifests itself in the classroom, and teachers must deal with it. Recall that Kerrie described the students at Clarke in Chapter 1 as "street smart" and "sexual."

Much has been written about what becomes of the self when the social context is unstable, when traditions are forgotten and institutions lack authority, and when ideologies are no longer able to capture imagination and story it. Persons and contexts evolve together; identity formation is "a process 'located' *in the core of the individual* and yet also *in the core of his communal culture*, a process which establishes, in fact, the identity of those two identities" (Erikson, 1968, p. 22, emphasis in original). Put differently, self is a "construction that . . . proceeds from the outside in as well as from the inside out, from culture to mind as well as from mind to culture" (Bruner, 1990, p. 108). Uncertain contexts and the absence of authority may thus prevent self formation, leaving behind a shattered self, a person who is no one and everyone (Glass, 1993). Without authority there is no possibility of community (Ehrenhalt, 1995) or of competance (Lasch, 1995).

Heightening this identity crisis is insistence in industrial democracies on "self-made identities" (Erikson, 1968, p. 133). This is the illusion that we can freely choose ourselves, that we are independent, unbounded selves, institutionally autonomous and free (Bellah et al., 1991). We are a people without histories — ahistorical beings, who live for the moment and are prone to display "cynical detachment" (Lasch, 1978, p. 95). Yet young people desperately need and want parameters, and for many, there are precious few of these. The young encounter too few common ideals or inspiring ideologies, beyond consumerism, upon which to ground identity; they fail to realize that they *are* because they are in relationship to others, to other selves and that history flows through them. Progressively fewer families are stable sources of meaning; they lack adults who young people can count on today and tomorrow, and whose lives stand for something larger than the individual self. Such people set and sustain standards of acceptable behavior and in doing so, they support teachers and promote education.

Bereft, young people often suffer from what Erikson so aptly described as a kind of "ideological undernourishment" (1958, p. 103); no big ideas grab them, orient them, and help them to find their way. In this situation, "committed identity becomes an increasingly arduous achievement" (Gergen, 1991, p. 73). Consider this: for boys, the increasingly common absence of a father and the domination of early education by even the most able women are troublesome, and so then youths seek identity elsewhere, in sports and through gangs. Academic performance, judged unmanly, slips (Elshtain, 1994) and teachers face the daunting challenge of trying to convince, sometimes bribe, boys to attend and to stay in school. Unfortunately, the appeal most often made, but too seldom convincing, is to consumerism — the ability to consume depends on getting a decent job which in turn depends on staying in school (Bullough, 1988).

A modernist looks for fixed identity, a North Star, and not finding one, feels adrift and may seek solace in an imagined past, when times and people were supposedly better. Simple and often technical solutions to complex problems are found appealing. In education the mythical "good old days" continue to shadow efforts at improvement. But the good old days were not all that good (Berliner & Biddle, 1995). When governors meet to discuss education, simplistic solutions to complex problems rule the day. They can imagine only two responses to the problems of education: national performance standards coupled with rigorous assessment, and increased use of technology to meet those standards (Diegmueller, 1996; West, 1996). The presumption is that testable national standards will impose order on a system recently run amuck. The governors' fascination with technology is grounded in a deeply embedded modern faith in science and technology to fix fundamental human problems. Ironically, while governors are eager to purchase gadgets, they are loath to support "long-range and ongoing professional development for teachers, buying and developing quality software, and ensuring technical support" (West, 1996, p. 22). Revealing their modern bias, educators are not seen as capable of adequately addressing the problems of schooling, and others, presumably more expert, are expected to step in and show the way. Modernists have faith in systems of control, and in experts — as long as they confirm established prejudices.

The Dangers

While we are not champions of the consumptive individualism of modernism that produces "bought identity" — "I consume, therefore I am" (Hartley, 1993, pp. 88–89) — neither are we enamored with the extreme relativism inherent in postmodernity (see Lehman, 1991). In a postmodern world, all voices are championed ("voice" is now the reigning metaphor) and no strong judgments are made about what is said. Everyone speaks, but no one, it seems, cares to listen or to be held accountable for what is said. Bellah and his colleagues (1991) powerfully illustrate this troubling

aspect of postmodern-mindedness when reporting the words of an Ivy
League graduate orator.

> They tell us that it is heresy to suggest the superiority of some value, fantasy
> to believe in moral argument, slavery to submit to a judgment sounder than
> your own. The freedom of our day is the freedom to devote ourselves to any
> values we please, on the mere condition that we do not believe them to be
> true. (p. 44)

Students want and need moral grounding; failing to find it, they sink into
cynicism. They need guides who will hold them accountable for their
actions. They need morally grounded, knowledgeable teachers, among
other caring adults who are engaged in and sustain the public world, and
who resist the urge to withdraw into the culture of narcissism (Lasch,
1978). Without them, nihilism raises its ugly, smirking head. An ethic of
tolerance supports a "culture of the indifferent" (Rieff, 1966, p. 12), which
endangers the very ideal of tolerance itself, as Walter Lippmann (1955)
argued long ago.

Lacking a common language of compassion (Greene, 1991) and affili-
ation (Bellah et al., 1985), the danger is that we will stop talking to
others different from ourselves, that we will turn away from the noise
and become unreceptive (see Noddings, 1984), no longer interested in
understanding others' views or connecting with them. Life becomes war-
like, reflecting a loss of faith in the future (Lasch, 1978). Seeking only
our own kind, we turn our backs to the other, and, no longer standing
face-to-face, totalize the other—stick the other into a convenient category
that can be dismissed or treated routinely (see Levinas, 1969) by some
"expert" somewhere. For teachers who turn their backs and forget their
moral responsibilities, children are consigned to categories and are lost in
the postmodern world, just as they have been reduced to labels and sorted
and tracked by the schools of the modern world. Indifference is the danger. In the postmodern world, it is easy even for teachers not to actively
care for the young because as persons they are thought of not as our
responsibility, but only their parents'. What is lost when one turns one's
back on others, however, is one's self: how teachers define themselves is
"to a great extent how teachers act in relation to others," especially toward
students (Soder, 1991, p. 301).

Recognizing that "not all forms of otherness and difference are to be
celebrated," the challenge, as Bernstein puts it, is to "*seek* for a type of
reconciliation of pluralization and differences without ignoring or repress-
ing the otherness of the Other" (1992, p. 313, emphasis in original). Teachers face the daunting moral, social, and practical challenge of honoring

student differences while simultaneously reconciling them. Border crossings are necessary so that students develop a sense of belonging, a concern for and understanding of the whole, and a feeling of being fully accountable for their actions. Taking a different cut on the same issue, Sarason, speaking as a psychologist, observes that studies of learning have been almost totally concerned with how individuals learn. The issue, he argues, is much broader and more fundamental: "In what ways should I think and act so that at the same time I recognize individuality I also recognize how, given the social nature of the classroom, those individualities can be interconnected or organized to contribute to the productive learning of others?" (1996, pp. 385–386). To do this, teachers must be capable and committed boundary crossers themselves, individuals who look beyond labels to see the people residing within them and who simultaneously see beyond particularity to commonality.

The stakes are high. Without reconciliation, public education is reduced to training; and civility, the foundation of democracy, becomes little more than a weak form of tolerance, a tourist's or wayfarer's ethic (Rieff, 1966). Tribalism is the victor — a withdrawal into sameness encouraged, ironically, by the champions of vouchers and school choice who have elevated selfishness and provincialism to the status of new democratic citizenship rights. Procedure replaces moral discourse and leaves behind a politics "concerned less with cultivating virtue than with enabling persons to choose their own values." Such systems inevitably lack the "civic resources to sustain self-government" (Sandel, 1996, p. 58).

ON TEACHERS FACING THE CHILDREN
OF THE POSTMODERN WORLD

Teachers teach themselves, what and who they are: "those of us who are teachers cannot stand before a class without standing for something. . . . teaching is testimony" (Patterson, 1991, p. 16). We are "selves only in that certain issues matter for us. What I am as a self, my identity, is essentially defined by the way things have significance for me. . . . [W]e are only selves insofar as we move in a certain space of questions, as we seek and find an orientation to the good" (Taylor, 1989, p. 34). The teacher's orientation to the good is central to what she or he does in the classroom and for children. It is also at the heart of what is taught, as we shall see especially in Chapter 5, when Kerrie's beliefs are explored. It matters a great deal what kind of person a teacher is, what her orientation is to the good, because who a teacher is inside school is also who she is outside it (Pajak & Blase, 1989) and because who she is is how she is related to others. Kerrie's sense of self was grounded in a profound service ethic. Without an understanding of this, it is impossible to understand Kerrie.

This is not to say that teachers do not change, however; they do. Identity is not a thing, but rather a way of being in and relating to the world, and just as the world we inhabit changes, so do we. Such changes are documented throughout subsequent chapters. Yet ultimately we cannot ever be fully certain who we are, even when the times we inhabit are relatively stable, as ours are not:

> [H]umans will always be in an important sense opaque to ourselves and to each other. We can never aspire to know who we definitely are because our assignable identities are so affected by the stream of historical events of which we are a part. . . . The understanding which we can have of ourselves is always 'in the middle of the way': there are no absolute beginnings and no absolute endings; there is no closure when we can know for certain who we are and what we have done. The process of understanding ourselves can never achieve finality, but is always unfolding and always being revised. (Fay, 1987, pp. 173–174)

In the next chapter we see, in three versions of Kerrie's story of becoming a teacher, how identities are "unfolding and always being revised," as Fay stated.

CHANGING CONTEXTS, CHANGING IDENTITIES

Contexts shape identity; they enable some institutional roles and self-understandings while inhibiting others. Schools were constructed and organized around a modern vision of education, one born of industrialism and factory work and committed to such metaphors for human relationship as supervision, discipline, and management (Bullough, 1994). Schooling, so conceived, denies otherness and encourages the development of teacher and student identities consistent with the modern emphasis on control, rationalization, and prediction, the stuff of social efficiency. It does this through established ways of speaking and acting, through accepted roles, relationships, and social practices such as standardized teacher evaluation, student tracking, age grading, homogenous ability grouping, and, in secondary schools, bells and forty-five-minute class periods. The day is rushed, yet time is wasted. The conclusion ought to be obvious: new identities, new and stronger moral relationships with children, require new institutions, yet the postmodern tendency is to flee from institutions, deny our complete dependency on them and their authority, and discount the hard work needed to re-create them.

As a preliminary move toward solving this conundrum, we need to shift our focus from the perils of postmodernism to its more compelling elements — the "ideas of difference, particularity, and irregularity" (Elkind, 1994, p. 12). These point toward a future within which even the most settled of teachers will be forced to acknowledge the inevitability of different kinds of student learning outcomes (despite the push for national standards), different kinds of progress, and, most important, different kinds of school contexts, ones that play to and enhance teacher talent and student ability. Such contexts are responsive to the differences among teachers, to their particularity and unpredictability, and not only allow but enable a broader range of "subject positions" and roles within the institution than formerly existed (Taubman, 1992, p. 229). They are also responsive to students and sharply focused on enhancing their learning (Louis, Marks, & Kruse, 1996).

The modern school treats all teachers as though they were alike, interchangeable; the postmodern school begins with the recognition that they are not. This recognition brings with it the possibility that within the classroom and the school, teachers will be able to integrate selves more easily as new opportunities for growth are made available and supported institutionally. The latter point is fundamentally important. Being allowed to be more of who they are, persons not playing a role but living a life, will reveal to teachers the untapped resources they have to make teaching more pleasureful and to meet their moral responsibilities of caring for and educating young people to overcome provincialism — to cross boundaries and to become increasingly competant.

This view of the future is quite at odds with the current effort to turn teaching into a profession along the lines of the high-status professions of medicine and law, a point to which we will return in Chapter 8. Inspired by modernism, this quest for expert standing will likely result in increased rationalization and standardization of classroom practices (see Labaree, 1992), an outcome Kerrie quietly resisted, and further separation of teachers from parents and students, thus undercutting "important connections between schools and their communities, leading to greater insensitivity within the school to the legitimate interests of parents and other community members in school affairs" (Zeichner, 1991, p. 367). Professionalism of this kind inhibits border crossing, heightens individualism, lacks moral authority, and, as Soder (1991) argues, rhetorical power, the power to convince others of the rightness of a view.

We suspect that few teachers actually enjoy the kinds of relationships the modernist view of schooling and professionalism support. Kerrie certainly did not, which is one of the reasons why she sought to increase her involvement in the wider educational community (see Chapter 8). This may be especially true of those who feel called to teaching as a form of service (Serow et al., 1994). Yet the entire institution and many influential policy groups help maintain these established roles and ways of thinking. Teacher unions are certainly culpable here. Modernist assumptions about efficiency and the need to monitor teachers strictly may make it difficult for many teachers to stay in teaching and to find pleasure in their work. Often such teachers enjoy teaching; they just find little opportunity to do it. Teacher development needs to be thought of in relationship to institutional change and culture building. As Fullan reminds us, "change is a journey, not a blueprint" (1993, p. 24).

Students rightfully expect instructional and content competence from their teachers, but they also expect to be greeted by a whole person, a caring person, one who knows who and what he is, who has moral standing, and who can be counted on to continue standing, face to face with students. Even when confronting doubt, such teachers have an "aura of certainty" about them (Floden & Clark, 1988, p. 519), which is important for their students. Knowing that the "remedy for unpredictability . . . is contained in the faculty to make and keep promises" (Arendt, 1958, p. 237), these teachers keep their promises. At the same time such teachers "never stop asking themselves what the nature of teaching really is . . . especially when they encounter 'difficult' youths or when they become unsure whether what they teach and how they teach is still appropriate for their students" (Van Manen, 1994, p. 141). Still, despite their doubting, they are constant — not fixed — so that their students might have a chance to figure out where they, too, stand, of how they are oriented toward the good (see Sherman, 1992). Such teachers recognize that it is "only in certain relational contexts that the thinking life, the developing identity, the moral personality, the emotional spirit, the educational learning, and the sociopsychological maturing of the young person occurs" (Van Manen, 1994, p. 141). Like Kerrie, they seek to provide such contexts, "communities of competence" (Lasch, 1978, p. 235). Teachers of this kind teach themselves; of that one may be certain — and their content is intellectual, ethical, pedagogically sensitive, and profoundly personal. It is content that transcends the technical and bureaucratic life of modern schools, with its assumptions that not all children can learn and that some must fail. Children adrift in a postmodern world — one of sometimes desperate uncertainties, where too few adults are willing or able to extend a firm but gentle guiding hand — discover in such teachers a reason for hope: for hopefulness is the only morally appropriate response to uncertainty (Elbaz, 1992). The message of hope is embodied in the teacher, personal and powerful:

> Hope does not demand a belief in progress. It demands a belief in justice: a conviction that the wicked will suffer, that wrongs will be made right, that the underlying order of things is not flouted with impunity. Hope implies a deep-seated trust in life that appears absurd to those who lack it. It rests on confidence not so much in the future as in the past. It derives from early memories — no doubt distorted, overlaid with later memories, and thus not wholly reliable as a guide to any factual reconstruction of past events. . . . Such experience leaves as its residue the unshakable conviction, not that the past was better than the present, but that trust is never completely misplaced either. . . . (Lasch, 1991, p. 81)

In firmly guiding the young, teachers teach hope and become part of the early memories — what will become the past — of the young. They prove they can be trusted and that justice will be served because they are adults who serve it, adults who have proved themselves worthy guides and faithful, if not infallible, judges for whom genuine human standards are taken seriously and respected but applied sensitively and intelligently, as demanded by an abiding concern for the individual child's future and particularity. Such teachers embody what is compelling in the postmodern view while striving to reconcile differences by helping others to cross boundaries, become engaged, and learn to forgive.

CONCLUSION

This is our orientation to teacher development, a product of having thought long and hard about teaching. First, by virtue of sharing a cultural context, each teacher's story contains both personal and public plot elements. Both are productive sources of insight about teaching and teacher development. Currently running through the story are postmodern plot elements that profoundly shape the contours of teaching. Second, development is always toward something. It is not neutral; it is value laden. We need to be clear about aims, about what visions of teachers and of teaching are embedded in teacher development efforts. Third, there is no development in the abstract; in its particularity, development is always for and about someone working in some place at some time with specific children and adults. It is about Kerrie working at Rocky Mountain Junior High School and later at Clarke Intermediate with dozens of students who brought to her classroom their own stories and ways of being in the world and with teachers who were similarly seeking to make sense of and find pleasure in their experience with young people and with one another. Fourth, the results of development are not predictable; rather, there is inevitably difference in outcomes. Finally, just as teachers differ, so will the contexts that enhance development differ in some ways, yet they will be alike in others. We will speak of commonalities in later chapters. We wish to stress here that teacher development is simultaneously concerned with the individual and with creating institutional and social contexts supportive of development. This includes establishing standards that are tied to a specific school community's effort to achieve reconciliation of differences as an affirmation of that community's identity, its shared moral standing and commitment to student learning (Bernstein, 1992). Such an affirmation reflects the members' orientations toward the good — orientations which, like the community's affirmation itself, are inevitably tentative but nevertheless morally justified, useful, and full of hope.

Questions for Consideration

1. Do you agree with the analysis? Is the role of the teacher getting more complicated? Why?
2. Consider your own orientation to the good. What kind of teacher are you? What is the self you teach? How is your life as a teacher connected to your life outside the classroom? Can young people count on you to be a champion of justice? Are you constant for your students?
3. Do you agree that teachers have an obligation both to honor diversity and to help young people to cross borders, to recognize commonality? If so, how do you meet this responsibility?
4. Assuming that you agree with much of the analysis presented of the current social context within which schools operate, can schools resist the negative influences of postmodernism, the slide into an extreme relativism? Conversely, can they not only cope with but build upon the positive aspects of postmodernism (difference, particularity, irregularity) and thereby enhance the quality of the educational experience of the young?
5. Assuming postmodern social trends continue: what changes in your own teaching role would you seek in re-creating the institutional life of teachers? What might be the impact of these changes on your students?

3

Teacher Development, Biography, and Narrative Reasoning

The power of stories as a means of studying teaching and of building pedagogical knowledge is now generally recognized and often celebrated (see Jalongo & Isenberg, 1995). Indeed, teacher development is best understood in relationship to biography, to the unfolding and telling and retelling of a life. Teachers share stories and in the sharing learn about teaching and about themselves as teachers. Stories also bear a good deal of a teacher's emotional life and bring pleasure and sometimes sweet release in the telling. It is important to pause and ask why one or another story is worthy of attention, and perhaps of publication. As a claim to uniqueness, the common appeal to "voice" simply will not do (Graham, 1993). Rather, like cases (Kagan, 1993), the stories that connect and speak to common teacher concerns invite engagement and reflection and perhaps even inspire laughter. Such stories invite border crossing, as discussed in Chapter 2, and carry normative value by illustrating patterns of thought and themes characteristic of the profession and of teachers working within particular contexts. Teachers see themselves in such stories, and in the seeing, make comparisons that stretch understanding and nudge along development.

Accordingly, some of the stories we tell here are ones that touch on issues common to teaching and experiences widely shared by teachers. Additionally, some stories are told simply because they must be told, because they are so central to who Kerrie is as a teacher and to her development as a teacher. We believe the stories contained here and in Chapter 4 nicely illustrate the role and power of narrative and narrative reasoning in teacher identity formation and their potential for encouraging teacher development. Not surprisingly, we often find out what we think about a person or an event when we tell someone else a story about it.

We will tell three edited versions of Kerrie's story of becoming a teacher. The first (1986) will conclude with a brief discussion of story elements and themes. Having told this tale, we will be in a position to consider some of the wider literature on the power and potential for encouraging development of stories and storytelling. The second version (1991) will also conclude with a brief discussion of story elements and themes. The third version (1995) then follows. Once all three stories have been told, we will compare and contrast them and react to one another's interpretations. This chapter, then, operates at multiple levels and involves a good deal of shifting between Bob and Kerrie's interpretations. The three versions of Kerrie's story were told to Bob in transcribed interviews. The interviews took two forms: open storytelling, where Kerrie was asked to "tell the story about how you became a teacher"; and a more traditional question-and-answer form, where Kerrie responded to specific questions about her development, often in relationship to other events in her personal and family life. For the second story Kerrie was asked to divide her experience of becoming a teacher into phases. The result was in some ways a less interesting story when compared to what Kerrie said when she told her tale more naturally, as a product of taken-for-granted narrative structures, but approaching the story in this way revealed new and unexpected insights especially important to Chapter 4. Finally, we should mention that the three versions of Kerrie's story told in this chapter serve as a backdrop and an introduction to the chapters that follow. In subsequent chapters we return to several of the issues raised here.

A FIRST TELLING, BEFORE THE FIRST
YEAR OF TEACHING, 1986

My mom was going to be a teacher, so [teaching] seemed like the direction to take as far as going to school. . . . I began to focus . . . upon English and history, which made me think, if I want to be a teacher, then I don't want to teach all the subjects. I wanted to teach junior or senior high. . . . [My mother] teaches second grade. [She's been teaching] about four or five years, not very long. She went back to school just a few years before I did. She just kind of set an example. . . .

High school teachers [also influenced me]. When I look back now and I think of the training I had, I look back at one high school teacher [who] taught me history. I think she is the one who I wanted to model [myself on]. . . . Yet when I look at her now, knowing what I know . . . she just lectured and showed movies. . . . She was young and single. She wasn't necessarily attractive. It was . . . her personality [that captured me]. . . . I don't know, why do you like one person instead of another? [History] was interesting to her. She didn't use notes much when she taught. . . . It seemed to [just] come from her; she knew [history]. We'd ask her questions and she'd know the answers. She'd recommend books to read . . . on the subject. She just seemed to represent history. Yet she wasn't necessarily a really dynamic teacher. . . .

The first history class I ever had that was just history was in seventh grade in Fort Riley, Kansas, where my father was stationed as an Army chaplain. I had Mr. K. This is where I fell in love with history. He told us there was going to be a test . . . I went home and memorized the unit. I got an A. I guess I've really liked history ever since then. . . . When I got to college I discovered [learning history] wasn't easy. It was more than [memorizing facts]—what is your interpretation, instead of my interpretation [of this topic]? . . .

[I thought of teachers] as rulers in their kingdoms, I guess. Sounds kind of funny. To me teaching is very territorial. They had a territory. It was theirs. They could rule it however they wanted within limits. They were the bosses. They could kick kids out if they wanted to. I guess I learned that [from sitting in classes as a student]. . . .

[I think] I always wanted to be a teacher. [Now that I think about it,] we played school all summer [when I was a girl]. Along with other things we spent a lot of time out at recess! . . . . My friends and I were all "teachers." We had a nonexistent class that we were handing out work to. Sometimes we'd drag in my girlfriend's brothers to be the students. They'd have to be sent to the principal all the time because they were bad. I see my daughter doing the same thing, [which] seems totally normal to me. . . . I liked organizing the things on my desk. Getting my mom to buy me a roll book. Going around looking through my house at things that I could put on my TV tray, which would be my desk. Lining up the chairs. . . . Writing on the chalkboard. All the teacher things. . . .

[As a student] I was always concerned about getting things in on time. [I was] careful to keep my eyes on my own paper so no one would think I was cheating. [I would] look over [at others students taking a test] to make sure I was not falling behind—or maybe to see if I was ahead. But not to cheat. . . .

I'm always afraid people won't know who I am. [Yet] they always do; they always know who I am. I don't know why . . .

I got in trouble once. It was when we moved [from] Kansas—Fort Riley. . . . I wanted to bring my friends in during recess and pull down the map to show them where I had just lived. I did. When we put it back up, I let go of it and the whole map came off the wall. The teacher walked in. I was sent to the principal. That was probably one of the most traumatic events that ever happened to me. . . . .

When I [imagine] the perfect [class], I used to see one where I was standing up at the front of the room talking and my students were just avidly watching me and writing down every word I said. I have had that happen before, so maybe that [dream was] kind of fulfilled. Now, I have a more activity-based scenario, where I am sitting there and my students are working at . . . different [learning] centers. . . . They are interacting with one another and they're having fun. They're being noisy. It's not boisterous, but it's not quiet, either. Everyone is busy and I'm sitting there watching them, because I've got them all trained so well. . . . They're busy learning. They're interacting. They're socialized. They're under control. . . . What I want to be able to do is to give of myself by teaching kids how to think—put things together; take things apart.

Themes and Elements

Kerrie's mother's influence on her decision to teach stands out. Her impact was subtle and powerful but is presented more as confirmation of the rightness of a decision already made than as an additional reason for becoming a teacher. Kerrie role-played teacher. She appears to have been "called" to teach, which is important to her story, just as the concept of a calling is important to the history of teaching (Mattingly, 1975): "In the strongest sense of a 'calling,' work constitutes a practical ideal of activity and character that makes a person's work morally inseparable from his or her life" (Bellah et al., 1985, p. 66). And further, compared to "non-called" teachers:

> . . . those who say they are called to teach display significantly greater enthu-siasm and commitment to the idea of a teaching career, are more mindful of its potential impact on other people, are less concerned about the sacrifices that such a career might entail, and are more willing to accept the extra duties that often accompany the teacher's role. (Serow, 1994, p. 65)

That teachers seemed powerful and in control to the young Kerrie seems to have been part of the appeal of teaching. Exactly why is uncertain, although it is tempting to speculate about the influence of Kerrie's moving around the country as the child of an Army officer and, as it turned out, a sickly mother who needed Kerrie to help with child rearing. Later, in high school, this theme takes a territorial turn and Kerrie expresses pleasure in the thought that she will be a "ruler" in a kingdom. In this kingdom, people would know who she was; she feared anonymity and sought confirmation of her value and worth to others. Her views of teaching shifted with experience, particularly after her student teaching, but the theme of being in control continues. The control becomes indirect, and she looks forward in her first job as a teacher toward having students engaged in learning as proof of having been trained well by her.

Kerrie's Reaction

Aside from the home and the classroom, where do women find a place of power and control? Women hold many positions: secretaries, policewomen, businesswomen, attorneys; the list is long and varied. While I was creative and ambitious, none of these careers appealed to me, nor were they within the realm of my experience. I knew I wanted to be in charge of something,

something that was of value and importance, yet I was also aware that I probably didn't have what it [took] to make it in law [school] or medical school. And so, following my mother's example and my childhood fantasies, I made the obvious choice—classroom teaching.

When Bob posed the question of whether or not I thought of myself as "called to teach," I was at first surprised. For me, "calling" has a religious meaning and I'd never related it to the work context. However, I was quick to realize that teaching was indeed my calling. I recognized that teaching and all it entails was more than just a good fit for me.

STORYTELLING AND NARRATIVE

We learn a great deal about Kerrie from this brief and initial story of why she became a teacher. We will learn more shortly as we explore the other two versions. What is most important is that we begin to see some of the value of storytelling as a means for studying teaching and teacher development. Who Kerrie is determines in good measure what she becomes as a teacher. In this section, we stand back and consider the sources of the power of stories and storytelling in human development more generally, which will provide useful background for our inquiry.

Robert Coles describes a transformative moment in his development as a psychiatrist that came after suggesting to a patient that she "just tell [him] a story or two." The suggestion required immediate justification. Coles (1989) writes:

> She looked at me as if I'd taken leave of my senses. I began to think I had: this was no way to put the request I had in mind. Why *had* I phrased my suggestion that way? I explained that we all have accumulated stories in our lives, that each of us had a history of such stories, that no one's stories are quite like anyone else's, and that we could, after a fashion, become our own appreciative and comprehending critics by learning to pull together the various incidents in our lives in such a way that they do, in fact, become an old-fashioned story. (p. 11)

Later he describes his realization that different stories are told to different people; that stories have a purpose, and that purpose is influenced not only by the teller of the tale but also the told — as listeners we "give shape to what we hear, make over [others'] stories into something of our own" (p. 19). Yet despite our connecting to others through stories, "each person's life has its own nature, spirit, meaning, and rhythm" (p. 90). By sharing stories, we learn about one another, and we especially learn about our-selves.

Much is at stake in the stories we tell, for in authoring them, or more appropriately, coauthoring them, we form a self (see Prawat, 1991; Witherell, 1991):

> We achieve our personal identities and self-concept through the use of the narrative configuration, and make our existence into a whole by understand-ing it as an expression of a single unfolding and developing story. We are in the middle of our stories and cannot be sure how they will end; we are constantly having to revise the plot as new events are added to our lives. Self, then, is not a static thing or a substance, but a configuring of personal events into a historical unity which includes not only what one has been but also anticipations of what one will be. (Polkinghorne, 1988, p. 150)

Within such stories, the self, as Bruner (1990) observes, operating as "nar-rator not only recounts but justifies [and] as protagonist is always . . . pointing to the future" (p. 121).

An often overlooked aspect of stories of self (recalling chapter 2) is that they represent a moral orientation to the world, stories that have woven into them a sense of the good — of what matters and has meaning and what does not: "To know who you are is to be oriented to moral space, a space in which questions arise about what is good or bad, what is worth doing and what not, what has meaning and importance for you and what is trivial and secondary" (Taylor, 1989, p. 28). Indeed, different conceptions of self go with different conceptions of the good, which is crucially impor-tant for teachers, since teaching is, as we have suggested, inevitably a form of testifying (see Patterson, 1991).

Even in a postmodern age, an orientation to the good and answers to the questions "Who am I?" or "Where do I fit?" come by virtue of our being born into narratives, cultural myths, and traditions, however frac-tured or firm. This occurs despite some social theorists' overconfidence in the power of the individual, as a self-determining subject, to re-create herself through self-estrangement (see Fay, 1987). Thus, "What I am . . . is in key part what I inherit, a specific past that is present to some degree in my present" (MacIntyre, quoted in Goodson, 1994, p. 35). This said, over time stories do unfold, and selves change despite inherited histories. Change is constant because events are unstable (see Griffiths, 1993). Nar-rative theology provides particularly powerful examples of change, often driven by a rejection of one's inherited stories and the cultural traditions that bear them, in which a new story is found gripping and the result is conversion, a transformation of self, a telling from a different and more compelling perspective, a changed reading of experience and of history (see McCollum, 1981).[1]

The unity of stories is largely a function of the narrative[2] "structure and strictures" (Thomas, 1993, p. 232; see also Witherell, 1991) and of the models of being (see Graham, 1989) made available within a given social context — society, school, family; ultimately, unity is imposed on experience.

> Stories involve choice, selection and emphasis in the service of coherence; they require structural features such as plots, beginnings, middles and endings; demand cause and effect, motivations and climaxes. . . . (Thomas, 1993, p. 232)

Like all tellers, Kerrie selected what to say and not say, when and how to say it or not say it, and in so doing she spoke for her familial, social, and cultural contexts — and through the languages[3] — that have shaped her life, bound her to others like her mother and former teachers, and given her direction and purpose. Also, unity is less a matter of discovering or uncovering a self than a reflection of surviving compelling memories and of patterning memories for the sake of creating meaning. Where there are no patterns, there is no story, no self (see Glass, 1993). Kerrie's self was grounded and patterned.

Inevitably the stories of self we tell are partial; one cannot possibly tell the whole story, and not merely because it is constantly evolving and we do not know how it will end:

> . . . all that I have undergone in the past is unavailable; what we can perhaps obtain is that which, according to a present perspective, appears to be rele-

---

[1]Ironically, critical social science seeks a similar outcome. "One of the therapeutic aims of critical social science is getting members of its audience to appreciate the real unity of their existence by convincing them to adopt a particular narrative account of their lives" (Fay, 1987, p. 71).

[2]Several authors distinguish among autobiographies, narratives, and stories. For example, Elbaz (1991) conceives of narrative as tending to "call on a conception of 'work' as a defined object with particular, formal qualities, an object which signifies something else in a relatively straightforward way and which is there to be consumed" (p. 6). In contrast, she asserts that "story is not linear and is less confined to a prescribed shape or form" (p. 6) and is therefore more open to change.

[3]"Languages" is used rather broadly to include music, dance, and symbols of various kinds, as well as the spoken and written word.

vant, whereas in the future, parts of a past that now seem unimportant may become central to an understanding of a history. (Elbaz, 1991, p. 5)

When reading this first version of Kerrie's story, one senses gaps, and questions come to mind. Why, for example, did Kerrie worry about whether or not others would know her? This seems important, especially when seen in the light of information that will follow later about Kerrie as a "loner," yet one who pushed herself to become heavily involved in the wider educational community.

In Western cultures, "occupation is a very important element in the definition of a self. . . . For teachers, the reverse is also true: 'the self is a crucial element in the way teachers themselves construe the nature of their job'" (Kelchtermans & Vandenberghe, 1994, p. 47). Indeed, teachers cannot hide themselves behind a professional persona; teaching is far too intimate and personal for such role playing (Thomas, 1993, p. 239), as Kerrie's story illustrates. The link between self and work is so fundamental in teaching that "everything a person has been and undergone in the past creates meaningful unions in his or her present experience of classroom situations" (Korthagen, 1993, p. 319). These "unions," what Korthagen calls "gestalts," refer to "the whole of a person's experiences with regard to a certain situation" (Korthagen, 1993, p. 319). Grounded biographically, they are the foundation of meaning making; embedded in stories, they enable the naming of experience and thereby link teacher commitments and actions to the lives of particular students. "The kind of teacher we are reflects the kind of life that we lead" (Connelly & Clandinin, 1988, p. 27).

The exploration and the sharing of narratives, what Van Manen terms "narrative reasoning" (1994), plays a central role in teachers' formation of a teaching self:

> Personal identity can be brought to self-awareness through narrative self-reflection. Self-knowledge not only assumes that one can establish one's own personal identity by means of stories, but also . . . that one can be accountable narratively for how one has developed as a person — for how one has become what one has become. . . . Self-knowledge is related to the search for one's own life story. Thus, by engaging in such narrative "theorizing" teachers may further discover and shape their personal pedagogical identity, and through such stories they can give accounts of the way they have developed over time into the kind[s] of persons they are now. (p. 159)

The story of one's quest to become a teacher is embedded in the story of one's life. This is a theme to which we will return.

Narrative reasoning provides an occasion for exploring stories, and not just in quiet moments alone, through "self-dialogue" (Jalongo & Isenberg,

1995, p. 88). When telling stories at lunch or over dinner, we hope that someone will listen and perhaps be empathic, amused, or edified by what we say. In the process our thoughts are clarified and sometimes tested. But when we reason narratively we seek something deeper — insight into and sometimes confirmation of who we are and who we are as teachers and what we are becoming and doing in the classroom. Narrative reasoning requires the comparing and contrasting of texts, storied experiences. Thus, stories "are both mirrors of our own practice and windows on the practice of others" (Jalongo & Isenberg, 1995, p. 174). Comparing and contrasting our story with others' invites consideration of the morality of actions, which speaks directly to who we are and of how we are oriented toward the good, and calls for consideration of the relationship between our self, as an expression of our higher aspirations and what we claim to be, and what we are or have become when teaching. Narrative reasoning makes us answerable to ourselves and others for what we are and are becoming, and in particular, for the quality of our relationship with the young people we teach. In some sense, we (the authors) became answerable to one another.

Additional contrasts and comparisons are also possible and desirable. Stories may be treated as data, as they are here, and comparisons made by those whose stories are told or by those who listen or read them for what can be learned about teaching and teacher development. Comparisons can also be made between stories and public theory, as we will see in Chapter 4. Events are interpreted through the stories we tell and through the beliefs embedded in and supported by those stories. Thus personal stories operate as private theories, and comparing and contrasting them involves a kind of theorizing, as Van Manen suggests. Coles (1989) observes that the "critical root" of the word "theory" is "'I behold,' as in what we see when we go to the theater" (p. 20). Comparing and contrasting personal stories to what others have beheld and judged important and made explicit is a powerful source of insight into who a teacher is and into how that teacher is developing.

We turn now to the second version of Kerrie's story, which was told in phases. Following this story, we will engage in narrative reasoning.

A STORY TOLD IN PHASES, 1991

[That first year of teaching] I watched C. [teach across the pod]. I did what she said. I modeled things that were modeled for me, pretty much. It took me a while, really . . . until my second year, to not be that follower. I changed through [the experience], but even now I still go back and in my mind I will say, "Well, how did C. do that?" I don't know why; isn't that funny . . . ? I could always see her class and how they were behaving. I still hold that up as the mark, even though [I felt let down by her at first]. She was still a very positive influence for me because she was a good teacher . . . I was so shaky on curriculum, even. I thought about moving to [a high school that had an opening], but I thought, "Oh, what would I do [with the curriculum]? I would be a first-year teacher all over again, [which was] scary, terrible.

Then I changed. I saw myself at the middle of the first year, adapting to the realities of student behavior and realizing that some problems can't be dealt with—you just kind of have to let them go. Well, they can be dealt with, but I couldn't deal with them yet—I [didn't] know what to do. . . . I'm that kind of person. If I can't deal with [a problem], I just put it away for a while and take it out periodically and see if I can deal with it. [Then], all of a sudden, I think, "Oh, it is so obvious, this is what I should be doing. . . . " I [realized] I didn't have to do everything the [way C. did]. . . . I was beginning to feel more empowered—the way I could manipulate [the situation], but still C. was very important to [me] all of that first year. . . .

[The] second year . . . [my] independence was growing, but at this point it was, like, okay, I've been through [the curriculum] once—I'm teaching the same thing all over again and I'll be able to make some changes now. . . . [I gave] more attention to ways of disciplining [students and to improving the] curriculum. . . . My third year [I labeled independent]. C. is no longer here. . . . I was able to adapt more [of the curriculum] because she was not there to judge what I was doing. . . . I felt [she] judged me. . . . I don't know why I didn't really feel comfortable. . . .

Fourth year, independent/master . . . [I was] more daring. Also, we had a new teacher come into our school [who was] a wild woman. Ambitious . . . that rubs off. . . . I see a lot of myself in [her]. She is just excellent. Now, that is not to say that she doesn't get herself into hot water, and when she goes deep, she goes deep, but she is just a wonderful model for teachers—popular with the students, fantastic with curriculum, daring. That helps me to see where I could go. . . . Anything that takes [me] out of [my] comfort zone is great. . . .

I still don't think I'm a master . . . but [I] have a lot of things in place. [For one thing,] in my fourth quarter last year . . . [I changed my entire program] after reading [Atwell's] *In the Middle: Reading and Writing With Students*. . . . That was like, throw out the English book, grammar book, and learn through writing. So all of a sudden I'm thinking, "Well, I haven't really mastered this yet." I'm still . . . learning; I'm sure this is not the last time this is going to happen. . . .

[I'm] student centered. . . . I still cajole them along, and we laugh and . . . have fun. It is not silent all the time, but I still am concerned. I want the kids to work. I want them to really be motivated to work, and a lot of that comes from me. . . . I want to have a loving environment in my classroom where my students can blossom. . . . I still get all the charity cases; when [there is] a kid who needs help, I get [him or her].

Themes and Elements: A Comparison

Kerrie was asked to tell her story in phases, as a way not only of updating the tale, but of seeing if her experience had any relationship to then recently published work on teacher life-cycles to which we turn directly in Chapter 4. This decision to impose an artificial structure on the story affected Kerrie's content decisions. She did not present herself as having "always" been a teacher but rather became one with her first year of teaching. This represents a dramatic change in the story, which is truncated and narrowed as a result of a researcher-imposed decision.

The power of C. to influence Kerrie's actions and feelings about herself are echoed in the first story by her desire to "make sure [she] was not falling behind. . . . " Gradually, she becomes more confident, more powerful, and with this growing confidence, she begins to realize the image of the "perfect" class as she expressed it in the first narrative, but she continues to compare herself to other teachers as a measure of her development.

The "calling" theme is evident in both the first and second interviews and takes the form of a service ethic. This is very important and speaks directly to who Kerrie is as a person, to her core beliefs (see Chapter 5). In the first, she expresses the desire to give of herself to students, while in the second, this theme is even more pronounced: She seeks to create "a loving environment."

The second story conveys a strong sense of a teacher who has hit her stride, enjoys her work, and feels she's making a difference in the lives of young people and is respected by her peers. There seems to be a clear line of development stretching between the first story and the second, illustrating the power of narrative to order experience, and for experience to enrich a narrative.

Kerrie's Expansion

Although my focus was narrowed by the labels I chose, it forced me to think about my teaching in new ways. While searching for labels, I thought back over my teaching experience, comparing myself to others with whom I taught and thinking about their actions in relationship to my own. Suddenly, in my eyes, the older man who taught in the room next door went from being a teacher with wisdom and knowledge to a teacher stuck in a rut, just waiting for retirement. At the same time, I realized that I had my own strong points, which I came to focus on increasingly. Eventually, these were the very skills which others valued in me as well.

Surely all teachers measure their development in some way. In the teacher education program I distinctly remember a discussion on what it meant to be a professional. Professionalism then became a touchstone for me, a kind of standard by which I measured my development and judged the actions of others.

Like other teachers, I knew there were many ways to judge success — the accomplishments and behavior of students, by the ability to achieve school goals, and by making comparisons with other teachers. When the "wild woman" came to our school, she captured my attention. A mature teacher, she was a professional. She was daring, flamboyant, and articulate — demanding and receiving the best from her students. I immediately recognized in her a standard against which to measure myself.

KERRIE'S MOST RECENT TELLING, 1995

My story goes way back, to playing school as a child. It was always fun to do that because my friend's mom was a teacher and she had roll books and things that we didn't have at our house. . . . She had an older sister who would play school with us, [which was] fun. I was a reader. . . . I always paid attention to my teachers in school and the different ways they taught. Unintentionally, without realizing it, I think I was tucking away what they did. Let me give you an example of that. When I was the chorister [in the youth program for my church], I would always watch to see how the [leaders] did things. So it was not hard for me when I became president. Yet I have other people say, "Gosh, I don't know what to do." [When I hear this,] I always think, "What do you mean, you don't know what to do? You have been a teacher for a year and you have been watching what [was done]. Duh! So I think that without realizing it, I tucked away things that teachers did, both good and bad. . . . I can think of teachers [I had]. Then my mom became a teacher; she went to school to become a teacher, and that set a good example for me. . . .

My story is unusual in that I got pregnant, then got married, then graduated from high school. But I was raised thinking that a college education and education in general were important. I knew I needed to pursue those things. My time line was just screwed up. I know my extended family was kind of surprised that I would go back and finish high school that year and then go on to college. To me, it has always been, well, what else are you going to do? . . . Then, with my mom finishing school and encouraging me to go to college, I jumped right in and did it—not without a lot of obstacles, but that didn't matter; that's just part of life, something's going to be hard along the way. . . . I am not a whiner. . . . I went to [a local branch campus] at night while my [two] children were young and studied during the day. That was very enjoyable and fit me perfectly because [classes were] small. . . . I really didn't have a good [idea of what college would be like]. After I had a zillion hours, having taken everything that there was to take, I finally needed to really [get the degree done], so I applied to go to the university during the day once my kids were in school full time. . . .

[The teacher education program at the university] changed my life. I felt a lot of security in the cohort. I met a lot of really good people who were influential. I did my student teaching and I felt like I did a pretty good job. I liked the way I was left alone by my cooperating teacher. I could be in charge of my own kingdom, even though it really wasn't mine. I borrowed it for a while. I liked teaching high school. . . . I think I was the first person [in my group] to get a job, and I was really excited. I lobbied for it. I called up the school district [offices] and told them . . . I would teach junior high. I don't know why I was so anxious; it was early in the year. I graduated in March and had that time to wait, wait, wait. During that time I did some substitute teaching, which was a good experience—to get into other people's classrooms and see how they ran them, what was lax, what was strict, just how different schools had different rules. . . . When I went to be interviewed at [Rocky Mountain Junior High School] in May, the teacher I was going to be [teaming] with came and talked to me. So I got to meet her. She said, "Contact me over the summer." I did contact her, but she really wasn't very friendly about it. I can understand this now, but she was less than cooperative about coming over to school and showing me around and giving me some materials that I was asking for. . . . I am optimistic, so I wasn't put off too terribly much. I liked getting a feel for the building and looking at my room and thinking about how I was going to arrange the chairs. . . .

I went back to the school itself in the late summer, and started decorating the room and organizing the chairs in nice straight rows. . . . It was a new school. . . . The walls went to the ceiling. They were carpeted panels. You could hear through them; you could knock them down if you really wanted to. The classrooms were in a pod, so [from my room I] could see [into other teachers' classrooms] and hear [them teach]. . . . It was not ideal, although it did help when it came to learning what other teachers were doing and how some of them behaved with their children, and how kids reacted to different teachers. I got to watch C. a lot. . . . I can't say that I patterned myself after her but I got to watch her teach what I will call "regular kids" and "honors kids" . . . . [With the honors kids] she was a little bit more rigorous and just moved them a lot faster. . . .

I can compare C. and her rigor now [after teaching for eight years]. What I thought was rigorous [then I now realize] was barely rigorous at all . . . but that is a whole other subject. . . . Eventually [she] left and I became a teacher of the honors track. I felt I was a very popular teacher there—well liked by the students, their parents, and the staff alike. I liked myself because I was creating an environment in which I would want my [own] children to be and in which I liked to be—one that was friendly, hopefully, to all students; a warm, fuzzy place.

Then the principal asked me if I would be the teacher specialist for the school, which [was] a partially administrative job—I did testing of students and really handled things that now [I realize] a principal, counselor, and a secretary would split if that position weren't there. . . . I worked on my master's degree. I took classes all along [while I taught], trying to help myself out with discipline, content matter, writing [issues]. I struggled with curriculum, trying to find a good, creative way to teach [areas] that are hard to teach, like writing. History and geography are pretty straightforward and you can do fun, creative things with those subjects. But when it comes to writing, kids need to write, and the only way they can learn to write is to write. . . . I was searching for something that was lacking in my curriculum. I really loved teaching in the core, especially when it [involved] three periods: English, history, and reading [taught to the same group of students]. It was wonderful to have those kids for three periods and be able to bring them around and give them a rounded education . . . it was great. I think that is the perfect [teaching] situation, but unfortunately [it isn't done anymore at Rocky]. Anyway, I went on to start my master's degree and I discovered Nancie Atwell and her writer's workshop [approach to teaching writing]. You teach them how to write by having them write every day and also read every day. That fit perfectly into the time I had. . . . If there was a real high point for me, really . . . teaching kids something that they couldn't get elsewhere, that was it. When those kids left me . . . they really had something. I had really given them a gift, but I was never able to do it again. . . .

I changed schools. . . . [At Rocky Mountain], I had really adjusted to the kids, and what they were like. . . . They are very different at [Clarke]. . . . [At Clarke] I couldn't have the students for the two periods when I needed to teach them . . . the transition wasn't smooth, anyway. I was finishing up my master's degree and decided that I was ready to go to a school closer to my home. . . . At the time I thought, why am I teaching these kids who seem so foreign to me [including the Cowboys, who were kind of a rural gang]. [Looking back,] I don't think of them that way. . . . Here [at Clarke, I taught] kids who are in my neighborhood, but half of the kids are bused in and are just as foreign as [some of the kids at Rocky] were, maybe even more so because many are inner city [kids]. We live pretty close to the inner city, but this little area seems more suburban. . . . Anyway, I [made the switch]. People would say to me, "Golly, it is hard [to move, isn't it?] You have built yourself a power base." I thought, well, if I could do it once, I could do it twice. That wasn't a concern for me at all. [I felt confident] about being a teacher and being experienced. So I moved to [Clarke]. I was very fortunate to get the job. Someone was taking a leave of absence for the year, so I took her position. It was great to be that close [to my house] and to see kids around my neighborhood—kids who go to the church I go to. I ended up teaching a lot of those students. That was nice. But it was an awful, awful year.

[I did not] have my own classroom. I taught English and history in a home ec room. I moved three times. . . . That was very difficult. You don't realize what . . . you have until you are off in someone else's room. The discipline isn't the same. The room doesn't reflect your personality. Maybe that is just me, I don't know. You don't have all of your stuff right at hand; it is kind of all spread around. You can't arrange things to your liking. . . . [There were other problems—] getting used to a new staff, meeting new people, trying to figure out new copy machines—just basic silly stuff. Having different school rules, different ways of handling things, crazy things like assembly schedules . . . the children were very different. I was used to dealing with a gang of [sorts], [the] Cowboys. Now I had many more racial problems to deal with. [The students] seemed to display more sexual savvy, that type of behavior. That was a struggle—to get used to what the kids were like. They are so diverse. We are talking about kids whose dads are millionaires . . . and kids who live [in the poorest sections of the city]. I mean, that is a lot, a big, a huge variety—half the population is bused in. That was very difficult to get used to.

I had to change my curriculum and take on geography. . . . I had really good support from the department at the school—very friendly; thrilled to share things . . . another huge obstacle, though, was shared governance. I have some really strong feelings about this. If I wanted to be an administrator and mess around with all of that, I would take administrative classes and make more money and do it. To an extent I can see why shared governance is good, but . . . I don't want to waste my time in this inefficient way to run things. Now, maybe people might say that it is unprofessional. . . . I am there to transmit knowledge and mostly to socialize the kids; that is what junior high is all about. So I am not a real fan of [shared governance]. I used to say, "Oh, if I were just at [Rocky Mountain Junior] and the principal could make this decision, not me, who cares?" We had to deal with silly things. There was a lot of fighting. Factions [developed within] the faculty. . . .

I came in with the new principal, a female principal. . . . [the faculty was] a group of more mature people. They [had] been together for a long time; they [were] not transient. . . . The "good ol' boys" ripped up everything the new principal wanted to do. . . . [For example,] the principal was talking about [how there would be a reduction of two teachers the next year]. She [said] if teachers [didn't] come back, we might be okay. The next day . . . [a] teacher who was supposed to retire walked into the faculty room during lunchtime and threw his lunch pail. I can still picture this. [Threw] it on the lunch table and [said], "I'll be damned if I'll make it easy for her!" I mean, he [was] just a jerk! . . . He was miserable. The kids [didn't] like him. He [was] sexist—the kids [would] . . . turn a paper from a girl in and it [would] get an A. They [would] take it back and erase everything and hand it in with a boy's name on it and it [would] get a C−. That [was] just how he [was]. He was a griper and a groaner and a contention maker. This [was] an example of [faculty] kicking against [the principal]. . . .

I spent the first year at [Clarke] struggling along, but still making a lot of friends among the teachers and students. I felt like I was getting somewhere. . . . Toward the end of the year . . . one of the teachers [in the gifted and talented program] was leaving. . . . I applied for the position. . . . I know the way to get to be at home someplace is to get involved, so that is what I do. I asked to be on the School Improvement Council. I volunteered for that the next year

and applied to be considered to be [one of the teachers in the gifted and talented program] and I was chosen . . . you know, I didn't have seniority and really probably shouldn't have gotten the job. . . .

The next year I had my own classroom, which was absolutely delightful. I
could rearrange my chairs the way I liked them . . . I liked more of a U so we
had more of an open space in the center . . . it kind of sets the stage for what
you want to do. [I like having] an open space in the middle for getting down
on the floor. . . . I decorated it the way I wanted, a nice classroom with an office, even, right across the hallway from the telephone and a beautiful view of
the gully, which is a real plus. Then I started working on the curriculum and
getting involved with [the gifted and talented program], which was a real eye
opener. It was extremely rigorous. I had excellent people to work with. But I
felt I had to be kind of low key, an observer. . . . As the year went on, I tried to
assert myself more and tried to make my presence felt a little bit more. I felt
like I was pretty good at accomplishing that slowly. [A program like that] is
not something you can jump right into. So that is what I did. I kind of made
myself at home and made good friends with some of the teachers . . . I felt
like I was fitting in really well and starting to know family names. That is really important when you are teaching, to get to know families. . . .

Then . . . this school year. I was excited about it because I was going to
be teaching geography . . . I had already taught geography for a year, and I
knew that I would be able to add more to it in the [gifted and talented pro-
gram] and add the curriculum [of that program] into the curriculum [of my
regular classes] as well. So I was really looking forward to that. Then, one day
my brother-in-law called me up and said, "I want to write a book, but I need
you to be the ghostwriter of it." I said, "What, come again? I have got a lot of
security and I make good money and you are going to have to pay me." That
is basically what I said. He said [he wanted me] to write it at night, at first. I
said, "You have got to be out of your ever-loving mind. It just won't happen because school is much too draining." So he is paying—actually, I suggested to
him a good, high salary, including career ladder money. [He agreed.] It was really hard to leave Clarke. We kept it quiet for a while. I still continued to teach
for a month after [he made the offer and I accepted it]. The principal let me go
very willingly, which was nice. She said if someone offered her the same opportunity she'd snap it up in a minute. . . .

One thing that I had been searching for and seeking is peace. You don't
find [peace] in a classroom full of thirteen-year-olds. Their language is so bad.
I was really tired—you know, it would be great if you could just go in the classroom and teach, but you can't. It is crowd control, and really, you are just socializing them and teaching them skills. If they pick up any [content] on the
way, that is purely a bonus. It is pretty frustrating. Still, [by leaving] I was giving up a lot. I had just established myself. I had a fantastic classroom. I had
many friends. The kids are great, they are . . . it is easy to sit back and look at
all of the pluses, but when I am driving up the street to run an errand and I see
some of these kids, I think, "Yikes, that kid could wreck a classroom in one
word, or one action." You know, that is where the trauma comes in. The

peace is not there. . . . [It is nice to be home] as opposed to [being with] kids who were using language I don't like, [who] won't stay in their chairs—and their parents are totally out of control . . . it is pretty hard, it is pretty scary, when I think about where our world is headed. . . .

It wasn't Clarke itself that made me decide to leave [teaching] . . . I felt good about it. But this was offering me a chance to be a writer and do something [else]. [It offered me] a new, totally different challenge, to help someone out and make good money doing it. You know, what made it easy was there really wasn't a risk [involved]. I have given up a year of retirement—[assuming I return to teaching next year,] my place is assured. . . . I still see kids [I taught]. I was walking the dog yesterday and I saw a kid who asked, "Is your book done?" "[When it is,] will you come back?" They still want me back. I was over there Wednesday helping with the musical and they still said the same thing—"You *will be back* next year? Well, can you come now?" You know, I don't miss it. I miss those warm fuzzies, but oh, man, there were so few of those. [The good things about teaching are] so much outweighed by the negatives. It is sad; I could cry, it is so sad.

NARRATIVE REASONING: BOB'S EXPLORATION

We get to know Kerrie from the three versions of her story. They illustrate how narratives operate in teacher thinking and serve as a means, by making teacher experience explicit, for teachers to consider their own beliefs and development and for teacher education researchers to gain a glimpse into teacher development. I begin with the second topic, but soon the two intertwine. What I have to say speaks both to general issues of concern to teacher educators interested in narrative and teacher development and to my personal interests, including my relationship with Kerrie. Beginning this way helps to illustrate a point made earlier in the discussion of narrative, that those who hear stories make sense of them in their own particular and peculiar ways. What grips me as I compare and contrast the stories, as I engage in narrative reasoning and make them meaningful in my own way, will be different from what others see. In this process, I am Kerrie's student; and she responds to me as a concerned and generous teacher.

Perhaps it is an obvious point that whose stories are told, and for what purpose, influences what is said, but it is also an easily forgotten truth. The most striking illustration of this in the three stories is when Kerrie revealed in the most recent telling details about her pregnancy and marriage. Other personal information was also shared, indicating that over time our relationship became more trusting. Her willingness to let me further into her story has helped me better understand the complexity of her actions and made me incredibly leery of those who would speak authoritatively for others. As she tells the stories she served for me, as Coles remarked, as both an appreciative and comprehending critic. She enjoyed telling the tales, but even while doing so she was aware of her audience and of how her remarks might be interpreted and misunderstood. Thus, as she criticized shared governance, she was well aware of how readers might judge her view unprofessional, and, anticipating this conclusion, justified her view in ways that would produce understanding and perhaps empathy from other teachers and certainly from me (this issue crops up again in Chapter 8). The act of justifying comes with being a narrator of one's own story. This is further illustrated in the third story, which is partly driven by Kerrie's decision to leave teaching and the need for the story to make sense in relationship to this decision — if not to justify it, at least to make it seem reasonable and ethical, and more than just a mad dash after money.

That stories of self represent a moral orientation is also well illustrated in each of the three versions. Kerrie spoke a good deal about what she wanted for her students and for herself. She sought to create in her classroom an "environment in which I would want my own children to be and in which I liked to be." It was to be a "warm, fuzzy" place where students would learn, where they would receive a "gift" of learning. Having often sat in her classroom, I know and appreciate what she means by "warm" and "fuzzy." I know the texture of her classroom well. As she said, despite her liking her students, she was troubled by some of their behavior, including swearing. She worried about the difficulty of some students' home lives. She celebrated other teachers' skill with curriculum and instruction and sought to learn as she could from those she admired. Prejudice for or against certain students — boys or girls — troubled her. And teachers who would not help a new principal solve school problems called forth anger and condemnation. Kerrie valued collegiality. She was, as Taylor (1989) would say, oriented in "moral space." Narrative reasoning provides a means for taking stock, for checking to see if the self that is being formed is consonant with the self that was imagined when one first began to teach (Pinnegar, 1996). A changed story may be in order.

As a child, Kerrie played teacher. As mentioned, she likely was "called" to teaching (see Serow, 1994), an insight that has led me in a new direction in my own thinking, a direction spurred on by our study of teaching and by watching my own young daughter play school with her friends. I connected viscerally with what she said. Kerrie was very aware of serving an "apprenticeship of observation" (Lortie, 1975); she learned to teach from observing teachers, for both good and bad: Some people are poor models of teaching. Moreover, she was encouraged by her mother to pursue teaching as a career. These factors profoundly affected her thinking about teaching and shaped her conception of her self as a nurturer, a person centered on service: "I want to be able to . . . give of myself. . . . " This is a central theme of Chapter 5, where we explore teacher beliefs. The pre-service cohort confirmed her self-conception, an outcome that pleases me, her former teacher. The most recent telling of her story, however, shows how experience and context can alter beliefs and commitments, however slightly, and how plot may change. For instance, as Kerrie spoke about the aims of teaching, her views changed. In 1986 she wanted to teach "kids how to think — put things together; take things apart." In 1991 she spoke of wanting "the kids to work" and for them to "blossom." But in Clarke, the new school, where she faced classes of inner city students for the first time, she stated that she was "there to transmit knowledge and mostly to socialize the kids; that is what junior high is all about." Yet at this point she also discovered that some young people can respond appropriately and well to an extremely rigorous curriculum, one more rigorous than she'd initially imagined possible when teaching the honors track at Rocky Mountain Junior High School. Thus her beliefs about what young people are capable of, both positively and negatively, changed as a result of her having changed schools and teaching assignments. Surely this is a common phenomenon directly related, for instance, to the problem of the nontransferability of expertise (see Bereiter & Scardamalia, 1993). Changing contexts result in changing stories, changing plots, and changing conceptions of self, a point of great interest in studies of teaching and teacher development.

The first and third versions of the story illustrate the unity that comes from traditional narrative elements — "a setting-complication-resolution structure" (Nespor & Barylske, 1991, p. 810). Kerrie chose what to tell or not tell and what to emphasize or de-emphasize even within the second version, when a phase structure was imposed by me. (More will be said of this second version shortly.) Narratively constructed, the past, it turns out, is dynamic, subject to renewal through ongoing interpretation. Reinterpretation reveals beliefs and produces new insights, new ways of understanding both teaching and oneself as a teacher. There is, then, a point to retelling old stories, as Kerrie was asked to do, but only when retelling involves reinterpreting; otherwise, stories may become fixed, and development may be arrested (Pinnegar, 1996).

It seems that Kerrie's last year at Rocky Mountain Junior High represented a kind of golden age of teaching that served as a basis for her thinking about her work at Clarke. The problems that arose at Clarke — from Kerrie's not having her own classroom; from how the day was organized into fragmented, short, instructional periods; and from Kerrie's confronting classes filled with a wide range of students, including large numbers of inner city young people — were quite foreign to her. Having once experienced a golden age — when she'd taught kids "something that they couldn't get elsewhere" — Kerrie was disappointed in her performance at Clarke and had a horrendous first year there, much worse than her very first year of teaching. The "golden age" influenced how she thought about present experience, just as present experience was the prism that produced the golden age. The story appeared to move toward resolution during the beginning of her third year at Clarke — when, out of nowhere, an offer came from her brother-in-law for Kerrie to write a book, something she longed to do — there is no "Hollywood plot," no happily ever after here (Connelly & Clandinin, 1990, p. 10). With this turn in the tale, Kerrie found herself needing to justify her actions to herself, but also to me, even as she anticipated a possible future outside of teaching — she was tired, desirous of peace, worn down by young people, and looking forward to writing and a better income. Yet she still felt the tug of the classroom and of teaching. This turn in the story-line disturbed me and left me puzzling what to do with our project. I understand her reasoning *better*, now that it has been made explicit, but I certainly don't *fully* understand. This, too, is an issue of profound importance to our inquiry: why would a talented and successful teacher leave teaching? Put positively, what might have been done to strengthen teaching's hold on Kerrie? How would the teaching context and the nature of her work have needed to be changed? These are crucial questions.

Kerrie's story nicely illustrates that the "kind of teacher we are reflects the kind of life that we lead" (Connelly & Clandinin, 1988, p. 27). The kind of person Kerrie is and the kind of life she has led come through clearly in each version of her story, and I am flattered to be included as even a minor character in it. Consider what she revealed about herself: she is not a "whiner"; rather, she is by nature positive and optimistic. Financially cautious, she is a risk taker in other arenas, someone able to "throw out the English book, grammar book" and develop a new program. Having completed a master's degree, volunteered for various school committees, and served as teacher specialist, she was academically and professionally ambitious, a point central to Chapter 8. She appears able to manage the dilemmas of teaching and set problems aside while still seeking solutions. Within the school community she was impatient with teachers who griped and resisted efforts to improve schooling. Yet she seems not to like conflict and to want to please and be recognized by others. Even while she expressed more than a little concern about the lives being lived by inner city young people and the negative effects troubled students can have on teachers and teaching, she liked young people a lot. Although she believed in getting involved in the school community, after years of teaching, she resented being forced to serve in ways that seemed tangential to what she viewed as the proper teaching role. This issue is crucial to understanding her decision to leave teaching. "Territorial" by nature, she liked to have the power to shape her work context. Yet despite having expressed confidence in her ability to teach young people, she accepted that there was much in that context over which she could have no control, no power. What she valued was a "warm, fuzzy" environment where students felt safe and cared for, but she found it increasingly difficult to create such a context. On leave at the time of the third interview, what she desired was "peace," a break from "crowd control." These statements reveal a good deal about Kerrie, and the complex and sometimes contradictory commitments she, and perhaps all teachers, hold. They also tell a good deal about why she left teaching. But they do not tell the whole story, a story that never can be told because it continues to unfold with each telling. As a researcher I find myself increasingly wondering how much of a teacher's life has been revealed to me in an interview, what kind of selection of data has taken place and for what purposes, and whether or not the person presented to me has a strong relationship to the one doing the presenting. After 10 years of working with her, I have a high degree of confidence that the person Kerrie presents to me is Kerrie. Perhaps there is no stronger argument for the value of longitudinal studies than this one.

From the perspective of my growing interest in teaching as a calling, one change is particularly interesting: the place Kerrie gave to her own teachers in each version. As her teaching experience grew, the importance of her teachers diminished; their place in the story was taken by colleagues from whom she learned a great deal. The nature of the influence of her colleagues is especially important to consider. The memories of teaching grounded in her experience as a student were frozen in time. She could return to them, ordering them differently or emphasizing different elements, but narratives of greater value had been forged through teaching and through observing her colleagues teach. With experience, memories of her teachers seemed to lose value, but not the internalized lessons about teaching she learned from them that lived on in her conception of herself as a teacher. Not only did she observe her colleagues teaching; she engaged in narrative reflection following the observations—she thought about what they did in their classrooms as compared to what she did in hers. In the early years this comparison was often unfavorable, and she felt uncomfortable and somewhat insecure: "I really didn't feel comfortable." In later years, however, the comparison often produced confirmation of herself, even while it still held the potential for personal and professional growth. Kerrie asked, "How would C. do that?" Moreover, her self-dialogue was complemented by her ongoing discussions with these teachers about teaching—she compared and contrasted texts with the "wild woman" and the result was an increased understanding of teaching and of herself as teacher.

NARRATIVE REASONING: A RETELLING BY KERRIE

An element of the story that is *not* related here is the impact of my work with Bob—an impact born in part of having long engaged in sharing and exploring stories. In our weekly interviews, he was very careful not to be critical of what I did. Instead, he would question me about my actions and motives, which, in turn, had the same effect as his advice might have had in the long run. As the months and years of our working together passed, I'd find myself wondering, "If Bob were here, what would his questions be regarding my teaching today?" This helped me keep a fresh outlook on teaching. If he had ever been critical or given me advice, I'd have become defensive, rather than reflective and aware of my motives. Ironically, the year I needed him most, my first year at Clarke, we were not actively working together.

What types of questions would Bob ask me that I later knew to ask myself? To quote Taylor (1989) again, "What is good or bad, what is worth doing and what is not, what has meaning and importance for you (and I would add, for the student), and what is trivial and secondary?" And as I recalled my work with Bob early in my career, the notion came clear to me that "I have a specific past that is present to some degree in my present." As I struggled through my first year at Clarke, I knew that though it might be difficult for me, it was still "good," "worth doing," and "meaningful and important." This knowledge helped me continue through adversity. I was more aware of my environment than I had ever been before—and I had been more than well aware of it in the open classrooms at Rocky Mountain. But at Clarke I was in an environment which was *not* warm and fuzzy. I was seldom able to establish the creative, nurturing atmosphere of which I'd been so proud at Rocky.

Although I *played* school as a child, I really *became* a teacher at about the age of eight. Since I'm the oldest of five children, six years older than the next child, I was given a great deal of responsibility for helping with child care at an early age. My mother was from a family of 13 children, and "responsibility" was always a big value for her. It was also one of the issues that pushed me out of the nest early. I felt that if I was going to carry a lot of responsibility at home, I might as well be in charge of a home of my own. By the time I was 16, after honing my skills for eight years, I had discovered that I was good at parenting. My personal identity, then, was one of nurturer and teacher—first to my siblings, and then to my own children.

When my children were in the upper grades of elementary school I took on the next logical "responsibility" and became the teacher of 70 seventh graders. Thus, my "substantial" or core self was right in line with my "situational" self (Nias, 1989). This certainly isn't meant to imply that the way was smooth, without its traumatic and dramatic moments, but it wasn't an extremely difficult transition, either. It seemed to be mostly a series of adjustments to working with a larger group, some of whom didn't always seem to know my (or anyone's) rules. I just expected that since I'd been able to create a warm learning environment in my parents' home and then in my own, I'd once again be able to create one in the classroom.

The first thing that struck me when I read the three stories was the insight I had started out with. In reading my words from nine years ago, I had to recall who I was then. My comment on the territoriality of teachers (assuming others are like me) caught my attention. I've already established that I am a territorial creature by admitting I wanted to start my own home at an early age. This made school a very appealing workplace to me. It also made life difficult when I moved to Clarke because I didn't have a classroom of my own. My first year of teaching, like every year after (except my first year at Clarke), began with arranging desks. I put them in straight rows at Rocky Mountain and kept them that way, moving them into temporary small groupings only until I began Writer's Workshop. Writer's Workshop brought about a total change in my thinking. I liked having the desks in a U formation. Students could easily see one another and we had an open area, like a stage, in the center. When I moved to Clarke, I could no longer arrange the room(s) to my own liking. I was in three different rooms each day and none of them was well arranged.

My territoriality came through in the stories when I commented on teachers as ruling their own little kingdoms. This came out in my first interview with Bob. I continued to think this way, although at different times during the next few years I often felt frustrated with myself for being a follower. I knew I was still learning about teaching and needed the security of watching and learning from others, especially C. But when C. left, I felt empowered and in charge. As difficult as my first year at Clarke was, it was nice to be able to close the door to shut the noise in or out. A closed door allows for some privacy and security when one is experimenting with unconventional ideas. In the exploration simulation "Galleons," for example, students throw wads of paper or paper airplanes into a garbage can to determine their "fates" for the day. Such actions, needless to say, may appear questionable to the casual or curious outside observer—teacher, administrator, or parent.

When Bob asked me to break my career into stages in the second interview, the first stage I outlined was that of follower. As I said, I learned a great deal from C. I was a follower and adapter. I still think of myself as one who doesn't reinvent, but I am *not* a follower. . . . I am an *observer*. While a follower will copy others exactly, an observer watches others, learns, and gleans the good. I tend to watch others: there were my own teachers, my teacher educators, and my children. Then I had watched the teachers I'd taught with, and early on I was indeed a follower. Later I learned from Nancie Atwell and implemented Writer's Workshop in my own way and to my own satisfaction. I continued to observe when I moved to Clarke—including paying attention to the relationships and factions among the teachers. When I started teaching in the gifted and talented program (AAP), I observed carefully. The AAP team required complicated planning among the four teachers involved. At first I wanted to understand the dynamics of the other three teachers' personalities. Then I slowly began to assert myself when I felt more confident about myself and my ability to contribute to the content and methods of teaching.

I noticed my initial workplace scenario. Although I had once valued a silent classroom, by the time of the earliest interview I had a realistic activity-based scenario where my students were working at a variety of tasks at an acceptable noise level. I understood the importance of routines, interaction, and socialization. Those were pretty sophisticated observations to be making at the beginning point of my career. People outside of teaching think that school is only about content. It is not, especially in the middle grades. I realized that as important as content was, it was only a vehicle for teaching students other things. It is amazing to me that the very scenario I outlined before stepping into my own domain was the one that would continue to characterize my ideal classroom. That "warm, fuzzy," busy scenario was to become a career touchstone for me.

I understand Bob's comparison of my three views of the aims of teaching. When I began teaching, my own two children were in the fifth and sixth grades. Possibly influenced by them, I saw my future students as needing basic skills, "how to think—put things together, take things apart." I hadn't let go of these aims by 1991; indeed, I'd *added* to them when I'd said I wanted my students to "work" and "blossom." My own son was in high school then and wasn't applying himself as well as he could have, and this was frustrating. Writer's Workshop influenced me as well. The only way this program can work is if the students apply themselves, if they work. I had seen my students "blossom" in my program, under the sunshine of praise from both me and from their peers. A synergy develops when Writer's Workshop is done well. By 1995, I was teaching geography and AAP at Clarke. I was looking for new ways to make the subject more "user friendly." I have always resisted the urge to be merely a "transmitter of knowledge." If a class could learn from playing a game instead of listening to a lecture, I created a game or contest. Still, subject matter needed transmitting. But even more than that, students needed to learn how to work with others in productive and healthy ways. At times I felt like a social worker. It's hard to focus on curriculum when you're faced with thirteen-year-old gang members who are breathing cigarette breath down onto your desk as you check their work.

At some point I began to think of myself as a student-centered teacher. I certainly hadn't started out that way. I think a teacher has to have a secure foundation and real self-knowledge in order to be ready to give to others. It took me a few years to gain that strength, to firmly know who I was. Here, too, Writer's Workshop played a part. It was a risky program, and because of my success with it I came to be admired. I felt good about myself. My students loved and respected me, my peers were impressed, even the district rewarded my efforts.

When Bob came to my room the next year, the desks were rearranged and class members were busy at work—writing. The change in desk arrangement was the outward sign of an inward change. I encouraged students to go in directions they were comfortable with—within reason. As a result of my trust in them, they felt free to take risks with their writing. When Bob asked me how I accomplished what I did with them, I answered, "By loving them along." The atmosphere was loving and creative. I realized that many other teachers didn't feel the same way about their students. I was willing to create lessons for which I could see a need as evidenced by problems in students' writing. I changed my plans. It was hard to monitor their needs and provide for them.

People often use the word "gentle" to describe me. It is not in my character to be generally hard-nosed. I mention this because as a result, and in conjunction with my teaching style, I often ended up with troubled students, almost right from the beginning at Rocky Mountain. It doesn't take long for counselors and principals to know where to send students who need special consideration. So I am student-centered.

Bob once asked me if I considered myself a "pleaser." I had to say yes. I work hard to fit in. But I also work hard to help others where I see a need, to be organized, to follow through on assignments, to accept responsibility, and to be friendly. These qualities have helped me build a power base. By the 1991 interview, I had worked myself into a position of enviable power in my school—that of teacher specialist. I hadn't lobbied for the job; it had been handed to me.

My colleagues thought I was crazy to leave Rocky, to leave such an easy job. But possibly that was just the point: it was too easy. I was just finishing my master's degree, my curriculum was on automatic pilot, I'd taken all the classes the district had to offer, and I was ready for a change. I felt my neighborhood *needed* me. I wanted to teach children I knew. It also didn't hurt that my local school district paid a lot better.

In retrospect, I see I had adapted to Rocky with little effort. Since I had nothing to compare it to, except for my experiences as a student, I took everything in stride. My two biggest complaints were the lack of classroom walls and the cowboys I taught. Cowboys are a rural gang; they have all the signs and behaviors of gang members. Now, in the new school, I discovered a whole host of differences, problems I needed to deal with. I felt comfortable around my neighborhood students, but the inner city students were just as troublesome as the cowboys had been, possibly even more so because I had to deal with them in the context of my own community. It bothered me that the silent majority of students who never gave me a moment's trouble had to suffer in silence while I disciplined the uncontrollable. Also, I had to adjust to a more mature faculty in a more well-established neighborhood. I had to earn the respect of both. The philosophies of the two schools were very different, too. In the new school everyone was expected to be involved in everything, and few teachers were compliant. In Rocky, few people were expected to be involved, and more staff members were willing to help out. This was a real eye opener.

Clarke practices shared governance. I learned that teachers aren't necessarily the best people to make administrative decisions. As the administrators of our classrooms, we don't ask students to be included in every decision we make. Sometimes a faculty is just too big for efficient decision making, where if one person disagrees nothing can get done. Many years ago, Bob and I agreed that teachers need to be more involved with the goings on in schools; after all, if they don't know the answers to the problems of schooling, who does? The problem is that when a teacher ends up on too many committees, morale suffers. It's too tiring and time-consuming and eats up precious resources that are needed for class preparation.

Rigor? It's rigorous to be a rigorous teacher! Rigor takes a lot of time for preparation, delivery, and then assessment. What I thought was rigor nine years ago I later discovered was busywork. Quantity and quality are not the same.

I loved teaching, even on bad days. Nevertheless, August of 1994 rolled around and for the first time in nine years, I wasn't ready for school to begin. I have nowhere to lay the blame. I had done a good job of guarding against burnout, which had been a cohort topic. I had watched teachers give up before my eyes and not understood it. Fortunately, I had never felt that way myself. I'd just felt the pressures of a "bad" crop of students (we'd been warned about them by their sixth-grade teachers), administrative problems, and teaming expectations. It all turned out to be a little much. While I would have cheerfully and capably kept plowing ahead, I was given a break by my brother-in-law, who made me the offer I couldn't refuse. It was hard to leave. I left students I loved and who loved me as a parent figure. While I have missed them and the warm fuzzies, and teaching, I seldom think of school at all. Sometimes I drive by it and realize that I'm just another member of the community who thinks about the school while driving by or when slowing down for a school zone. I don't know yet if that's enough for me.

A Brief Reaction From Bob

What Kerrie has written illustrates nicely the importance of narrative reasoning as a means for studying one's own practice and nudging along development. Narrative reasoning draws on a fundamental insight about learning to teach, as Pinnegar states: "When a story is reinterpreted it becomes not just a new story but a new experience" and we learn, as she asserts, "*in* experience," not *from* it (1996, p. 13). Interrogating our own stories and engaging in self study purposefully and systematically is one of the most promising means available for fostering teacher development, when teaching is understood as a profoundly personal art form, an expression of a self evolving, as testifying. It is an approach to encouraging teacher development that is too often discounted or dismissed, in part because teacher experience is either ignored or underappreciated in typical development programs, when it should be a central element in teacher education both pre- and in-service (Bullough & Gitlin, 1995).

Narrative reasoning is also a means for identifying issues important to teacher development. Of particular interest are those tied to the interaction between a teacher's life and beliefs, and her work conditions. It is in this interaction that we find a fuller understanding of Kerrie's decision to leave teaching.

Questions for Consideration

1. When you tell a story of your life, of the evolution of your decision to become a teacher, what themes stand out, what critical incidents or important events or people? What factors were most influential in shaping how you think of teaching and yourself as a teacher? How were they influential?

2. As you read the first telling of Kerrie's story, were memories stirred? What similarities to your own story did you notice? What differences?

3. Were you "called" to teach? If so, how did you know you were called? How does being called influence your teaching?

4. Can you break up your own career into phases, as Kerrie did in her second telling? What phases would you use? How would you characterize your current phase? Where are you heading developmentally? (What do you think will be your next phase?) Do you like where you seem to be heading? Assess the trajectory of your career.

5. If you were to write or tell a teaching narrative, what hopes for yourself and for your students are revealed? What do these reveal about your place in your school and your developmental stage?

6. Much of what teachers become comes from observing other teachers and from how teachers are perceived. What do others perceive from watching you? Is this how you want to be perceived?

7. In telling a narrative of your development as a teacher, what has changed over the years? Are you pleased with the changes? How has the context within which you have worked either enabled or limited these changes?

4

Narrative Reasoning
and Public Theory:
Teacher Life Cycles and
Developmental Stages

Besides interrogating one's own stories as a means for encouraging development, stories can be compared and contrasted to what others have beheld and judged important and made explicit. As embedded in narrative, private theory can be compared and contrasted to public theory (see Griffiths & Tann, 1992), which often takes a propositional and impersonal form. Yet embedded in the propositions of public theory there often resides a kind of story (see Bullough, 1996). This is not surprising. To account for events, to explain them, involves linking actions and establishing relationships among actors even when the actors are nameless, faceless, and representative of central tendencies, a tale about how people often act under certain conditions. Through comparing and contrasting stories and public theory, both can be illuminated and seen differently, and self-knowledge can be extended. Drawing again on Coles's imagery, the outcome is that our field of vision is enlarged and we are able to engage increasingly complex problems and see new possibilities for solving them (see Prawat, 1991).

In this chapter, we engage in narrative reasoning as a means for testing public theory and for enriching private theory, both important aspects of teacher development. Through this process, we believe the gap between private and public theories can be narrowed even as their differences are heightened, an outcome that has important educational consequences and speaks to the question "How can research be made meaningful for teachers?" The importance of making such comparisons is hinted at in the second version of Kerrie's story, which was told in phases, and the way in which the story was fundamentally changed by the phased structure.

Given researcher interests and the nature of public theory, it is easy to neglect or discount teacher experience or to accord it too high a status and to ignore the tensions between that experience and public theory when such tensions hold potential for illuminating and perhaps correcting misperceptions, misunderstanding, and false beliefs. As presented here, narrative reasoning lends authority to teacher experience (see Munby & Russell, 1994), while providing means for exploring it. All three stories presented in the preceding chapter will be drawn upon here and points of similarity and tension will be identified.

Huberman's life-cycle work was selected for analysis because of the light it sheds on teacher development generally and on mature teachers specifically. Other theories could have been selected for analysis, including stage theories or even instructional theories because they also can be easily slipped into a narrative form, usually as a case in this instance, and teachers frequently think with cases when making instructional decisions. At the conclusion of the chapter, we will include a brief discussion of Ryan's stages of teacher development (1986) because they were used to organize the data reported in *First Year Teacher: A Case Study* and because there has been some controversy surrounding the value of such theories for understanding development (see Grossman, 1992). Shortcomings of the approach then will be noted. However, we wish to underscore a general point, that each of these theories can be useful to teachers as a fruitful means for thinking about their development and the trajectory of that development. This is precisely how we use Huberman's (1989) stages in this chapter, as a means for thinking about Kerrie's development, while simultaneously illustrating a particular version of narrative reasoning. Finally, we should mention that Chapter 6 touches on David Berliner's studies of teaching expertise and stage theory (1986, 1988, 1990, 1994).

LIFE CYCLES AND TEACHER DEVELOPMENT

We begin with a brief overview of Huberman's work. Huberman describes the career pathways of teachers in terms of phases, starting with two rough categories: easy or painful beginnings. Kerrie's beginning was easy. "Easy beginnings involve positive relationship with pupils, manageable pupils, the sense of pedagogical mastery, and enthusiasm" (Huberman, 1989, p. 42). The themes of this period are "survival" and "discovery" (p. 33). Between the fourth and eighth years of teaching, a second phase begins, "stabilization" or "stabilizing." "The theme invariably contains two features. . . . The first has to do with pedagogical stabilizing: feeling at ease in the classroom, consolidating a basic repertoire, differentiating materials and treatments in light of pupils' reactions or performances. The second feature has to do with commitment to the profession . . . " (p. 42). From stabilization, Huberman concludes that teachers move (in six to ten years) in different directions, toward experimentation or reassessment. He describes experimentation this way: "Once a basic level of classroom mastery is achieved, there is a need for refinement and diversity. On the one hand, informants come to see that they can get better results by diversifying their materials and their modes of classroom management. On the other, they feel the stale breath of routine for the first time" (p. 43). Reassessment "is a phase with multiple scenarios. . . . For some, it is the monotony of daily life in the classroom, year after year, that induces reassessment and self doubts. For others, it is a disenchantment with the outcomes of successive reforms, in which they have participated energetically, that sets off the 'crisis'" (Huberman et al., 1993, p. 8). Drawing on others' research, Huberman and his colleagues (1993) notes that:

> . . . the deepest *crisis* period in men began at age 36, and lasted as long as 55. The problem appeared to ride, above all else, on questions of professional advancement. 'Am I going to climb up the career ladder? Do I want to spend the rest of my life in the classroom?' On the other hand, the analogous moment of self-doubt in women tended to come at a later period (around 39 years of age), was shorter in duration (until age 45) and appeared less connected to professional successes *per se* than to unwanted aspects of the job definition or to unpleasant working conditions. (p. 9)

MAKING COMPARISONS AND TESTING THEORIES

Kerrie came to teaching already thinking of herself as a teacher, one who would create an active classroom, where students were busy learning and interacting and were well behaved. She enjoyed easy beginnings as she assumed a teaching role at Rocky Mountain Junior High School. The themes Huberman identified of survival and discovery are both evident in her story, although her survival within the classroom appears never to have been a serious issue. She was "shaky on curriculum" and uncertain about appropriate student behavior. During the early years of teaching, Kerrie discovered a good deal about teaching and about herself as a teacher. Some of what she learned came from observing and openly borrowing from C., the more experienced teacher who had played a part in hiring Kerrie. She learned about her students and about how to design a curriculum that would engage them appropriately. Gradually her independence and self-confidence grew and she became "more daring." And just as Huberman suggests, she began "consolidating a basic repertoire, differentiating materials and treatments in light of pupils' reactions or performance" (1989, p. 42).

A dramatic change followed. Long having been unhappy with her writing program, but uncertain what to do about it, she encountered Nancie Atwell's (1987) book *In the Middle: Writing, Reading, and Learning with Adolescents* and discarded her entire program, and with it three years of curriculum work. At this point in the story, signs of the experimentation phase noted by Huberman are evident, and the timing appears about right. So far, the three versions of Kerrie's story fit relatively comfortably within the theory.

A surprising turn of events follows at this point in the story, events which move Kerrie's career path outside Huberman's scheme. Kerrie was very satisfied with her program and making good progress toward mastering it when she decided to change jobs. She stated that she wanted to teach at a school closer to home, work with students whom she assumed she already knew, and looked forward to an increase in pay. Her move to Clarke Intermediate School, and the reasons given for the move, touch on Huberman's discussion of "reassessment." Clearly she was not bored with her work at Rocky Mountain, but she wanted a change nonetheless. To this point in the story, Kerrie's career path appeared to move from stabilization to experimentation to reassessment. This is an unusual path. Kerrie's reassessment, however, is not about whether to teach or not; that came later. Nor did she raise career advancement questions, which were satisfied by Kerrie's being appointed a teacher specialist by Rocky Mountain's principal. Nor was she unsatisfied with the work. These are all questions the theory proposes.

She simply was ready for a change, a new challenge, and she wanted to work nearer home. Later we will return to this point.

As an experienced teacher, Kerrie felt confident about the move to Clarke. Nevertheless, she was severely tested by the teaching conditions she encountered there, including a change in subject areas, not having her own room, and her unfamiliarity with inner city students, a problem she had not anticipated, given that she lived in the neighborhood of the school. As Huberman observes (see 1989, p. 54), context changes represent an issue he could not fully address with his data and contextual changes are central to Kerrie's experience. A tension emerges.

Despite her strong experience as a teacher, because of conditions at Clarke, Kerrie had an "awful, awful year." In many respects, she was once again a first-year teacher facing the problem of learning how to teach a different group of students; it was a painful beginning. The themes of discovery and survival return, although they are encountered from the perspective of a teacher who had already succeeded in one teaching context, and this is a dramatic difference that added to her disappointment. Near the end of the first year she began to stabilize, learning how to work effectively with the students, and began to feeling more at home within the school. Accepted within the gifted and talented program, and finding herself dependent on the experienced teachers within it, she found herself in a subordinate position: "I felt I had to kind of be low key, an observer. . . . " The program was, she said, "not something you can jump right into." It appears as though before Kerrie was able to stabilize, before she had settled fully into the school and had consolidated a basic repertoire for engaging inner city students, she found herself in an experimentation phase, with all its uncertainty. Then, suddenly, near the beginning of her third year of teaching at Clarke Intermediate, just when she seemed most confident about the geography curriculum and appeared to be stabilizing, she was offered the opportunity to change careers. With this offer she reassessed her commitment to teaching. Prompted by the offer, and consistent with Huberman's research, as noted above, she reflected on her work and the teaching role she occupied and entered a crisis, brief and intense. Observation notes taken at the time indicated that Kerrie seemed distant and somewhat disengaged from teaching as she considered her situation, her future, and her brother-in-law's offer. She took a leave of absence. She emphasizes that she did not seek to leave teaching, but that working conditions and growing frustrations with teaching made leaving attractive when the offer came. Recall her statement that she was "seldom able to establish the creative, nurturing atmosphere" in Clarke that she'd created at Rocky Mountain Junior High School.

The pace of these changes is dizzying. No one could have predicted the offer from her brother-in-law, or the rapid changes in teaching assignment. However, the potential of such changes to undermine teacher competence are well understood, although often undervalued (see Yee, 1990). The direction of Kerrie's career path seems less linear than circular; she spins outside the expected pathways, although some of Huberman's language remains helpful for thinking about her experience. She seemed to go through spirals — sometimes very tightly wound and compressed — of stabilization-experimentation-reassessment, sometimes stimulated by personal decisions, such as to discard her established curriculum in favor of a variation of Atwell's Writer's Workshop, and sometimes prompted by contextual changes, like the reassignment to the gifted and talented program.

The patterns of Kerrie's development enrich understanding of life-cycle research by pointing to the importance of context and of individual commitments and actions to the direction a career takes and to the reasons teachers act and move from one phase to another. At the same time — and if we now think of theory as Coles did, as a means for orienting vision, for seeing differently and more broadly — knowledge of life-cycle research brings with it the possibility of enriching understanding of Kerrie's and other teachers' stories. Thus, when considered in relationship to public theory, individual stories may take on additional meaning both for readers of those stories and for those whose stories are told. Each brings a different truth to the study of teaching.

"A career . . . is constructed through continuous processes of personal negotiation and interpretation within a work setting" (Yee, 1990, p. 121). When seen through life-cycle research, the negotiation of Kerrie's career, her story, takes on additional meaning. Even when the fit is not a good one, Huberman's concepts are potentially enlightening; they point in the direction of issues and concerns pertinent to her feelings of self-worth as well as to her future development as a teacher. We believe the same is likely true for exploring other teachers' stories of development. Moreover, as Kerrie suggests, they may have value even for beginning teachers. This is most certainly the case for Ryan's stages (see Bullough, 1989) and Berliner's stages of teaching expertise.

INTERROGATING THE STORY AND DIGGING DEEPER

Comparing Kerrie's story of development with life-cycle research leaves some questions unanswered, questions which become occasions for digging a little deeper into the private theories or beliefs that grounded Kerrie's classroom actions and moved her development along pathways that sometimes parallel and sometimes depart from those proposed by life-cycle research. Since the spirit of narrative reasoning is conversational and fluid, we took the opportunity to pose a set of questions of the sort that we have often explored through interview and in discussion. The questions were intended not only to keep our conversation about teacher development going, without which understanding is not likely to deepen, but to reveal more about the personal theories that underpin teacher understanding and action, generally. Self-knowledge does not come easily; it is only hard won, even though it is inevitably limited. Several questions came to mind; three were asked.

• How did Kerrie know that it was time for a change, that stabilization needed to give way to experimentation? Knowledge of this kind — self-regulatory knowledge (Bereiter & Scardamalia, 1993) — is extremely important for fruitfully and intelligently directing one's development as a teacher.

• Were there times when the pace of change was too rapid, and if so, what means were used or would have been helpful for better managing the context to achieve desired ends? Teachers often think about development in personal terms, without fully attending to context. Asking this question seemed particularly important, given the role unfavorable work conditions ultimately played in Kerrie's decision (indeed, in many teachers' decisions) to leave teaching (Boyle et al., 1995) and how burnout is often thought of as an individual failing, a matter of a candle flickering and dying out, rather than a systemic failure (Bullough, 1989). Thinking about teacher development contextually is central to long-term professional growth, as will be discussed later.

• What has Kerrie learned about herself and teaching as a result of her reassessment of commitments? Taking stock from time to time, pausing to consider where one is and where one is heading, is crucial to future development. It is a matter of becoming a student of one's own development.

Rather than discuss these questions in interview, Kerrie wrote about them and we discussed what she wrote. Although it is time consuming, writing is a powerful means of achieving greater self-knowledge and clarity.

Kerrie Elaborates

How is one to know what other teachers are experiencing except through gossip? (And gossip may be a form of narrative reasoning, where stories are compared and much is learned.) Maybe it would have been beneficial for us to consider in the cohort [preservice teacher education] the stages a teacher is likely to experience throughout a career as a way for thinking about our own development. But we didn't.

What prompted me to change, to experiment? No matter what goals a person has, you can handle only so much at a time. So while I realized within the first couple of years that I was doing a poor job of teaching writing—in fact, not really teaching it at all—I knew it was a challenge for another day. Once I had the basics down—knew what my routines would be, knew my content, had a discipline style I could live with, and felt comfortable with the myriad chores an educator has to do—then and only then could I feel ready to experiment. After all, I had to have something to experiment with. There always came a time when I felt compelled to make a change, when things would get a bit too tidy—that was the time. Also, I was always taking classes and thinking about teaching, so I was prepared for moments of inspiration, when I would have an epiphany, a feeling that was impossible to ignore.

I have occasionally tried to move my students along too quickly, then have had to stop and regroup, slow down, or go back to recover ground. As I look back, it seems I may have moved myself too quickly or been moved too quickly, but school circumstances often limit opportunities. After my first difficult year at Clarke, it would have been a good idea to try a second year in my own room and see what adjustments I could make to the curriculum, and to learn more about the students. But I didn't see those as options. The context required something else. First of all, we were being moved into teams. I would be the geography teacher on a geography-English–pre-algebra team. This would have given me six straight periods of the same preparation, a job I didn't relish. (I like variety.) Second, AAP was expanding and a position was open. Opportunities like that don't come often and have to be taken when they arise. I had taught in a gifted and talented program at Rocky Mountain and knew the rewards that come from working with bright, motivated students. Third, the school district would pay for my gifted and talented teaching endorsement. There seemed no other choice but to move quickly, even though I would not say I had stabilized.

As difficult as my first year at Clarke was, I had two open periods, one for personal preparation and one for team preparation. Although I was teaching a new subject, geography, the other teachers in the department helped with curriculum and I had my writing and reading programs well enough in hand that I often had some free time at the end of the day. This led me to volunteer to be history department chair for the next year. The next year came and I soon found myself spread too thin. Aside from these voluntary assignments, I was on the seventh-grade team, which required a lot of coordination among the three of us. I had to prepare for AAP and was taking gifted and talented endorsement classes. Toward the end of the year, I also helped with the production of the school musical after school. By the end of the year I knew I had taken on more responsibilities than was wise. I made a pact with another teacher to not volunteer for *anything* extra. The only problem was that once I was seen as capable and helpful, I would never be quite as free again. Pleasing others has its consequences.

I have had two chances at a new beginning. Compared to other first-year teachers, I definitely had an easy beginning at Rocky Mountain, then continued to make improvements over the years. When I moved to Clarke, I *expected* to have a second easy beginning. But both Bob and I label it a painful beginning. I have thought about that. I had come so far in my professional development, I expected to pick up at Clarke where I had left off at Rocky Mountain. By Huberman's (1989) definition—"positive relationships with pupils, manageable pupils, the sense of pedagogical mastery, and enthusiasm"—the move to Clarke was a second good beginning; at least, it was no worse than the first year at Rocky Mountain. Then where does the "painful" label originate? I had become a good teacher at Rocky Mountain; the difference was that at Clarke *I* knew things could be better than they were, even if the students did not know. Although it was a painful beginning for me, it wasn't a difficult time for my students. To all outward appearances, the curriculum was top-notch and classes were well organized and routinized. I suffered through an adjustment period; it was a time of discovery, as Huberman suggests.

I find it interesting that Huberman seems to speak of reassessment somewhat negatively. Reassessment need not be negative. In fact, I found myself reassessing continually. Monotony or repetition is part of teaching, thank goodness! That very quality allowed me to free up my energies for curriculum development or to experiment with discipline. While I can see that not all teachers want to spend their lives in the classroom, especially due to difficult working conditions, they have the option to do as I did—make a change, switching schools or grade levels.

It was not difficult working conditions that led me to change schools. I think it was the opposite. I was successful at Rocky Mountain, and I wanted to apply that expertise more closely to home. While Huberman cannot fully explain why teachers make changes, and Bob states, "she simply was ready for a change, a new challenge," I do know why I changed. Reassessment caused me to take a look at my context, both at school and at home. I felt the pull of my neighborhood. For me, I felt that I'd practiced on strangers and now I was ready to teach the people I knew. Again, context is important.

At both Rocky Mountain and Clarke, teaching became a better job for me as time went on. Viewed from the outside, it seems obvious that teaching would get better because of the amount of time I spent improving my teaching skills and getting to know the student population better. While this is true, there are other reasons perhaps of greater importance—my growing friendships with the staff in each school, my knowledge of school policies, my involvement in each school's activities, and so on. Basically, I came to feel at home at school. In answer to the last question, the more involved I became, the happier I was at school. Being happy at school comes through in the classroom. I could tell that my students respected my involvement in the school community. Having their respect added to my feelings of having power and contributed to my desire to improve as a teacher. I can't help but compare myself to the teacher I referred to in the 1995 version of my story, the one who was ready to retire. He was miserable and uncommitted, and so, in turn, made his students miserable. They felt no commitment to him or his classes. In contrast, I was happy and committed and my students responded to me accordingly. I was in teaching for the long haul or I wouldn't have changed schools in the first place. I saw myself making the change early in my career and then becoming an institution at Clarke. Whatever problems came my way due to the move I accepted because I thought I would have plenty of time to work them through down the road.

PERSONAL THEORIES, PERSONAL COMMITMENTS

Here we learn a bit more about what Kerrie believes motivated her and what inspired her to action, and as a result we get a fuller view of the person embodied in the teacher role. Kerrie is not a worrier. She set problems aside, like her unhappiness with her writing program — "a challenge for another day" — until she had the energy and knowledge to respond fully. But if worrying was not a source for motivating teacher change, what is? Kerrie responded: when things got "a bit too tidy," she changed. She changed when she became too comfortable, but from what she writes, she seldom was comfortable; stabilization was rare. She took courses, pursued an endorsement in gifted and talented education, and sought out and responded to opportunities for an expanded teaching role presented by the context. She seemed to be a risk taker who was ambitious and who liked and needed "variety" in her teaching assignment. Happiness came from involvement in the local school and wider community; feelings of being alive and mattering come for her through service, a central value we will explore more fully in Chapter 5. She had high expectations for herself, which helps account for her feelings of going through a second "painful beginning" upon her move to Clarke. And we learn that what her students thought of her — especially that they respected her as a teacher and community member — motivated her to improve her practice and extend her involvement in the school. In this she undoubtedly was quite typical; good teachers care what their students think.

Taken together, these beliefs or private theories played a central role in Kerrie's development as a teacher. Without attending to them, it is not possible to understand much of her behavior, and yet such qualities necessarily are ignored by stage theories of teacher development, which generally fail to explain movement from one stage to the next just as contextual variables are typically missed.

NARRATIVE REASONING REVISITED

Narrative reasoning may take different forms. Here we have interrogated stories as data and in relationship to public theory to illustrate a type of narrative reasoning that we believe has the potential for enabling teacher development and to introduce a theory of teacher life cycles that we found useful for exploring Kerrie's experience. The use of narrative as a means for exploring, testing, and ultimately generating public theory is too little understood. We believe it holds great promise as a means for encouraging teacher development but also as a means for generating public theory when themes are identified that cut across stories or patterns emerge that reveal common elements in teachers' experience of teaching. In turn, as we noted, public theory can call attention to unrecognized story elements, illuminate private theory, and be a means for reconsidering storyline or plot. Public theory, for example, may provide a language useful for exploring experience, and through the use of this language, aspects of that experience are revealed for the first time and increasingly sensitive and ever finer discriminations may be made that enhance understanding. Such concepts as "easy" and "painful" beginnings and "stabilization," for instance, proved useful for both of us as we explored Kerrie's stories. In short, public theory, although frequently discounted by teachers as irrelevant to practice, is a means for gaining perspective and for encountering and then posing new questions about one's development as a teacher.

The power of narrative reasoning is not always fully evident, however. Its influence is often subtle, indirect, private, or unrecognized. This is one of the reasons we thought it important to share a few of the effects we experienced from writing this and the preceding chapter, and of engaging in narrative reasoning.

Kerrie. One of the great lessons I learned from Nancie Atwell is that writing is recursive. A writer revisits the written piece many times through the drafting, editing, and publishing process. What I should have seen was that teaching is also recursive. I mastered some teaching techniques each year only to get a new group of students the next year that gave me a new set of problems to deal with. I've revisited old problems and thought of them in new ways and with differing outcomes. One issue stands out: although I was taught to weigh the consequences of my actions, when it comes to teaching, I realized I took advantage of what was directly before me rather than thinking about the consequences. This is a problem. I reacted to my context. This tendency had an impact on me during my second year at Clarke, when I really took on too much. If I go back to teaching, I'll be slower to jump into the middle of things. I'd like a year to get back into the curriculum, to get to know the students and new programs. Plenty will come my way without my seeking it.

The bottom line is that telling my story and comparing versions was good for me. Personally, I don't care much about how it helps the teacher education researcher community; it's the person in the classroom who counts for me. I became aware of the value of my story during my first year of teaching. Bob's questions forced me to reflect on what I did and why I did it. The value of sharing stories continued to linger with me over the years. One day when I was teacher specialist at Rocky, I watched a gifted first-year teacher leave the building in tears. I saw the need to form an informal group of first-year teachers (there were seven that year) into a support group of sorts. I realized that they were going through what I had gone through five years earlier, but with no Bob to talk to. Together they made it through that first year and much of what we did was to share and compare stories, mine and theirs, and that's powerful.

Bob. Over the years, I thought I had come to know Kerrie quite well. Nevertheless, our latest interview and what she wrote brought new insights. For instance, I hadn't fully realized how my interviews with Kerrie had influenced her thinking, that she used my questions as a means of reflecting on her practice. I found myself thinking about my responsibilities as a researcher in slightly new ways as a result of this insight and worried anew about the interpretations I have made of her work and about how we work together. I must admit, when she told me that she planned to take a leave of absence from teaching, I struggled to understand her feelings. Initially, I experienced a rush to judgment. As I have read a good deal of the literature on teacher burnout and retention, my initial reaction was to try to fit her experience into a familiar category, Yee's "good-fit leavers" (1990), for example. I should have known better. Rather than listen to her, I grabbed a bit of public theory to explain what was going on. But she did not fit the category, at least, not completely, and now I better understand why.

By my thinking about Kerrie's story of her development in relationship to life-cycle research, particularly about the tensions, my understanding of the importance of context has been sharpened, especially with respect to how limited the opportunities for change often are and how teachers must work very hard to take advantage of them. As already noted, Kerrie's story, and particularly her discussion of how she came to think of herself as a nurturer, has heightened my interest in teaching as a calling, and in the relationship between mothering and teaching, which we will explore in Chapter 5. This has had a profound impact on my work. I found myself engaging in another form of narrative reasoning—I compared my first-year experience and my decision to leave teaching and return to graduate school with Kerrie's story. I discovered that one major difference between us was that I failed to get involved in the school community and left teaching feeling quite alienated from other teachers. In contrast, and ironically, Kerrie got heavily involved and was overwhelmed and left. Nevertheless, this was a painful personal insight into who I am and into who I was as a teacher. These are but a few of the outcomes of our venture into narrative reasoning; others will follow.

IN CONCLUSION: STAGES, ONE MORE TIME

Data for *First Year Teacher* were organized around Ryan's stages of teacher development. Drawing on and extending the work of Fuller (Fuller & Brown, 1975), Ryan (1986) proposed four loose but identifiable stages: A "fantasy" stage, a "survival" stage, a "mastery" stage, and an "impact" stage. During the fantasy stage, the neophyte imagines what teaching will be like and dreams about being like the wonderful teachers of her past. The fantasy is interrupted by student teaching but returns for those who continue in their resolve to become teachers. The transition from student teaching to a first job often proves shocking. The beginning teacher quickly discovers that in various ways past experience has been inadequate to the job; the fantasy crumbles and the survival stage begins, a fight for one's professional life as problems with discipline and management intensify. For most beginning teachers, Ryan asserts, the survival stage is over by midyear. For many, like Kerrie, it ends earlier, much earlier. The three stories provide ample evidence of the utility of Ryan's categories for thinking about teaching and teacher development.

The mastery stage is the "craft stage, where the new teacher begins to learn the craft of teaching in a step-by-step fashion" (1986, p. 14). Having generally gained control over discipline and management problems, the beginner focuses, more or less systematically, on the improvement of particular instructional skills and on curriculum issues. At this stage, achieving improved student learning replaces achieving good student behavior as the dominating concern. A teacher reaches the "impact" stage, which corresponds roughly to Berliner's "proficient" stage (1986), when she is on top of her game, when she understands what needs to be done to engage students in learning and does it — declarative and procedural knowledge are joined, and the result is student learning. This stage comes, if it comes at all, after a few years' experience.

Ryan's first three stages accounted rather nicely for the data gathered during Kerrie's first year and one half of teaching, or so it seemed while we were writing *First Year Teacher*. The "mastery" stage seemed to come into play before the Christmas break. Still, a warning was offered:

> There is a tendency among those who use stages as a means for thinking about human development — and among their readers — to reify the stages, that is, to assume they are actual things with clearly discernible boundaries. Nothing could be further from the truth. Human development defies easy categorization. It is seldom smooth, never conflict free, and frequently characterized by backsliding. Such is the story of Kerrie's first year of teaching. (Bullough, 1989, pp. 17–18)

The three versions of Kerrie's story suggest that perhaps an even stronger qualification was needed; stage theory has several limitations, some of which are revealed by checking the theories against teacher experience, as we have done here.

A few issues deserve mention. While it is true that for many beginning teachers, discipline and management problems arise early and play a central part in their development, much depends on how these two concepts are understood and how the problems associated with them are framed, as well as the kinds of systems schools have in place to address them. Such problems might originate in lack of knowledge of various kinds, of student ability and modes of learning, of appropriate instructional procedures and routines, of institutional roles, of content, and of self, or from a simply horrible teaching assignment. As we discovered, the move to Clarke Intermediate and encountering a new set of students actually resulted in Kerrie's becoming concerned about discipline problems after she had long since set them aside at Rocky Mountain Junior High School. Lack of knowledge about students was a major contributing factor to this apparent developmental slippage — which was painful *because*, based on her prior experience, she knew that her classes and her teaching could be much better than they'd been at Clarke and because she did not know the students as well as she'd thought she would. Stage theories tend to underplay context, and contextual differences — class size, student behavior, teaching assignment, presence or absence of collegial interaction, school and district policies about discipline, and even, as we have seen, the failure to have one's own classroom — are crucial to the direction of development and to determining what development takes place. As Rich observes, speaking of stages related to teaching expertise, "within each stage stability is assumed. The individual is placed in a particular category of expertise with little concern for the arena where the expertise is played out" (1993, p. 138). The linearity inherent in stage theories presents some problems. Grossman (1992), for example, observes that management, instruction, and curriculum issues are often and necessarily addressed simultaneously, and not sequentially, by beginning teachers; such decisions are of a piece, interwoven, inseparable. A concern for technique — how to gain control — does not necessarily precede the concern for the moral dimension of the teacher-student relationship. Clearly this was the case for Kerrie, although management problems initially demanded most attention.

Stage theories are descriptive and fail to account fully for movement from one stage into the next. In Chapter 6, this issue will be addressed directly through the work of Bereiter and Scardamalia (1993) and in relationship to the emergence of teaching expertise where idiosyncratic personal qualities of the kind mentioned above and contextual factors both prove important. They are always important, and they deserve careful consideration by individual teachers as they ponder where they are developmentally, where they are headed, and how their work is both constrained and enabled by the contexts within which they work. As Bereiter and Scardamalia imply, not all teachers are equally committed to teaching, and not all are concerned with improving their practice; who teachers are as people and what they believe about themselves and about teaching and learning either encourage or discourage development. Narrative reasoning helps identify these and other shortcomings associated with using stages to make sense of teacher experience while potentially revealing possibilities.

If these difficulties are genuine, what, then, becomes of stages and stage theory as means for understanding teacher development? They remain what they have always been, loose conceptual tools for thinking about development, albeit in general terms; they are heuristically useful, as Kerrie suggests, and this is important. But one must be wary. Models frame problems, and in framing them, offer preferred solutions that exclude other, perhaps more promising, possibilities for understanding: "A theory can be used to kill facts or create them" (Rieff, 1966, p. 84). One sees what one looks for; beliefs guide action. Stages tend to mask the mystery and majesty of human development, which must not be forgotten in attempts at sense making. Narrative reasoning, when public theory is confronted by the authority of teacher experience, returns a measure of the mystery.

Questions for Consideration

1. How does your career pattern fit into the cycles suggested by Huberman? Are there parallels between your career and Kerrie's? What are they? What factors have prompted changes in the direction of your career? Have you experienced periods of stabilization and experimentation? Does stabilization sometimes last too long, making you feel as though you are in a rut? If so, what might help you get out of it and feel more alive professionally?

2. Kerrie was asked to respond to three questions, two of which follow in revised form: How do you know that it is time for a change in your teaching, that stabilization needs to give way to experimentation? Are there times when the pace of change is too rapid for you, and if so, what means do you use or would you like to use that would allow you to better manage your work context to achieve desired ends?

3. Do Ryan's stages accurately describe your experience as a teacher? If so, can you identify the factors that have influenced movement from one stage to the next? What are they?

4. What place does public theory have in your thinking about teaching and learning? Do you find that public theory influences private theory? Is the converse also true? Do the private theories you hold influence your views of public theory? What is the nature of this influence? For example, do your private theories prompt you to discount public theory? If they do, how might this be a problem? Or do you seek to create a conversation between public and private theory of the kind characterized by narrative reasoning? What is the proper relationship between public and private theory?

5

Changing Beliefs and Changing Teaching Metaphors

Teacher beliefs and teacher practice have a dynamic relationship; beliefs shape practice (Zahorik, 1990), but practice also shapes belief (Grossman & Stodolsky, 1994). Similarly, school contexts, including students, who represent the most influential contextual component, the one that matters most to teachers (Lortie, 1975) and institutional arrangements shape both beliefs and practice, enabling and limiting meaning and action. Given the complexity of these relationships, it is difficult to know quite where to begin to sort them out, but sort them out we must if a richer understanding of teacher development is to result from our inquiry.

We begin with beliefs. Some years ago Gary Fenstermacher (1978) suggested that the aim of teacher education is to influence the grounds upon which teachers make decisions, to encourage "reflection on the bearing of facts upon the learner's beliefs" (p. 168). In some fundamental sense, then, teacher development is about developing beliefs, perhaps changing them, perhaps strengthening, refining, or discarding them (Borko & Putnam, 1995). Moreover, school improvement is dependent on just such an outcome (Prawat, 1992).

In this chapter we focus on developing, changing, and discarding beliefs about teaching. Our aim is not only to illustrate how beliefs are necessarily at the center of virtually all discussions of teacher development, including shared teaching stories, but also to show how extraordinarily complex and difficult it is to change beliefs, when change is deemed desirable, even while recognizing that teacher growth is dependent on just such an outcome. The challenge for teachers — and for those who work with them — is to progressively overcome the blindness of belief, to confront the ways in which interpretations grounded in belief mask the educational possibilities residing in teaching situations. Just as teachers hold beliefs, beliefs hold teachers.

Necessarily, a rather lengthy discussion of the role of beliefs in human thought and development follows. It will serve as a context for exploring aspects of Kerrie's teaching experience and development.

ATTITUDES, KNOWLEDGE, AND BELIEFS

There is a great deal of confusion about just what a belief is and about the relationships among belief, attitude, and knowledge (Pajares, 1992). Linking cognition with action, Charles Saunders Pierce defined belief simply as a disposition to act. Later definitions have become more elaborate: "beliefs are thought of as psychologically held understandings, premises, or propositions about the world that are felt to be true" (Richardson, 1996, p. 103). While helpful, such definitions do not end debate; they merely signal its beginning (Pajares, 1992).

Green (1971) offers a useful point of departure for distinguishing belief from attitude:

> . . . it seems true that whenever a person holds a certain belief, he must also take some attitude toward that belief; and that attitude is always itself capable of formulation as a belief. It is a belief about a belief. (p. 42)

From this view, attitude touches on the affective component of beliefs: that beliefs bring with them emotional as well as cognitive content (Richardson, 1996). (We will return to this point shortly.) But attitude reaches beyond belief and is more encompassing:

> When clusters of beliefs are organized around an object or situation and predisposed to action, this holistic organization becomes an attitude. . . . Beliefs, attitudes, and values form an individual's belief system. (Pajares, 1992, p. 314)

The relationship between belief and knowledge is a complex one, and a source of considerable confusion and disagreement (see Pajares, 1992; Richardson, 1996). The word "knowledge" is often used in confusing ways (Fenstermacher, 1994). At times knowledge and belief appear synonymous, as though the way in which a belief is held, or a strong commitment to it, makes it true to the holder regardless of the presence or absence of supporting evidence.

Beliefs are held in two ways—evidentially and nonevidentially (Green, 1971, p. 48). The difference is crucial to our inquiry. To hold a belief evidentially is to have grounds, reasons, and evidence for holding it.

Such beliefs, as Green observes, "can be rationally criticized and therefore can be modified in the light of further evidence or better reasons" (1971, p. 48). In contrast, beliefs held nonevidentially,

> without regard to evidence, or contrary to evidence, or apart from good reasons or the canons for testing reasons and evidence . . . cannot be modified by introducing evidence or reasons. (1971, p. 48)

Beliefs held evidentially may count as knowledge, as something "known," while those that are not similarly supported remain merely beliefs.

We immediately run into problems, however. Much of what a teacher "knows" is tacit, embedded deeply in practice as "implicit theories" (Clark, 1988) and embodied, and not readily available to recall. Moreover, as Polanyi argued, our deepest beliefs, the foundation of knowing, cannot be "asserted at all" (1958, p. 60). Truth originates in "joint human awareness" (Erikson, 1975, p. 181). Serving to orient us to the world and at the center of self, these beliefs make knowing possible yet are themselves unknown—beliefs about the world, about its orderliness and predictability. This dilemma—that the boundaries separating knowledge and belief blur—is the basis for research into teachers' "practical knowledge" (Elbaz, 1991) and "personal practical knowledge" (Connelly & Clandinin, 1990). Such knowledge is not only personal; it is idiosyncratic and contextual, and it counts as knowledge because in fundamental ways, beliefs operate like knowledge: " . . . when a person believes something, he believes it to be true or to be a reasonable approximation to the truth" (Green, 1971, p. 43). Yet such views of knowledge are not without their own problems: if the boundaries separating belief and knowledge are removed completely, knowledge is reduced to belief, perhaps opinion, when most certainly not everything teachers believe can stand scrutiny or would be recognized as knowledge. Beliefs can be false. As justified true belief, knowledge, even though inevitably partial and provisional, bears greater truth value.

Like all humans, teachers seek to maintain their beliefs, even those that others might readily judge false. Academics are no different (Hamilton, 1996). Like any other system, above all else we seek to keep ourselves in "an ordered state" (Csikszentmihalyi, 1993, p. 20). True or false, we invest emotionally and intellectually in our beliefs and in how they are organized, and part of their power comes from this investment. For instance, research on attribution theory convincingly shows that people "respond not to actual stimuli but to what we think caused them" (Hunt, 1993, p. 428). Put simply, we see what we expect to see, given our beliefs. Cognitive psychologists have taken this insight further, noting that "all too often we notice and add to our memory store only what supports a strongly held belief, ignoring any that does not" (Hunt, 1993, p. 546). In short, humans seek confirmation of beliefs, resulting in a "confirmation bias," the basis for the self-fulfilling prophecy: "beliefs influence perceptions that influence behaviors that are consistent with, and that reinforce, the original beliefs" (Pajares, 1992, p. 317).

At first glance, this tendency may be judged negatively. However, more thoughtful consideration leads to a different and educationally very important conclusion: confirmation is essential to being human and is inevitably sought, given the self-referential nature of selfhood and consciousness:

> Unyielding as beliefs may be, they provide personal meaning and assist in defining relevancy. They help individuals to identify with one another and form groups and social systems. On a social and cultural level, they provide elements of structure, order, direction, and shared values. From both a personal and socio/cultural perspective, belief systems reduce dissonance and confusion, even when dissonance is logically justified by the inconsistent beliefs one holds. . . . People grow comfortable with their beliefs, and these beliefs become their "self," so that individuals come to be identified and understood by the very nature of the beliefs, the habits, they own. (Pajares, 1992, p. 318)

Humans face the problem of maintaining a sense of personal coherence, a sense of sameness, a feeling of being a "me," while having to respond to a dynamic and uncertain social context, as discussed in Chapter 2. To do this, some screening of immediate experience is necessary, screening that helps to establish and then maintain a sense of self:

> the essential tension inherent in selfhood dynamics, allowing one to experience more than one perceives and to perceive more than one attends to, makes it possible that in any situation we are all in a position to experience much more than that which would be required at that moment to maintain our own consistency in that situation. (Guidano, 1991, p. 70)

The very process of self-formation means that individuals not only do engage but *must* engage in self-deception at some level merely to manage the constant challenges to self. This is true even when the boundaries of selfhood are relatively flexible, as in a postmodern age.

Beliefs are unyielding because they are interlocking, clustered, and organized into systems, a "personal meaning organization," that is not a thing, but rather an unfolding mode of being in the world, a process aimed at "continuity and internal coherence" (Guidano, 1991, p. 33). Beliefs are "acquired as parts of a belief system, and when they are modified, they will be modified as parts of a belief system" (Green, 1971, p. 42). Changing a fundamental belief, then, is extremely difficult because related beliefs — perhaps attached to a particular attitude, which in turn is attached and sustained by other attitudes, each bearing some, perhaps very strong, emotional value — are influenced. Thus when fundamental beliefs are challenged, the challenge, whatever its source, is taken emotionally and perhaps cognitively as an attack on the self; and the initial reaction generally is to shore up the system, even at the cost of engaging in a counterfactual defense, and in self-deception. Moreover, because belief systems are lived out and with other people, changing beliefs may require changing relationships, and these changes are also resisted. Others expect us to be as we have always been to them — their identities are tied up in the predictability of our actions. From the perspective of object relations theory, changing relationships requires a change in the self — the self is a "graduated and interlocking series of relationships" (Scharff, 1992, p. 13).

The conclusion is forced upon us: despite the Western celebration of the power of reason, it is most likely the emotional effects of situations that trigger discontinuity, or perhaps it is the duration and intensity of challenges that prompt change, rather than the weight of a well-articulated, carefully argued, and evidence-laden case. Proof is found in the relative ease with which contradictory beliefs often are held simultaneously. The most sensible and best supported of arguments can be dismissed almost without thought when, for instance, such matters as religion — representing deeply held beliefs — are discussed. As John Dewey (1922) wrote: "Man is not logical . . . He hangs on to what he can in his old beliefs even when he is compelled to surrender their logical basis" (p. 224).

Having said this, we ought not be too harsh when deciding that someone else holds contradictory beliefs they ought not to hold, when a teacher believes in equality of opportunity, for example, yet teaches in a gifted and talented program, as Kerrie did. Such contradictions are deeply embedded in schooling. Teachers commonly face the dilemma of being committed to serving individual students yet feeling similarly committed to enforcing subject matter curricular standards. "Unable to serve two masters at once, most teachers emphasize one or the other factor in their instructional planning" (Prawat, 1992, p. 361). They compartmentalize beliefs and separate them from one another, yet the tension often remains. Beliefs are held at different levels, some close and others relatively far removed from conceptions of self, and with differing degrees of commitment. Some apparently contradictory beliefs may not be held strongly and are relatively easily altered or discarded when confronted. Other beliefs are context specific, and conflict is avoided by one's merely shifting contexts — leaving a school or changing grade levels, for instance. Some beliefs are contradictory, reflecting fundamental tensions in schooling. While St. James believed that purity of heart is to will one thing, humans simultaneously will many things.

CHANGING BELIEFS

Perhaps no other topic is of greater importance to teacher development than how beliefs change, or how change can be encouraged when deemed desirable. Despite their resilience beliefs do change, and something akin to a conversion experience is not always necessary. Humans are more than just creatures of habit, deeply rutted in routine, staid and stable; we are also "unfinished animals, constantly in the process of change and development" (Ornstein, 1993, p. 8). Moreover, the contexts within which we mature and develop are dynamic and, as already noted, they constantly challenge established ways of being in the world. What prompts change in beliefs?

Addressing this question requires standing back a bit and considering further just what kind of creatures we humans are. Already we have discussed how we are storytelling beings who make sense of experience by generating narratives within which we play central parts and how growth can result from exploring the stories we and others tell about ourselves and about teaching. Such activity is both cognitively and emotionally engaging. In fact, the stories we tell are not only means for making sense of experience, but also for holding onto our conceptions of our selves — and sometimes we lie to justify ourselves. Changing stories indicate changing selves and changing beliefs (sometimes stories endure too long and are told too often, indicating arrested development). Fundamentally, we are creatures who construct meaning in context and in relationship to others, and who, in the constructing, develop and change over time. We are thinking creatures, and thinking, as Boyd Bode remarked long ago, is the "finding and testing of meaning" (1928, p. 10). This is what we are. Despite how difficult it is to alter beliefs, there is no reason to despair.

Theorists working within a "constructive-developmental" tradition, who draw and build on the work of John Dewey, George Herbert Mead, and Jean Piaget provide especially fruitful directions for approaching the question of what prompts change. Kegan (1982), for one, reminds us that humans do not just seek self-confirmation. When conversing with the world, we are sites of "ongoing tension between self-preservation and self-transformation" (p. 45). Usually we seek growth, and a few of us seek "transcendence," to go well beyond ourselves and to integrate our goals with larger goals, like the "welfare of the family, the community, humanity, the planet, or the cosmos" (Csikszentmihalyi, 1993, p. 219). Echoing themes discussed in the previous chapter, we do not only seek to assimilate new phenomena to our current belief systems; we also engage in accommodation and create new beliefs, new ways of being in the world in response to new experience. Sometimes these changes are more or less forced upon us. At other times they are openly sought, part of a quest for understanding and perhaps, as will be discussed in Chapter 6, expertise. The entire process is characterized by periods of relative stability and of distress:

> Piaget's work has demonstrated . . . that this conversation [with the world] is not one of continued augmentation, but is marked by periods of dynamic stability or balance followed by periods of instability and qualitatively new balance. These periods of dynamic balance amount to a kind of evolutionary truce: further assimilation and accommodation will go on in the context of the established relationships struck between the organism and the world. (Kegan, 1982, p. 44)

The force behind human growth may well be hard wired: a drive toward inclusion, intimacy, and connectedness, on one hand, met by a similarly powerful drive toward autonomy and individuation on the other. The two exist in shifting patterns of temporary balance, enabled and limited by the kind of institutional and personal supports encountered in family, school, and work, and by the internal workings of an organism literally condemned to make experience meaningful—which is to say orderly and sensible.

"All growth," Kegan asserts, "is costly. It involves the leaving behind of an old way of being in the world. Often it involves, at least for a time, leaving behind the others who have been identified with that old way of being" (1982, p. 215). It involves increasing complexity and overcoming simplicity (Csikszentmihalyi, 1993, pp. 157–159). And it may bring with it a crisis of meaning: "All disequilibrium is a crisis of meaning; all disequilibrium is a crisis of identity (what is the self?)" (Kegan, 1982, p. 240). *Not* growing, however, is costlier still. A temporary balance may become a permanent one as institutions sustain and support a set of comfortable, historical relationships, often in favor of separation over integration, where talent goes undeveloped but work is predictable, all too simple to challenge our abilities. Immediately we think of the Marxist and neo-Marxist critiques of 10 and 20 years ago, where deskilling of teachers and other workers was a recognized outcome of the quest for control and predictability in the workplace (Apple, 1979, 1982; Bullough, Goldstein, & Holt, 1984). Little concern was given to human development and even less to making work more interesting and more complex. Productivity suffered. Worker satisfaction dropped. Institutions stagnated.

At this point, it is necessary to return to the distinction introduced earlier: beliefs may be held evidentially and nonevidentially. In their Reflective Judgment Model, King and Kitchener (1994) show how beliefs may be supported in different ways. These differences have importance for considering how beliefs might be changed and the role reason might play in bringing about change. Their model posits a developmental progression in how ill-structured problems are solved and how solutions are justified. Teaching, of course, is fraught with ill-structured problems. Initially, for young children, beliefs are merely accepted and unexamined: they just *are*. Later, justification is authority based; one believes something because an authority asserts it is true. Still later, in what King and Kitchener characterize as a "quasi-reflective thinking" stage, "knowledge is uncertain and knowledge claims are idiosyncratic to the individual since situational variables . . . dictate that knowing always involves an element of ambiguity" (1994, pp. 14–15). Relativism deepens, and eventually individuals justify beliefs by "rules of inquiry for [a particular] context and by context-specific interpretations of evidence." At this point, "beliefs are assumed to be context specific or are balanced against other interpretations" (1994, p. 15). In the "reflective thinking" stages,

> Beliefs are justified by comparing evidence and opinion from different perspectives on an issue or across different contexts and by constructing solutions that are evaluated by criteria such as weight of the evidence, the utility of the solution, or the pragmatic need for action. (1994, p. 15)

In the last stage,

> Beliefs are justified probabilistically on the basis of a variety of interpretative considerations. . . . Conclusions are defended as representing the most complete, plausible, or compelling understanding of an issue on the basis of the available evidence. (1994, p. 16)

At the later stages it would seem that a line is crossed between belief and knowledge. What is significant, however, is that recognizing how beliefs are held and with what degree of commitment influences profoundly how or whether they will be changed. Moreover, the Reflective Judgment Model reinforces an important developmental point, that timeliness of a challenge is critical to its having its desired effect. The concern for timeliness led to what Piaget dubbed the "American problem" — can development be speeded up? While this issue remains lively, it is certain development can be arrested, which is the much more important point for this inquiry.

Beliefs grounded in authority are susceptible to some kinds of challenges but not others. Similarly, beliefs underpinned by a weak relativism may appear to be easily changed, when all that results is that a new belief is added alongside an old one and assigned to a specific context within which it is judged relevant. Last, when beliefs are held in the strongest sense evidentially, the commitment one holds is less to the belief than to a larger goal, perhaps of understanding or to one's own professional and personal development. Commitment to such a goal overrides commitment to the beliefs in question. Thus better arguments or more compelling data are embraced, and adjustments in beliefs follow. Such teachers want to develop — they *believe* that the outcome, the risk to self, will be worthwhile: "The learner, like the discoverer, must believe before he can know" (Polanyi, 1958, p. 208). Possessing a relatively stable identity, a secure sense of self, is likely a precondition to having and expressing such courage. Recognizing these differences presents a serious problem for teachers and teacher educators: not everyone will seek self-development. Kitchener and King (1994) quote Rest on this point:

> The people who develop . . . are those who love to learn, who seek new challenges, who enjoy intellectually stimulating environments, who are reflective, who make plans and set goals, who take risks, who see themselves in the large social contexts of history and institutions and broad cultural trends, who take responsibility for themselves and their environs. (pp. 174–175)

Environment can do much to stimulate development, but not everyone can or will respond. Furthermore, individual temperaments differ dramatically and these differences matter a great deal. Consider: introverts tend to hold beliefs with deeper conviction than do extroverts, those with "uninhibited temperaments" (Kagan, 1994, p. 253). When one is deciding how to encourage teacher development, individual differences, human particularity, must be carefully considered; unfortunately, this seldom happens.

Cognitive psychologists have given some general guidelines on how beliefs may be changed, but these suggestions come primarily from studies of students, not adults. This is important because of the likelihood that adults are much more heavily invested in their belief systems than are younger people. At the same time, some adults are capable of functioning in ways that facilitate change, like those who King and Kitchener (1994) studied, who scored at the upper levels of their model and were judged "reflective." Pajares (1992) nicely summarizes the current wisdom on conceptual (read "belief") change:

> Beliefs are unlikely to be replaced unless they prove unsatisfactory, and they are unlikely to prove unsatisfactory unless they are challenged and one is unable to assimilate them into existing conceptions. When this happens, an anomaly occurs—something that should have been assimilable is resisted. Even then, belief change is a last alternative. . . . A number of conditions must exist before students find anomalies uncomfortable enough to accommodate the conflicting information. First, they must understand that new information represents an anomaly. Second, they must believe that the information should be reconciled with existing beliefs. Third, they must want to reduce the inconsistencies among beliefs. And last, efforts at assimilation must be perceived as unsuccessful. (p. 321)

BELIEFS AND EDUCATIONAL PRACTICE

The relationship between beliefs and educational practice is "relatively unexplored territory in research on teaching" (Grossman, Wilson, & Shulman, 1989, p. 31), although there is some evidence that teachers develop teaching styles congruent with their beliefs (see Zahorik, 1990). Part of the difficulty is that beliefs can only be inferred (Pajares, 1992) and causal relationships are elusive. But it is generally agreed that beliefs strongly affect behavior and that their influence arises in part from the way in which they operate as presuppositions that determine what is perceived and how it is perceived and as hypotheses that establish boundaries for what is understood as reasonable and proper action. Conversely, practice shapes belief; changing practice may precede changing beliefs (Richardson, 1996). An example of this dual influence of belief on practice and practice on belief comes from a year-long case study (Bullough & Knowles, 1990) of a second-career teacher, "Lyle," whose beliefs about students changed as a result of an extremely negative teaching experience so that he came to define them as "beasts," animals who unreasonably challenged authority and who were unable to govern themselves. The impact of this belief, and others connected to it, dramatically influenced Lyle's classroom practice:

> The more negative Lyle became toward the students the poorer became the quality of his planning, or so he reported, and the worse became his relationships with students. When teaching, he would simmer internally over student misbehavior and suddenly would explode at a student's acting out in ways that just moments before had gone unacknowledged. He would single one

student out of a number of misbehaving students for ejection from class. . . .
[C]lasses often seemed tense and uneasy and he was deeply troubled by how
events were unfolding. To his chagrin, teaching had become a form of warfare. (p. 108)

Believing students were beasts, Lyle became unable to recognize or hold
onto contrary evidence, that some students were not beasts, and the available range of possible responses to off-task student behavior was severely
constricted. The beast metaphor brought with it a deeply troubling but
compatible teacher role, one Lyle felt compelled to play out. Beliefs about
students and beliefs about teaching come together, inseparably linked —
students are beasts; teaching is warfare, a battle to gain and maintain
control. Besides being a battle ground, the school also became a zoo.

Beliefs of various kinds powerfully influence practice for both good
and ill. In the section that follows, we explore clusters of belief associated
with Kerrie's conception of herself as a teacher, grounded in the metaphor
"Teacher is mother." Data will be drawn primarily from interviews and
observations conducted during Kerrie's first, fifth, and eighth years of
teaching. We then turn our attention to teacher expectations. We focus on
these two areas of belief not only because the data speak powerfully to
them but also because of their central place in teacher development.

TEACHER IS MOTHER

Metaphors prove a useful means for making explicit and then exploring
beginning and experienced teacher beliefs (see Bullough & Knowles, 1991;
Bullough with Stokes, 1994; Munby, 1986; Tobin, 1990). This is because
metaphors serve as the "basis of the conceptual systems by which we
understand and act within our worlds" (Taylor, 1984, p. 5); they represent
a "unique and enduring and irreplaceable way of embodying the truths of
our inward lives" (Abbs, 1981, p. 491). Changing metaphors signal changing beliefs and practice. The approach is a hopeful one that has found a
place in training people for the ministry (Brewer & de Beer, 1991) and in
efforts to improve the quality of university teaching (Barnes & Goodhue-
McWilliams, 1992). There have been good results in teacher education as
well: "In staff development programs that focused on teacher metaphors,
teachers adopted new metaphors and teaching practices changed along
with the metaphors" (Richardson, 1996, p. 112). Moreover, a focus on
metaphors draws attention to both beliefs and the contexts within which
teachers seek to express them. It is important to note that teaching contexts
may be supportive of and hostile to different types of metaphors, so hold-

ing a metaphor must not be confused with enacting it; institutions, after all, are characterized by their role preferences (see Tobin, 1990; Bullough with Stokes, 1994).

Representing clusters of beliefs and operating as general beliefs themselves, metaphors function at different levels in teacher cognition: "While metaphors may be both 'surface' and 'deep' . . . it is the deep or 'structural' metaphor . . . which gives greatest shape to our understanding and perception of social situations" (Grant, 1992, p. 434). Deep or root metaphors, which are "often discovered through storytelling," as our inquiry well illustrates, serve as the basic organizers of understanding. Central to self, these metaphors are most difficult to change but are also of most importance to teacher development.

The power of root metaphors in Kerrie's thinking about teaching was readily apparent early in our study. In our earliest interviews, she spoke naturally of teaching as an extension of mothering, of nurturing and caring for young people: "I was a mother." Such beliefs were deeply embedded in her life history; she found herself doing a good deal of mothering of her siblings even as a small child. As with many female teachers, mothering, although a complex and deeply contradictory relationship with children (see Casey, 1990), was a central part of her life and worldview. For men, the relationship between fathering and teaching is also often close and positive (see MacDonald, 1994; Pajak & Blase, 1989). In this section we explore the development of Kerrie's mother metaphor over the several years of our study and the beliefs associated with it. As a first-year teacher she initially made teaching meaningful through this metaphor; it was through it that she judged the effects of her instruction and the quality of her relationships with students.

Kerrie drew on her experience as a mother throughout her first year and one half of teaching to frame and then address many of the ill-defined problems she faced. But mothering came into play even before she'd met her first class at Rocky Mountain Junior High School. Having student taught high school history, she realized she knew relatively little about seventh-grade students, yet she needed to plan a program for them. To do this, Kerrie necessarily drew on beliefs about what students would be like and these came primarily from her experience as a mother, even though her children were then younger, one in fifth grade and the other in sixth. Based on this experience, she characterized seventh graders as "naive, shy, know-it-all brats (laughter)!" How did she know this? "From my children, I guess. Not that they're the wonder kids, or anything. But they're kids. I have thought about their friends, too." Although their influence diminished throughout the first year, her own children served as the lens through which she made curriculum decisions. Believing that if *they* liked a book or understood an assignment, her students would as well, she moved ahead confidently.

The power of this metaphor and of the beliefs associated with it was readily apparent in how Kerrie thought about her classroom and the kind of learning environment she wanted to create: Class was to be "'like a home,' affectively: warm, supportive, caring, but not a womb" (Bullough, 1989, p. 54). Similarly, like others holding such beliefs (see Cole, 1988), she wanted the class to be "like a big family," like *her* family, where individual family members were invested in, cared about one another, and had a good time: "We will all be happy," she said. Class would be "fun." She liked the classroom best when it felt "snugly," "peaceful," which happened most often when she was reading to the students or they were quietly working at their desks. Mothers, Kerrie thought, modeled virtue: "'I always just thought it was every teacher's responsibility to [serve as a model of decency]. I guess I think everyone should do that, it's part of their job. Aren't we supposed to be . . . pillars of the community?'" (Bullough, 1989, p. 98). Even at this early point in her development, Kerrie understood teaching in moral terms, and that teachers teach themselves: "We can only teach out of our own being— there is nowhere else to teach from" (Abbs, 1981, p. 495).

Consistent with her mother teaching metaphor, Kerrie was sharply focused on serving students. With her she brought into the classroom an enduring belief in the value of service and a service ethic grounded in intimacy and connection with others (Noddings, 1984). It was an ethic of engagement rather than of tolerance; she remarked in an interview a month into her first year of teaching: "I'm more concerned about what is going to be best for the students than for me, usually." As with most other teachers, Kerrie's motivation to teach was deeply and biographically embedded in her need to care for the young (Perry & Rog, 1992), and recalling injustices suffered in school by her own children, to make a difference. This need was at the center of her conception of herself, a point we shall return to later because of its importance to understanding how and why Kerrie changed. However, as a matter of religious faith, she understood that service is not one-sided; as Coles (1993, p. 177) argues, something is given and something is gained, a self. As previously mentioned, Kerrie felt called to serve (Serow, 1994).

Throughout the fall of Kerrie's first year of teaching, she mothered her seventh-grade children as they made the transition from elementary school to secondary school. She bonded to them and they to her. She felt very possessive of individual students: "I don't want to let them go." She found herself protecting individual students from hurt and heartache. For instance, in October she noticed that two girls were picking at and teasing another, particularly shy, girl. Kerrie intervened in the situation: "'If they ever [pick on you again,] will you please tell me? . . . If they ever do anything, if you have to, stand by my desk, come and stand there. Even if I'm helping other people, just stand there and wait and I will know that something is bothering you. If you want to talk, that's fine. I can handle that. . . . ' She was quivering ninety miles an hour, not crying." This commitment to students had unanticipated consequences: within weeks of Kerrie's starting to teach, word got out that she was willing to take "difficult" students into her class. This was the beginning of a career-long pattern: "there's a new kid I have in the morning class who has moved up from sixth grade. He's a seventh-grader who was held back last year. . . . Guess who got him? Bleeding Heart."

Problems With Mothering Metaphors

To be sure, mothering is a common metaphor, particularly among elementary school teachers. Elementary school has long been a female world, and as women increasingly replace men as administrators, it is becoming even more so. Long emotionally dependent on women, young children often expect to be mothered by their teachers, even while sometimes resenting it (see Grumet, 1988). Seventh grade represents a transition year and is often experienced as a move from mother to other teaching metaphors — ways of relating to teachers, including male teachers — by students. As such, teacher-student relationships become increasingly complex and uncertain. That mothering itself is a deeply contradictory metaphor, not only for young people but for those who seek to enact it, adds to the complexity. Contradictions abound.

Spencer (1986) observes that teaching is fraught with contradictions, especially for women teachers. Some of the contradictions she identifies relate directly to the difficulty of enacting a mothering or parenting metaphor, and, more generally, to the struggle to establish and maintain a stable teaching identity. Given that students serve as a "critical reality definer" for teachers (Riseborough, 1985, p. 262), and that students are the object of teacher nurturing, it is not surprising that they are the source of much inner turmoil.

> One of the reasons teachers cite for choosing teaching as a career is that they like (or love) children. The implication is that "children" means *all* children. However, teachers find that *real* children in *real* classrooms are not always lovable — or even likable. (Spencer, 1986, p. 10)

And further:

> Among the reasons teachers choose teaching as a career is that they want to "help" people, particularly children. They anticipate that rewards will be intrinsic and that pleasure will be derived simply from watching children learn. They find, however, that [not] all children . . . want to learn and that [not] all children are . . . desirable people with whom to work. For most teachers, intrinsic rewards are minimal. . . . (Spencer, 1986, p. 9)

Needing to love the unlovable and finding themselves having to punish those they wish to comfort and care most about tears at teachers, and they speak in contradictory terms, as Kerrie sometimes did:

> [I] think of how [I] want [my] own children to be treated. Somebody loves these kids. They deserve [love] most of the time; they all deserve it some-time. . . . [Really,] whether they're always . . . deserving it, the love is still there, even though they're in trouble. . . . I want them to feel that, but, you know, it's pretty hard to do. God might have it down pat. I do not.

Love-inspired acts greeted passively or perhaps met with hostility dampen even the most generous spirit. For Kerrie, nothing caused more anguish, nor ultimately prompted more reflection, than having to "be hard on a student I truly liked."

Contradictions of this kind may weaken beliefs and role commitments, as powerful emotions are released, but they do not necessarily undermine strongly held conceptions of self as teacher, one's deepest beliefs. However, they are not the only factors that might challenge a teacher's beliefs about self-as-teacher and prompt change. The unbounded nature of teaching places never-ending demands on teachers who choose or are compelled to recognize them; the demands of parenting are similarly unbounded and exhausting. For teacher-mothers, the demands can be overwhelming—"For those who sustain the emotional and physical lives of others, there is no time out, no short week, no sabbatical, no layoff" (Grumet, 1988, p. 86). A teacher's desire to nurture her students may conflict with her commitment to her own children at home, who need not only their mother but an *energetic and engaged* mother. Guilt often results (Spencer, 1986; Pajak & Blase, 1989). For single mothers, the dual burden of mothering at home and at school can be especially debilitating, as a case study conducted by Bullough and Knowles of a divorced mother of five children well illustrates:

> While nurturing was at the center of [Barbara's] self-understanding and was
> the source of her greatest pleasures as a parent and as a teacher, the personal
> costs of maintaining a parental understanding of teaching were beginning to
> be too high. She could not continue as she had been doing; there was nothing
> left for her to sacrifice but her family and her health. Facing growing physical
> and mental exhaustion, coupled with concern about the welfare of her own
> children, Barbara gradually accepted that there were limits to how far she
> could or should sacrifice for the students. There simply was no end to the
> needs of the young people and no possible way for one person to respond to
> them all. [She had] become so involved with the students that she thought it
> proper to take shopping, with the mother's permission, one of her female
> students who had problems with personal hygiene. Something had to give! . . .
> [F]earing that her own children might suffer because of her dedication to
> nurturing other people's children, and finding in her own children's well-
> being the source of her greatest pleasure, Barbara began to draw a line indi-
> cating how far she would get involved in the lives and problems of her stu-
> dents and how much she would do to satisfy their never-ending needs.
> (Bullough & Knowles, 1991, pp. 132–133)

Generally speaking, the aim for both male and female teachers is to
"integrate their identities inside and outside of school" (Pajak & Blase,
1989, p. 301). To do this requires setting boundaries and sometimes reconsidering and backing away from commitments, altering some beliefs.

Shifting and Changing Metaphors

Like other beginning teachers, Kerrie experienced the "reality shock" that
characterizes the survival stage of teaching discussed by Ryan (1986). Kerrie moved quickly and relatively easily through this stage, which ended by
Christmas break of her first year of teaching but left behind a subtly
different teacher. For a time in the fall of her first year of teaching, as we
wrote in *First Year Teacher*, Kerrie struggled with who she was as a
teacher:

> Having to be a "bitch" and a policewoman made it difficult for her to express
> herself as she saw herself — a warm, loving, caring, easygoing, teacher-
> mother — and to establish the kinds of relationships with students that she
> found most satisfying. "It just drives me crazy that kids can't respond to love.
> Why can't people respond to someone who shows love in the same way as they
> respond to someone who shows strictness?" She kicked students out of class —
> "since the first of October I've just been kicking them right out of class" — but
> was troubled by doing so. (Bullough, 1989, p. 28)

She was troubled by the fact that she was acting in ways contrary to deeply
held beliefs about herself as a person and as a teacher — her metaphor. She

was heavily invested in her metaphor, and a challenge to it threatened other related beliefs and produced turmoil. She struggled intensely to realize and sustain her metaphor. Her success in teaching depended on such an outcome, since it was through the beliefs connected with her metaphor that she ultimately judged her practice. These beliefs governed how she felt about her work and about herself as a teacher.

As Kerrie got on top of management and curriculum issues, especially by planning more carefully for management, achieving consistency in rewards and punishments, routinizing the classroom, and identifying appropriate content and activities to engage the students (see Bullough, 1989, pp. 30–36), she became better able to create conditions within the classroom that supported her desired relationship with students. Improving teaching skills were crucial to this outcome, as was the help other teachers gave in clarifying the boundaries of acceptable student behavior. Reflecting on this time, Kerrie writes:

I can still picture my first year when at the end of seventh period I tried to quiet the class for afternoon announcements. It was a daily battle. Finally a girl named T. would stand up and scream, "Shut up!" at the top of her lungs. It was always effective, but certainly not desirable. Taking the advice of another teacher, I took T. into the hall and told her that as much as I appreciated her effort, I needed her to let me be the one in charge of quieting the class. For me, mentally, this change turned the tide. I was in control.

In addition, Kerrie participated in numerous in-service classes offered within the district that proved helpful. She got involved in professional association activities, that culminated in her election as association building representative at year's end (see Bullough, 1989, pp. 101–102). This involvement brought her into contact with teachers from around the district with whom she could discuss her concerns and seek, and sometimes give, advice. With increasing skills, Kerrie was better able to adjust the context to be more supportive of her values. At year's end she remarked: "Sometimes the answer is not changing yourself; the answer is [to] change the environment." Nevertheless, Kerrie's mother metaphor began evolving subtly, even though only a few aspects of the metaphor itself proved unsatisfactory at first.

[*Has your role changed, the way you see yourself as a teacher?*] I would say it's filling out. Things get added in. (Pause.) I don't even know how to say what's filling out, or anything about it. It's hard to say. [For one thing,] I guess I see myself more as a disciplinarian than I had before. There's just . . . more coming into it, it's getting to be a harder (more complicated) job.

As teaching became more complicated, Kerrie felt less like a mother and more like a teacher. A few students, very unlike her own children who were "usually obedient" directly forced change:

> S. just won't respond . . . he's just gone absolutely out of control. I don't know what to do with him. I've spoken with his dad. His dad said he is sup-posed to be on Ritalin. Hyper. [The father said,] "I will not put him on the drug." I said, "I can understand that, but you've got to work with this child." When he goes home there is no parent there until . . . 6:30 or 7:00 at night. He doesn't ever do any homework. He doesn't do anything, ever, ever. I don't know what to do with him. I have sat him right there facing my desk and he doesn't do any better. He'll distract me sitting there! I can sympathize with the poor kids sitting next to him. I can't isolate him. He doesn't do anything.

Kerrie resented having to babysit such students; mothering was more than babysitting. She expected her students to behave like her own children: "I trust them to make their own decisions about what they want to do. I don't want to tell them what to do. I want them to decide. I've brought [my own children] up to be [that way]." She discovered there were serious limitations to using her own children as the basis for making teaching decisions, and she used them less and less as the year progressed.

By spring, her classes were well under control. She could discipline students and be tough if she had to be without damaging her relationship with them. Mostly, her year's experience confirmed the basic value of her metaphor, and of the educational power of loving young people: *"Is it possible to love them into decent behavior?* Yes, I think it is. Teachers do it." But she recognized its limitations. In late spring she expressed the belief, for example, that she was sometimes too tolerant of student misbe-havior, and not demanding enough: "I wish I were more demanding. I don't think of myself that way very much."

There are two aspects of teachers' service ethic, an affective dimension and an academic one. The first requires that teachers care for all students as individuals and be responsible for them, and the second that students need to learn when they are in school. Kerrie was concerned primarily about the first, but also about student academic performance. It was with almost motherly pride, for example, that she reflected at year's end on her students' progress, beginning by speaking about one of the most difficult ones she'd taught all year:

> Look at the difference between how he was at the beginning of the year, when he was an absolute [pain]. I look at him now . . . he is so much improved. The sad part is [that] his eighth-grade teachers won't know he is improved. But then it made me look at my other students and how far they have come. It's

not even academics I'm thinking of. It's them. Their control of themselves and how they respond in class and behave toward others. . . .

Her pride was in how they had matured as people, socially and academically. They were her children.

Kerrie in Her Fifth Year of Teaching

In the fall of 1991, after a three-year hiatus, we resumed our inquiry. Kerrie was still teaching at Rocky Mountain Junior High School, in the same classroom, although she no longer taught the same students for three periods, including English, reading, and social studies. Instead, she taught two groups of "advanced" students for two periods each, English and reading. She spent two periods of the day carrying out duties associated with her position as Teacher Leader. Having reorganized the curriculum around Nancie Atwell's Reading and Writing Workshop, Kerrie spent less time in front of the class than she had previously. Mostly she "conferenced" with students on their writing, which included editing and discussing pieces of writing; taught what she called "mini-lessons" on common writing problems such as punctuation; and read to the students from novels, re-creating the "warm, fuzzy" times that she'd most valued during her first two years of teaching. For their part, students spent most of their time writing, discussing their works in progress, or peer editing. The atmosphere was one of productive independent and small group work. During weekly observations, the classroom was always busy, often buzzing, and mostly productive.

We discussed how Kerrie thought about herself as a teacher and whether or not the mother metaphor still held sway.

KERRIE: Mother is definitely still there, but there [are other metaphors]. Guidance counselor, coach . . . an advocate. . . . [But] being a teacher for this length of time has taken over. When I begin to have problems, when [I'm] pondering about a child, that's when [my thoughts] become most tempered by the mother part [of teaching]. Then I think, "Oh, that really wasn't very fair," or I feel really good about how I handled that person.
BOB: Is there any time when the teacher role shows up in your mother role [at home]?
KERRIE: Yes, yeah — when I want [my children] to perform better and they say, "You are just acting like a teacher." They do, they are aware of that. But I don't do that a whole lot. I think they see it. I know it is there.

BOB: When you walk into the school, do you put on a teacher hat?
KERRIE: [No]. I think it is just me, all the time. . . .

As Kerrie talked about what gave her the most pleasure, her focus
was sharply on student learning, that the students engaged the content
appropriately and well and were learning. Warm and caring relationships, and a class that would be "like a family," were still highly valued,
but student engagement mattered most of all. This represented a subtle
but significant change:

Engaged is really it for everything. I look over [and see] this child is writing.
These two are conferencing; they are engaged. They might look off task to
you, but they are doing the right thing. . . . Also, they feel pleased. They are
so happy when they come up and we've conferenced and I say, "Okay, this is
your grade. You've done such a good job. I'm so impressed with how you are
doing." . . . They are just thrilled with their progress. I have kids saying, "This
is the best class I've every had."

Although Kerrie felt less motherly toward her students than she had
during her first years of teaching, a few students still called her "Mom."
She thought this natural, even pleasing: "It doesn't bother me at all. When
they call me Grandma, I will get worried [laughs]. My mom gets called
Grandma all the time, but they will say 'Mom' [to me] and they just laugh.
I'll tell you what, it is flattering to me in that . . . that is a word that
would come out to address me. That means they are feeling comfortable
around me." Some students, however, most easily called forth the mother
in her: "Especially these really bright ones. . . . I want to hug them."
    At this point in Kerrie's development, her fifth year of teaching, she
had settled into a comfortable teaching role and style. Although the
mother metaphor persisted, it weakened.

PRINCIPLES, BELIEFS, AND METAPHORS

Settled and secure as a teacher, Kerrie thought less and less about teaching
as an extension of mothering. To understand how she thought about teaching required revisiting our earlier work together, reviewing observation
notes, and conducting additional observations and interviews. In addition, for this second round of data gathering, a series of twelve videotapes
of Kerrie teaching were made that provided her the opportunity to talk
about teaching, what she was doing in class and why. These conversations
were recorded and transcribed and later analyzed for insight into how

Kerrie was then thinking about teaching and about herself as teacher. As noted previously, beliefs are usually inferred, and much of this analysis sought to identify what seemed to be the underlying beliefs of Kerrie's practice (see Bullough with Baughman, 1993).

A cluster of principles were identified which seemed to serve as the basis of much of her decision making. Beliefs of various kinds underlie the principles, and underneath them all resided Kerrie's service ethic. Taken together, these principles and the beliefs that sustain them formed a coherent and mature, although not entirely explicit, philosophy or ideology (Zahorik, 1990) of teaching, a "living educational theory" (Whitehead, 1989). Captured in shorthand phrases, they often cropped up in interviews as explanations for an action as well as in informal conversations. Some of them arose directly from Kerrie's beginning conception of teaching as mothering, while others represented a consolidation of gains made initially through trial-and-error approaches to teaching coupled with internalized insights gained from in-service courses and especially from engaging in a five-year-long conversation about teaching with other teachers and as part of our study of teaching and teacher development. They operated as tried-and-true principles, serving as taken-for-granted and proven teaching theories, evidentially grounded through teaching practice over an extended period of time: "They worked."

Echoing the values of mothering, the first principle identified was, "Love them along." As Kerrie stated:

[A lot of my success came from] learning how to deal with the students and to treat them the way they need to be treated—positively. I call it "loving them along," because that is what works for me. I want to have a loving environment in my classroom where my students can blossom.

The beliefs underpinning this principle reach back to parenting and to the first weeks of teaching, and to Kerrie's consistent desire to be loving and to create a loving classroom. Similarly, the second principle dates from her first weeks of teaching: a classroom should be a warm, fuzzy, place, like a family, where students feel loved and cared for. However, she later added the notion that the classroom should be more than a family; it should be a caring community where students feel connected and responsible for one another. In some respects this adjustment represented an extension of Kerrie's longstanding interest in cooperative groupwork.

A third principle was captured in the sentiment "I feel 'like I am very much a student-centered teacher.'" Student success and the building of self-esteem were primary values, evident in curriculum decision making, grading, and discipline and management decisions where adjustments were made to individual students. The fourth principle was that "skills, taught out of context, are nothing." This was a lesson learned through in-service courses but realized most fully when Kerrie implemented Reading and Writing Workshop, which involved teaching grammar and spelling through writing and reading. Previously, spelling was taught separately and students were tested on Fridays. This change was an answer to a long-term and very frustrating problem noted as early as February of her first year of teaching: "[Grammar] is in the book and is something they learn; they do it on their papers, but it doesn't go into their minds at all." A fifth principle, representing her growing understanding of how young people develop, was that at the end of seventh grade, a student "ought to look like an eighth grader." By this she meant that it was her job to help the students mature intellectually and emotionally, which was a source of great personal satisfaction. Although she could not express in detail precisely what an eighth grader "looked like," she knew, and she also knew what it would take on her part to nudge a student along in this direction — this transformation did not just happen.

A sixth principle grew directly out of Kerrie's first year of teaching when she discovered that almost despite herself, the negative views she held of a few students at the beginning of the year changed by year's end: "[At an in-service meeting] one of the teachers said, 'You know, those kids, the ones you have all that trouble with, those are the ones who are breaking your door down the first day of school next year to come in and see you. That's really true." The principle was to be "tolerant" and not "write anyone off." The addition of the phrase, to not "write anyone off," separates Kerrie's positive conception of tolerance from the more negative view of it as an expression of indifference. That she consistently accepted into her classroom students whom other teachers sought to avoid stood as strong evidence of her commitment to this principle and its related beliefs.

Two phrases, when combined, formed a seventh principle: "I take teaching seriously" and "I see myself as putting all I can into teaching." Later we will explore professionalism. Here we need mention only that this principle speaks to Kerrie's expectations for herself and for other teachers, that she believed good teaching was the result of hard work and that teachers were obligated to help one another to improve. Examples of this commitment abound: During her last two years at Rocky Mountain Junior High School she routinely made her files available to other teachers; actively participated in and took leadership for a school-wide peer evaluation program; attended and presented at a variety of professional meetings; and organized a support group for first-year teachers. In these and in many other ways she sought to assist others to improve their practice as she sought to improve her own.

Numerous beliefs gather around and underpin these principles, each operating as a well-tested hypothesis. Briefly: loving students is the most effective way to get them to behave, to feel positive about themselves, and to perform academically. Feeling cared for (in class) and connected to teachers and classmates, belonging to a kind of family, encourages appropriate behavior and motivates students to work harder and more productively. Motivation is in some ways tied to the production of a curriculum that is interesting and fun for students, that is developmentally appropriate. Students need help seeing the connections between what they are expected to learn in school and what they need to do. They need opportunities to apply their learning in ways that are meaningful to them; otherwise, they are not likely to learn at all, and teachers have wasted their time. Students do change and mature, and the results are often delightful. If adults stick with young people, even those who are often "nasty," and keep seeking the students' best interests, some students will learn and positive relationships with teachers will result. Growth for teachers comes through working hard at becoming a better teacher; anything less lets young people down and makes teaching less interesting and challenging than it should be. Underlying all the principles is the belief that to teach is to serve. Kerrie's experience at Rocky Mountain Junior High School supported these beliefs; as part of her belief system, the principles were, for her, emotionally charged, and since they'd been tested and found to be true, they counted as knowledge about teaching.

These are among the principles and beliefs Kerrie took with her when she moved from Rocky Mountain to Clarke as she began her sixth year of teaching. Developed at Rocky Mountain — an essentially middle- and working-class suburban school — her beliefs faced a severe test in the very different urban context of Clarke.

Not Much Mothering Here

When Kerrie left Rocky Mountain Junior High School, she demonstrated many of the qualities associated with teaching expertise (Berliner, 1990, 1994). It is important to mention this here because in retrospect, she identified her last year at Rocky Mountain as her best year of teaching, a teaching "utopia," she said. Her lessons were purposeful; they flowed easily, seemingly effortlessly, to their conclusion. Transitions were nearly automatic, so that lessons appeared almost seamless. Kerrie easily handled unexpected events. For example, when students who had agreed to read their writing to the class backed out at the last moment, she was unflappable. Without missing a step, she changed plans and launched into a new activity.

She easily categorized problems and framed solutions. For instance, when viewing a videotape of her teaching for a think-aloud exercise (after noting a few students on the video who interrupted a conference she was conducting with another student), Kerrie remarked,

[They will continue to do this] until everyone has gone through the cycle (writing, peer conferencing, teacher conferencing, publishing, following Atwell's program) a couple of times. They [will] get it, but it takes a long time. Some kids haven't gone through [the cycle] yet.

What might seem to be a problem to an outside viewer of the tape was barely a concern for Kerrie, who understood the issue contextually and deeply. After noting an area or two that she thought needed work, particularly to improve her conferencing skills, she exclaimed, "It [her taped teaching] looks good, doesn't it? It looked really good. I look like I know what I'm doing all the time. I can't help but think, I would love me so much [as a teacher] if I were a seventh grader" (laughs). She was at the top of her game that last year at Rocky Mountain. She loved her work, and the students were performing at high levels. And she was a very popular teacher, one often sought out by students between classes and before and after school.

Instead of teaching English and reading to "advanced students," as she had at Rocky Mountain, when Kerrie moved to Clarke she taught six periods of social studies and English. She became a traveling teacher; without her own classroom, she remarked, she did "not [have] that warm, fuzzy feeling all year." It was a difficult first year at Clarke, but it got better as Kerrie made friends among the faculty and began fitting in, even though she felt like a novice teacher all over again. The students were dramatically different from those she had taught at Rocky Mountain, and this proved to be a source of considerable difficulty—made all the more challenging when a decision was made to mainstream all resource students. "I look back and I think I was adapting a lot to the way they behaved. . . . I didn't know them, I hadn't seen them before."

These children were not the "naive, shy, know-it-all brats," she anticipated the students would be at Rocky Mountain. Compared to the students she mothered at Rocky Mountain, these young people were more diverse, and often much poorer; they seemed more mature and the range of ability levels was broader. When, during her second year of teaching at Clarke, she began teaching in the AAP, that range of ability levels broadened even further. AAP students were young but very sophisticated, and privileged: "I read a story last night that a kid had written about this ship he'd been on. I thought, I want to [travel like] that." These students were selected for the program because they fitted a "star profile"—they had high test scores and involved parents, and they were highly motivated and "obedient": "They hardly need you. They need you for direction and that is it. You're a facilitator. . . . " Teacher was facilitator, not mother. On the other extreme, in addition to the mainstreamed students, including young people with severe behavior problems and limited intellectual abilities, were those from some of the roughest and poorest neighborhoods in the city, "gang wannabes" who were "street smart." Kerrie mentioned that the students did not mix across groups and that some students' behavior was surprising:

They snipe at each other during class all the time. They don't let up. . . . That stops a lot of teaching because [I'm] so busy just dealing with kid problems, with attitude problems. . . . Plus, . . . they're very sexual. It's unreal. . . . I had to have the counselor come in and talk to them about sexual harassment. . . . They're just very blatant about the things they say to each other. . . . I had a kid . . . who looked at a girl and sat there and pretended to masturbate [while] looking at her. That got everyone's attention, including mine!

Neither the wealthy kids nor the tough, inner city ones seemed to need, or apparently want, mothering. Working with them accelerated Kerrie's move away from mothering, a change that was also prompted by changes in her own life. Her own children were out of school, and her relationships with them had become more adultlike. Also, Kerrie was older. She still cared deeply about the students but no longer felt she needed to "love them along," according to the first principle. Rather, she encouraged student independence, particularly with the AAP students. Observation notes indicate that she seemed somewhat less engaged personally with the students and was sometimes distant and businesslike — more a manager than a mother. Certainly she was less physical, seldom touching a student, as she commonly had in her first years of teaching. This is not to say that Kerrie's belief that teachers must care about their students had changed; rather, it indicates that what counted as caring changed somewhat. Although she regretted how rarely she felt that "warm and fuzzy feeling" of her second principle, she became more interested in having an academically productive class, warm or not — although, sometimes it *was* warm. Her desire for productivity was especially strong in those classes where students were difficult to keep on task, and in AAP, where children were often aggressively self-confident and parents were pushy and demanded that their children perform at high levels and get good grades. The aim was to keep students working, and this was evidence of caring: "[Pleasure] comes from seeing them learn . . . I love it." Consistent with her third principle, Kerrie continued making individual adjustments, particularly in response to her developing understanding of what individual students were capable of doing. In the most difficult-to-manage classes, she increasingly emphasized whole group instruction. AAP students, in contrast, were given numerous curricular choices. The fourth principle, that skills must be taught in context, was much in evidence in Kerrie's classes as she sought to make the curriculum relevant. The fifth principle — that at the end of seventh grade, a student should "look like an eighth grader" — no longer applied. Kerrie taught some eighth-grade classes and AAP included a mix of seventh- and eighth-grade students; the expectation was that the older students would help socialize the younger ones into appropriate behavior. She sought to prepare the eighth-grade students for high school, which meant that she needed to place a greater emphasis on academic development over social development. The sixth principle, of tolerance and of refusing to write off any student, was challenged.

Sometimes I just want to say, "Everyone who doesn't want to stay [in class], go. Okay, now, everyone else, we are going to have so much fun." If only we could do that, it would be great. I don't know what we'd do with the kids in the hall because there would be an awful lot of them.

Yet despite these feelings, in not a single set of observation notes is there any evidence of Kerrie's ever giving up on a student — of acting punitively, for example. Indeed, she continued to accept the students other teachers avoided, a tendency which eventually proved costly, as we shall see in Chapter 7.

That Kerrie's principles should have changed so dramatically signaled a change in her beliefs about teaching, a change that undoubtedly affected her feelings about remaining in teaching. Clearly she felt much less like a mother. Her students played no small part in prompting the change, although there were many additional influences.

So, what happened to . . . mother?
Oh . . . that's part of teaching, [but I've changed]. It's age coming on. . . . I used to be a lot sweeter and I could put up with a lot more crap [from students]. These days it's like I can't stand this, sit down and be quiet, get out of my face, I'm not going to talk endlessly to you. I've got at least two boys. . . . Every time I've said something and given instruction [one of them] comes up to get something [and asks], "Is this it? Is this it?" I'm to the point now [where] when he comes up, I say, "Stop, you heard me, figure it out or go ask someone else, I don't want to talk to you." . . . I'm not as nice as I used to be.

A RETURN TO THE LITERATURE ON CHANGING BELIEFS

Earlier we quoted from Pajares's summary of the research on how beliefs change:

> Beliefs are unlikely to be replaced unless they prove unsatisfactory. . . . A number of conditions must exist before students find anomalies uncomfortable enough to [make them] accommodate the conflicting information. First, they must understand that new information represents an anomaly. Second, they must believe that the information should be reconciled with existing beliefs. Third, they must want to reduce the inconsistencies among beliefs. And last, efforts at assimilation must be perceived as unsuccessful. (1992, p. 321)

As mentioned, much of the research on conceptual change focuses on students, and we are interested in adult learning. The difference now becomes readily apparent. Embedded in this quote is a view that belief change is highly rational, as though one sits down, reviews a list of beliefs, checks off those that no longer are serviceable, and changes them or decides to resist change. When dealing with misconceptions of science, for example, something very roughly akin to this might actually transpire, and teachers are well advised to plan instruction in ways that challenge their students' mistaken beliefs. But what happens when it is adult beliefs we are interested in, and when the beliefs being challenged are not the relatively superficial ones, but deep ones, like Kerrie's conception of herself as a mother?

The evolution of Kerrie's mother metaphor and the beliefs attached to it represent real changes in some aspects of how Kerrie conceived of herself as a person, not only in her identity as a teacher but in her self. No specific event or factor produced the change, although evolving life circumstances and altered work conditions played important parts. Moreover, no staff developer could have designed a program with such outcomes in mind; rather, they happened in the course of living a life, aging, and selectively responding to dynamic and unpredictable situations at home and at work. That selves and professional identities change is certain, but teacher identity needs to be understood in relationship to living a life and forming and seeking to maintain a self within shifting contexts.

Service remained at the center of Kerrie's conception of herself as a person and as a teacher. But as we have seen, over time, that strongest of beliefs to which she was most committed emotionally and intellectually no longer found their fullest and richest expression in mothering young people. For her self-preservation, her service beliefs gradually took other forms—pushing students to perform at higher levels academically, for example, and then taking private pleasure in their intellectual growth.

The data indicate that Kerrie's quest to continue to be of service to her students, who at Clarke showed little need for mothering, necessitated discarding the metaphor and altering some of the beliefs clustered around it. Academics became much more important:

I gained a sense of responsibility about the education I owed my students. I never felt that my students learned enough to be prepared for the future. Academics became very important to me, and as the socialization aspect became increasingly difficult, especially with mainstreamed students, all too often I lost patience, finally getting a glimpse of what burnout was all about.

To continue to be herself, she had to change herself, but she did not set out to do this; it happened as a consequence of living and trying to make sense of her life in unpredictable circumstances. Service had oriented her to the world, but what counted as service changed even as serving became more difficult.

Again we return to points made in the introduction to this chapter: as noted, humans do not only seek self-confirmation; we are also sites of "ongoing tension between self-preservation and self-transformation." Holding steady to a service ethic which grounded her and was even deeper than the mother metaphor—perhaps it is Kerrie's most fundamental belief—allowed her to accommodate other beliefs, to shift commitments, while still being at her core herself, one who engaged in service to others; this was a unity born of responsibility (see Morson, 1986). Around this most fundamental of beliefs, other beliefs within the wider system of beliefs changed, sometimes only slightly; without change the organizing hub of service could not itself have remained steady. There was no conversion experience, but there was growth and professional development, which necessitated, as suggested by object-relations theory, leaving behind some ways of being in the world and of relating to others, including her students. Growth is always costly.

TEACHER EXPECTATIONS

We will round out our inquiry into Kerrie's changing beliefs by briefly exploring teacher expectations. This section is included not only because of the importance of teacher expectations in promoting or inhibiting student learning, but for insight into the place of evidence in changing teacher beliefs and teachers' attitudes toward evidence and data gathering. The message in this section is a very positive one about teachers and their openness to change.

"*Teachers' expectations* are inferences that teachers make about the future behavior or academic achievement of their students, based on what they know about these students now" (Good & Brophy, 1994, p. 83). They are, then, beliefs about students, hypotheses. Teachers hold expectations for groups as well as for individual students. We have already noted that Kerrie was uncertain about what to expect from students prior to her first year of teaching and before beginning to teach at Clarke Intermediate School. She spent much of her first year of teaching discovering what the students could and could not do. In February of her first year of teaching, for example, she remarked:

It's beyond me. I don't know why they don't know [what they don't know]. [It] shocks me. I hope they know all the things I'm teaching, like how to put words into syllables. [Then I discover] they cannot. They don't even know how to clap syllables. That's something I wouldn't even [have thought about].

She found the entire process "baffling" and began planning under the assumption that they would know very little: "Then I can go faster if they all get it or know it already. I plan that they won't know it, that I'm going to have to explain [everything] in detail." She was finding out just what a seventh-grade student tracked in the lower ability group could and could not do, did and did not know. She felt frustration, for at times she concluded they might not be trying: "Sometimes I just think these suckers are lazy! They don't want to understand." She decided, however, that the problem was hers. For instance, she admitted that a book she selected was simply too difficult: "I gave the kids the books [to read] and told them to read chapter one and answer the questions. . . . They were too hard." They failed because of an inappropriate decision Kerrie had made, not from lack of effort.

A great surprise came early in that first year when she discovered that, contrary to her expectations, she had to plan carefully for management. She believed that a fun and interesting curriculum would by itself prevent off-task behavior — that students would behave and stay on task. She was wrong, as she reminisced five years later: "[Needing to plan for management] just went over my head. Part of my problem was that I thought I was going to be so great that I wouldn't have to worry about discipline. . . . I've learned a lot [since then] . . . prevention is [the key]." Near the conclusion of her first year of teaching, she reflected on her problems with management and commented:

Next year it will be much easier to say, "These are the rules." At the start of the year I could set a rule and I didn't know if it was going to last or not. I didn't know if it was a good rule or not. Now, I know. . . . I can predict, so failure comes down a little bit and I get success sooner.

Gradually, trial-and-error approaches to problem solving gave way. Kerrie began to be able to see through her students' eyes and to anticipate problems. She adjusted her expectations accordingly. She reported monitoring her own actions: "I have to stop and say, from these kids' point of view, if they're used to answering questions in less than whole sentences and now I'm expecting them to write a long paragraph, 'that's not fair.'" A change in procedure or in the curriculum was needed.

Like many teachers, Kerrie expected boys to misbehave more often and with greater severity than girls, and observation notes indicate she was correct. "*Boys are worse than girls?* Well, yes they are. I can't think of any [serious problem students] I have who are girls. . . . Maybe there are some. I'm sure they are there, [but] I think they're much less common. You know they're there. It's like, why are there more men in prison than women?" Yet observations indicate that although she spent much more time disciplining boys than girls, she seemed to relate well to both and to delight in each group's accomplishments.

Once comfortable with her understanding of what was reasonable to expect from a group of students, Kerrie began to focus on what seemed reasonable for individual students who fell outside the norm, and she engaged in what she called "troubleshooting," helping individual students:

I give them all a standard set of expectations. I hope that those are pretty clear to them. Then individually, when I'm grading things subjectively, that's when [I make] a differentiation between the kids.

Some children, her "lost sheep," needed special help and encouragement:

I have one little girl who is absent every other day because her mom works and someone has to take care of the kids. She is being robbed of her life. All I can do is help her and say, "It hurts you so much to be absent every other day." . . . All I can do is help those I can. Sometimes I'll ask them, "Why didn't you get this done?" [or] "Why didn't your mother sign this?" "Well, I haven't seen her since Sunday." You only know by asking. [Sometimes I make exceptions.] It's the feel I get from the kids. It takes time [to know what to do]. Some of them I'm still zoning in on—zeroing in on them. I know they have problems, and it takes time to find them out.

As indicated earlier, beliefs may be either well or poorly supported evidentially. Based upon their review of the relevant research literature, Good and Brophy (1994) report that "studies of in-service teachers' achievement expectations for their actual students do not reveal much evidence of grossly biased judgments." They assert:

> . . . most impressions that teachers form from interacting with their students are based primarily on students' participation in academic activities and performance on tests and assignments rather than on physical or other status characteristics. More generally, most teachers' perceptions of students are largely accurate and based on the best available information, and most of the inaccuracies that may exist are corrected when more dependable information becomes available. (1994, p. 94)

Further, they argue that different kinds of treatment of individual students is necessary and appropriate at times, especially when recognizing that those most in need of help are least likely to ask for it. The difficulty is to "determine whether a teacher is challenging a student below, at, or above the optimal level" (1994, p. 96). To make a judgment of this kind requires intimate knowledge of a student and of the possibilities for learning inherent in a given educational context.

That teachers are generally open to evidence contrary to their expectations and frequently make adjustments in expectations suggests that there may be more openness to changing beliefs among teachers than is commonly assumed — at least, some kinds of beliefs. The intensity with which Kerrie sought to understand her students' strengths and weaknesses, especially those students judged to be of low ability and tracked, in order to establish an engaging program of study, supports this conclusion. She actively sought data that would help her make the best decisions she could for her students by reviewing student work for common errors, meeting frequently with students to discuss their performance, and conversing often with parents, even inviting some parents to visit the classroom and assist her. Being open and attentive to data that were contrary to expectations — and in the low-ability group there was a good deal of such data — produced some surprising results that helped sustain her tolerance principle. Some students who initially did little work turned around, and Kerrie's expectations rose as a result: "I think of K. He has really come up in the world this year. He started out below zero and he's up to a C. He's in resource." Some students improved their behavior, much to Kerrie's surprise: "A lot of the ones that I used to just really [dislike because of how they behaved] — the girl who dyed her hair [and tried to be seductive] — I really like her now . . . I really do like her. She's tried very hard and she's come a long way this year. . . . She has changed." A willingness to attend to data implies a willingness to risk being proved wrong. It is the higher moral purpose of needing and wanting to provide the best possible education for young people that makes this possible.

CONCLUSION

Beliefs change, but not all changes are for the good. Positive beliefs about students, for example, often change in the face of constant and contrary student behavior, and guilt results (Spencer, 1986, p. 170). Some beliefs are highly resistant to change. If it were otherwise, the people who enter teaching would likely not be the people we would want to teach our children. Steadiness is a virtue: teachers need to stand for something students can count on.

Given what is known about beliefs and belief formation, it is the height of folly to assume that change in any fundamental beliefs is likely to result from involvement in the kind of in-service programs that are often provided for teachers, the kind which involve a few hours of being talked to and of participating in groupwork of one or another kind. Kerrie's movement away from mothering as the essence of service took place over a period of years and represents an outcome of a purposeful and sometimes painful attempt to become a better teacher and to make sense of life in changing circumstances. The course of her development was not laid out in advance but evolved as she sought to better realize herself in the classroom and with and for young people. Change took place within the continuity enabled by Kerrie's being a person centered on service and willing to risk beliefs in order to serve ever more effectively.

Aside from programs that aim to strengthen teachers' content area knowledge which may undermine misguided beliefs or misconceptions, we have come to doubt the value and the wisdom of teacher development efforts that aim at fixing teachers. A more respectful approach to teacher development is needed. Teachers are adults. Who they are as teachers is deeply embedded in who they are as people and in the kinds of lives they lead and have led. A change in deeply held beliefs is not likely to result from participation in in-service programs. Only frustration and disappointment will follow. Instead, we suspect that significant positive changes in belief are byproducts of living within challenging yet supportive environments over extended periods of time and with others who themselves are engaged in the quest for personal and professional development. We suspect that the proper goal of formal programs of teacher development is to help teachers, in Bode's sense of the term (1928), to think together especially about their work contexts in ways that will make them ever more meaningful and increasingly congenial to personal and professional development. Thereby they may become part of the unfolding of a collective moral life and the building of a more fully educative community, a community of competence. This is but to say, that in teacher development, as in all education, the ultimate resides in the immediate (Erikson, 1975, p. 247). Too often this point is forgotten.

Questions for Consideration

1. Kerrie's root metaphor for teaching was "Teacher is Mother." What is your root metaphor? How is this metaphor grounded biographically? How does it influence your thinking about students, learning, content, and the purposes of schooling?

2. Assuming you have identified a root metaphor, what are its weaknesses, its gaps?

3. Over the years you have taught, have your metaphors for teaching, learning, and students changed? Change would be indicated in the language you commonly use to talk about your work. If change is noted, how have your metaphors changed? Are the changes positive? Negative?

4. Kerrie's philosophy of education was captured in a few brief statements of principle. Can you similarly capture your philosophy? What principles underlay the decisions you make in the classroom? Are you proud of your principles? Do they result in a quality education for young people? Do they accurately represent what you care about most and value most as a teacher?

5. What place do service and a service ethic play in your conception of yourself as a teacher?

6. If you have changed teaching contexts, including grade levels, how did the change effect your thinking about teaching and about yourself as a teacher? In comparing the two contexts, what factors proved most influential in changing your views?

7. Have you changed over the years? What effect do your age and number of years of teaching experience have on your current views of teaching? Has your behavior changed as you have matured? If so, how? Are you pleased with the changes?

8. Have you found yourself resisting efforts of others to implement new programs in school or to change the program in some way? Have you

felt threatened by such efforts? If so, why have you resisted? Why have you felt threatened? What, specifically, was threatening? What is revealed about you as a teacher by the answers to these questions?

9. Do you hold contradictory beliefs about teaching? If so, what are they? Are these contradictions sources of difficulty or uncertainty in teaching? How do they impact your practice?

6

Pushing Boundaries and Developing Expertise in Teaching: Three Problems

This chapter focuses on the development of expertise in teaching. Two general questions frame our discussion: how do teachers become expert? And how is expertise encouraged? To address these, we will explore Kerrie's response to a set of three complicated educational problems. But before we turn to our analysis of her experience, it is necessary to provide a brief overview of a slice of the recent relevant research literature that will help situate this part of our study of teaching and teacher development.

EXPERTISE: AN OVERVIEW

Much of the work on teaching expertise has involved making comparisons of novices and expert teachers and noting differences (see Berliner, 1986; 1988). However, how expert teachers become expert, how and why they move from "rule-based behavior to understand[ing] the relevance of context and the constraints it imposes on . . . behavior [to] fluid performance based on intuitive understanding" (Genberg, 1992, p. 491), has remained an elusive question. Yet it is a crucial one for teachers, teacher educators, and others interested in teacher development and school reform. Our experience resonates with the arguments of Bereiter and Scardamalia that expertise is more a process than an end state. It is "a venture beyond natural abilities" (1993, p. 4), one that involves boundary pushing, as Hugh Nibley suggested several years ago:

> Only if you reach the boundary will the boundary recede before you. And if you don't, if you confine your efforts, the boundary will shrink to accommodate itself to your efforts. And you can only expand your capacities by working to the very limit. (quoted in Gillum, 1993, p. 220)

"The career of the expert is one of progressively advancing on the problems constituting a field of work, whereas the career of the nonexpert is one of gradually constricting the field of work so that it more closely conforms to the routines the nonexpert is prepared to execute" (Bereiter & Scardamalia, 1993, p. 9). When facing problems that exceed capacity, experts, like nonexperts, simplify the problems, but they do so "to the minimum that their knowledge and talent will permit" (1993, p. 20). Put differently, experts work at the upper edge of their competence; they push boundaries ever outward, as Nibley suggests. Practice does not make perfect; Aristotle told only part of the story: "For the things we have to learn before we can do them, we learn by doing them . . . " (in McKeon, 1947, p. 331).

When looking for expertise, "we have to find it in the ongoing process in which knowledge is used, transformed, enhanced, and attuned to situations" (Bereiter & Scardamalia, 1993, p. 46). Formal and tacit, or hidden, knowledge — teacher beliefs — play pivotal roles in the development of expertise. Informal, impressionistic, and self-regulatory knowledge also come into play, in addition to the more obvious declarative and procedural types that enjoy such high status with university-based teacher educators (see Eraut, 1994). Informal knowledge refers to "educated common sense" (Bereiter & Scardamalia, 1993, p. 51), impressionistic knowledge to ones' feelings about things, and self-regulatory knowledge to how experts know themselves — it is "knowledge that controls the application of other knowledge" (1993, p. 60). Situational knowledge and knowledge of processes or skills are also important, as we shall see. The key difference between experts and nonexperts is how this knowledge is applied:

> There is something experts do over and above ordinary learning, which accounts for how they become experts and for how they remain experts, rather than settling into a rut of routine performance. . . . Experts . . . tackle problems that increase their expertise, whereas nonexperts tend to tackle problems for which they do not have to extend themselves. (Bereiter & Scardamalia, 1993, p. 78)

Moreover, once a problem is solved, experts reinvest the energy saved in "progressive problem solving" (1993, p. 82).

In this process, what a context demands of a teacher, and the structural and personal support that is available along with the teacher's individual traits, matter a great deal. With respect to the former: "it seems that our skills develop up to the level that is required for the environment . . . " (Bereiter & Scardamalia, 1993, p. 91). With respect to the latter: "persistence, industry, and desire for excellence are relevant," as are innate talents (1993, p. 43). People reinvest their energy in progressive problem solving for various reasons. One is "flow," where investing in "the process of expertise . . . actually *feels* good" (1993, p. 101). As Csikszent-mihalyi (1993) argues, humans "experience enjoyment when we take on a project that stretches our skills in new directions, when we recognize and master new challenges. . . . [J]oy comes from going beyond what one has already achieved, from mastering new skills and new knowledge" (pp. 175, 177). The emotional aspects of developing expertise seldom receive attention, but they are central to its development. Teachers take pleasure in being able to nudge their students along to new heights and in knowing that they have played a prominent role in what has been accomplished. Such motivations are central reasons for becoming a teacher.

Another reason is that the context supports the development of expertise. An unchallenging and unsupportive context, representing a "mismatch between opportunities and abilities leads to a progressive atrophy of the desire for complexity during the course of a lifetime," and without this desire, expertise becomes only someone else's dream (Csikszentmihalyi, 1993, p. 203). Contextual issues will be important throughout this chapter but will be discussed extensively at its conclusion and in Chapters 7 and 8.

A third reason acknowledges that there is a "heroic element in expertise . . . which is not an explanation of why people put effort into the process of expertise, but rather an acknowledgment that the other explanations do not quite do the whole job" (Bereiter & Scardamalia, 1993, p. 102). Put starkly,

> it is easier to develop selves around goals that lead to stagnation rather than to grow[th]. Fear of losing control over one's psychic energy is perhaps the strongest reason why so many will turn their attention inward, and try to defend the self while remaining oblivious of the potential for involvement that surrounds them. (Csikszentmihalyi, 1993, pp. 245–246)

A FOCUS ON EXPERTISE

If expertise is a process, then longitudinal case studies of teacher development, ones that attend to changes in contexts and persons over time, are an especially promising means for increasing understanding rather than the more common and narrower focus on cases, individual problems, or specific tasks (see Eraut, 1994). The decision to focus on expertise in this chapter came from Kerrie switching schools and teaching assignments, and in recognition that, as Berliner notes, expertise is highly context dependent: "knowledge is, for the most part, contextually bound" (1990, p.

10). As previously noted, Kerrie taught her first six years at Rocky Mountain Junior High School, a suburban middle- and working-class school. The last two years she taught there, she was recognized as an expert teacher (see Bullough with Baughman, 1993), and demonstrated many of the qualities associated with expertise, as Berliner (1988) characterizes them:

> The experts are not consciously choosing what to attend to and what to do. They are acting effortlessly, fluidly, and in a sense this is arational, because it is not easily described as deductive or analytic behavior. . . . Experts do things that usually work, and thus, when things are proceeding without a hitch, experts are not solving problems or making decisions in the usual sense of those terms. They "go with the flow". . . . (p. 43)

At Clarke, Kerrie's principal nominated her for teacher-of-the-year honors. In Rocky Mountain, her classes were often seamless, and at times teaching seemed effortless, even though clearly it was not.

DATA GATHERING AND PROBLEM FOCUS

The initial observational focus was to understand what was transpiring in Kerrie's classes, but also to identify characteristic instructional patterns and patterns of interaction—what Guba (1978) calls "recurring regularities." In addition to weekly observations, eight geography periods were videotaped for analysis. For this aspect of our study, an attempt was made to understand how Kerrie's performance was different from, yet similar to, what was observed at Rocky Mountain Junior High School, and to identify central problems that captured or demanded her attention and energy. Patterns were compared and differences were explored in interviews, which proved to be a means for illuminating the influence of contextual factors on Kerrie's development. This is important because the stability of expertise is often assumed, and contextual influences are underplayed in discussions of teaching expertise (see Rich, 1993), just as they often are in discussions of stages of teacher development as noted in Chapter 5. Interview transcripts were viewed as potentially factual statements and as cultural artifacts (Silverman, 1993, p. 100). As such, here as elsewhere, comments made in interview were tested against classroom observations. As cultural artifacts, statements were viewed as representing shared ways of making meaning representative of a particular context. This is important, because although there is much that is common to schools—the patterns of action and interaction that distinguish school from other forms of institutional life — contexts differ, and from this difference there arise situations and ways of responding to these situations that are unique and potentially limiting or challenging, providing new opportunities for teacher development. Thus teaching at Clarke Intermediate School presented new as well as familiar situations to Kerrie. In responding to these situations, she drew on past experience gained at Rocky Mountain Junior High and beliefs as well as resources — ways of framing and responding to problems — made available to her within the new context.

This chapter concerns three problems. A fourth problem, teaching classes composed of increasingly diverse students, will be the subject of Chapter 7. Following Bereiter and Scardamalia, a problem was defined as existing "whenever there is a goal which we do not already have a known way of achieving" (1993, p. 82). We focus on multiple problems because problems interact and affect how or even *if* a teacher will address them. This point emerged early, and is very important to understanding the unevenness of teacher development.

The first problem is a carry-over from Rocky Mountain Junior High School and represents Kerrie's career-long effort to create better ways to teach writing. The second focuses on planning for the Accelerated Academic Program (AAP) that Kerrie taught at Clarke in the afternoon as part of a four-person interdisciplinary team. Bob had been observing in Kerrie's classroom for nearly three months before fully realizing how different Kerrie's planning was in the AAP program as compared with her other planning, and that she was expending an extraordinary amount of energy in the effort, energy likely taken from other activities. Finally, the third problem arose as a result of Kerrie's having been assigned to teach geography, a subject new to her, one she'd studied but had never anticipated teaching.

As these problems were identified, adjustments in data gathering were called for. Interviews and classroom observations were generally adequate for addressing the first and third problems but not the second. Accordingly, arrangements were made to have the AAP planning meetings audiotaped for the purpose of discourse analysis (see Silverman, 1993). Bob realized that there were dramatic differences not only in the amount of talk generated by each team member, but in the roles they played in interaction and in the types of issues or concerns that demanded their attention. From these initial impressions, and through the process of constant comparison (Glasser & Strauss, 1967), Bob identified a set of categories and created a simple matrix for analyzing the tapes (Miles & Huberman, 1984). Categories were created that sought to get at the purpose or function of a statement. For example, was the intention of an utterance during a planning meeting to set the agenda, defend a point, or present an idea? (A statement was assumed to be a complete thought.) In addition, tapes were analyzed to identify types of questions asked by participants. These were coded by noting whether the information sought by the questioner was to understand *what* needed to be done, *why* it needed to be done (its purpose), and *how*, *when*, and *by whom* it should be done. Questions were coded that sought *confirmation* or *clarification* of a point or idea or to *challenge* a point or idea. With very rare exceptions, these categories captured the questions posed during planning meetings. Finally, to get a rough measure of the amount of participant talk, at ten-second intervals the speaker's name was noted and for each speaker a percentage was calculated of total tallies. The assumption was that the analyses, when combined, would provide a reasonably accurate description of the roles played by participants in each planning session, and further, that by comparing the results of the coded planning sessions, changes in team members' roles and in their understanding of teaching AAP students might be revealed. Bob wondered if he could track an increase in expertise by a team member in planning sessions, and if so, whether it would alter team member roles. In part this is a concern because small group role specification typically increases over time and groups become more highly organized (see Slater, 1965). Kerrie faced a choice: either she could become increasingly involved and influential in planning and force the team to adjust to her, or she could accept a passive role, one necessitating little boundary stretching.

School Contexts and Background: A Brief Recapitulation

At this point, it might be helpful to revisit briefly the contexts within which Kerrie taught. At Rocky Mountain Junior High School she taught two groups of seventh-grade students reading, social studies, and English in a core. Later, social studies was removed from her teaching load and she taught English and reading to the same students in two-class-period blocks. Given this arrangement, Kerrie was able to integrate content. At Clarke she was hired to teach social studies — including geography — and English. During her first year there she traveled from room to room, which was disorienting, but during her second year, she was assigned her own room. Clarke was an ethnically and socially diverse urban school that drew students from among the wealthiest and poorest neighborhoods in the city. Half the student body was bused to school. In contrast to Rocky Mountain Junior High's faculty, which was young and rather transient, Clarke's was stable and mature.

Clarke was committed to a middle school philosophy that included a commitment to integrating content across the disciplines and to inclusion.

During her first years of teaching, Kerrie worked with the average- and low-ability classes but eventually began teaching the "Advanced Core" — reading and English. She enjoyed this work. Clarke had its own version of an advanced core, but it was smaller, more exclusive, and tied to the desire of some parents to have a gifted and talented program in the school. In contrast to the Advanced Core at Rocky Mountain Junior, AAP teachers designed the curriculum from scratch. During her second year of teaching at Clarke, Kerrie was chosen along with another teacher to join two highly experienced veteran teachers to be part of the AAP team.

A Biographical Note. Kerrie moved to Clarke during her daughter's junior year in high school. Her son had already graduated from high school and was working. While in some respects her home obligations had lessened from what they'd been while she'd taught at Rocky Mountain Junior High, other and different personal obligations increased in intensity. These need to be mentioned here because the amount of energy a teacher has and how it is invested in teaching needs to be considered in relationship to her life inside and outside the classroom. After all, a teacher's life, like that of any working mother, is not neatly segmented (see Spencer, 1986). Kerrie was not only a teacher, she was also a wife, mother, "housekeeper — I hold things together," primary president (head of a religious organization responsible for instructing and providing activities for children 11 years old and younger), and much more. Balancing the demands of these roles at times proved difficult. Winter, she noted, was an especially trying time. Having started a new business, her husband was often away from home and working with people Kerrie did not know. In response, Kerrie found herself worrying about their marriage relationship and seeking ways of strengthening it. Her position as primary president was also demanding:

One of my problems is that both of my counselors have three or four children and babies—so I have to pick up a lot of their slack. I kind of resent this sometimes. . . .

To make matters worse, her father began undergoing chemotherapy for cancer, and her mother needed considerable emotional support. Given these demands, Kerrie, like other teachers, made decisions about how and where she would invest her energy. Since the work of teachers is unbounded and can easily consume all of one's energy, these decisions have a direct bearing on the development of teaching expertise, a point too seldom recognized (Eraut, 1994). As mentioned, expertise needs to be considered in terms of the interaction between person and place.

Three Problems

Teaching Writing. During Kerrie's first year of teaching at Rocky Mountain Junior High School, feeling swamped by the demands of developing a curriculum for the first time and learning new skills associated with instruction and classroom management, she compromised the desire to have students write extensively and rewrite their work. Having compromised a fundamental value, one stressed in her subject area university methods courses, she felt guilty, but she saw no alternative: "The classes are too large . . . I don't have my kids write much, [I can't because I take] so much time correcting it." Five years later, she reflected on this decision and remarked: "It is like, well, I [didn't] know what else to do, so I'm going to continue on and do the best I can and refine the things that I know I'm doing well" (Bullough with Baughman, 1993, p. 88). Put succinctly, she lacked formal knowledge of ways of teaching writing that might have been suitable to the context while requiring minimal time and energy to learn and implement. Unable to adequately address the problem, she set it aside for a time.

Early in her fourth year of teaching, Kerrie attended an International Reading Association conference and obtained a copy of Nancie Atwell's book *In the Middle: Writing, Reading, and Learning with Adolescents* (1987). As she read it, lights went on. She saw within Atwell's program, Reading and Writing Workshop, the possibility of shifting her program toward a writing emphasis and decided to change her entire curriculum. Her uneasiness with how she had been working came out: "It was like I would add a new really neat trick [to my program], but it still didn't do [what I wanted]. It didn't take those kids to where I knew they needed to be [in writing]."

In the spring term of her fourth year of teaching, Kerrie creatively implemented as much of Atwell's program as she could. She remade the program to fit her context and values. Atwell emphasized students writing, then editing and critiquing one another's work, but she asserted that the teacher should do the final editing. Kerrie saw no reason for that; instead, she met with students, and they did the final editing together. Completed works were photocopied and "published" by displaying them in a public place in the room and originals were placed in student portfolios, as Atwell recommended. But contrary to the program, Kerrie included the study of novels by the entire class rather than focusing exclusively on individual student reading. Like Atwell, she noticed common error patterns in student writing and organized "mini-lessons" to address them. Sharing many of Atwell's beliefs about teaching and learning to write, she closely followed her suggestions on how to organize a class for writing. Class began with students briefly reporting on what they were working on, then determining whether they needed teacher conferences; then came the grading, with an emphasis on progress and goal setting. Reading and Writing Workshop ran smoothly during Kerrie's last year at Rocky Mountain. Students learned a great deal about writing, and their performance was up.

The program change surprised several of her colleagues, who admired what she had been doing. By shifting her program, she took a direction dramatically different from the other teachers in the department. A few parents complained, wondering how their children could possibly learn the rules of grammar in the new program, as they had in the old. Nevertheless, committed to improving student writing and confident in her teaching ability, she persisted, while her colleagues continued as they had before, unaffected by Kerrie's new program.

The teaching schedule at Clarke was less compatible with Reading and Writing Workshop than was the schedule at Rocky Mountain Junior High. At Clarke, Kerrie taught social studies and English, not reading, which meant a significant reduction in the amount of time she had to work with students on writing, and Reading and Writing Workshop was time intensive. As a "roving teacher," she did not have her own classroom, which meant there was no place to display "published" works. The English teachers shared a planning period and a textbook, and the expectation was that Kerrie's curriculum would represent departmental priorities. These problems, coupled with others associated with learning how to work within a new context, forced her to compromise. Kerrie tried combining reading and writing in one period, a suggestion made by Atwell, although never implemented by her, but she could not duplicate her success at Rocky Mountain. Frustrated and disappointed, she divided the week into reading and writing days and gave up trying to develop an integrated program. Seeing no alternative, she expended her energy elsewhere: figuring out how things worked in the new setting, finding her place, and getting to know inner city students. She was not concerned about developing expertise, per se. Her thoughts were on other, more pressing concerns. It was a very difficult year: "The first year at the school was hard. I had to make a lot of changes in one year, and it was hard."

Her second year at Clarke brought another change in schedule, and Kerrie taught eighth grade for the first time. She was determined to emphasize writing more than she had with her seventh graders the year before. But how to do it? Drawing on the experience and personal knowledge she'd developed at Rocky Mountain, as well as her increasing situational knowledge of Clarke students and how they learned, she decided to emphasize journal writing, along with frequent and more traditional writing assignments. In addition, she decided that before work was turned in, students should share it with others in the class, receive feedback, and engage in rewriting. She began routinizing the students to this process the first week of school, as she had done during her last year at Rocky Mountain: "Okay, you're going to do peer response," Kerrie would say, reviewing the procedure. On the board she wrote:

Peer Response

1. Partners
2. 1st person reads aloud, 2nd person listens, takes notes
3. Trade

"Last," she'd say, "you need to read one another's paper and give feedback, so try and pick someone who is smarter than you . . . tomorrow you will write the final copies."

In addition, Kerrie gave specific lessons on the parts of speech. Feeling pressure to prepare the eighth graders for high school, Kerrie taught them grammar on Mondays. Trying to make writing more interesting, she varied the writing assignments. One day, for example, they wrote "picnic poems," which were copied on paper plates that were then stapled to a wall over a red-and-white-checkered plastic tablecloth. Occasionally, students went to the computer lab to work on their writing. (The lab was available five days a term to each teacher.) They did this in addition to reading and reporting on books through a variety of means like the Clarke Filmstrip Festival described in Chapter 7, an idea first developed at Rocky Mountain.

Over the Christmas break, looking ahead to the rest of the year, Kerrie deliberated long and hard about the English curriculum. The role of deliberation in developing expertise ought not be underestimated (Eraut, 1994). Despite her struggle to find ways for teaching mainstreamed students, and her difficulty with some of the boys in the class, she concluded: "If I really believe in writing, then that's what I'd better be doing [with that class]." She rethought the curriculum in light of her prior experience with Reading and Writing Workshop at Rocky Mountain and the previous year at Clarke, what the students had thus far accomplished, and the energy she thought she could put into the effort. Writing, she decided, would become the central focus of the class for the rest of the year. This decision was eased by her increased knowledge of district priorities — student writing ability was tested — and of what other teachers within the building were and were not doing. She discovered, for example, that the computer lab was often available to her and her students beyond her allotted five days.

After Christmas, Kerrie contacted other teachers and made arrangements to use the computer lab for much of the rest of the school year. This was possible because just one other teacher was using the lab at that hour, and he needed it only occasionally. A chart went up on the wall:

What Writers Do

Rehearse (find an idea)
Draft one
Confer
Draft two/revise
Confer
Decide the content is set
Self and group edit
Teacher edit
Final copy—publish

A new daily schedule was established: after giving students a list of types of writing assignments that would have to be completed during the term, class began, as at Rocky Mountain, by Kerrie's quickly reading the roll and noting what students were working on. The wall at the back of the room was set up for publishing (posting) student work. In addition, she began teaching the students new routines. For example, she expected students to read some of their written work to the class:

We have a problem with students leaving for the computer lab and not return-ing [to read their work]. It's okay; I want you to work in the lab, but some peo-ple [still] need to read their writing to us, so we'll [have] to do that at the start of the class [not the end]. Is anyone ready to read to us?

Given the make-up of the class, even minor adjustments in routines were difficult, but Kerrie persisted in refining her program while struggling to help every student.

With these changes, Kerrie recreated at Clarke several of the features of her writing program at Rocky Mountain. There were, however, important differences—new problems—that stretched her teaching skills and understanding. Given greater time constraints and the availability of a computer lab, she found her approach to conferencing with students changed. Instead of calling students to her desk and talking through each student's paper, Kerrie had conferences take place at computer screens.

She read the writing on the screen and gave feedback, and later checked to see if changes had been made. Conferences were brief, involved less coaching and goal setting, and seemed a bit less intimate than those held at Rocky Mountain. Kerrie found them less personally satisfying but saw no reasonable alternative. This was made necessary not only by time constraints, but also by the need to carefully monitor a few students who sometimes roamed the classroom, seeking opportunities to cause trouble, and a few mainstreamed students who had difficulty staying on task. Generally, greater emphasis was placed on self-and-peer editing, which can have positive learning effects, as Kerrie noted. In fact, Kerrie did not want to see a piece until after the student was well satisfied with it.

In addition, the students seemed to require considerable help identifying topics, and a few students needed much teacher direction. Accordingly, some assignments were very specific, like writing a cinquain (a five-line stanza). Listed on the board:

Cinquain

Title, 2 syllables.
Description of title, 4 syllables.
Action about title, 6 syllables.
Feeling about the title, 8 syllables.
Synonym for the title, 2 syllables.

Others, like making a map of the neighborhood, were intended primarily to stimulate thought and to help students who had difficulty getting a writing topic. These were subtle but important changes without which this shift in Kerrie's curriculum could have caused more problems than it solved.

The importance of formal knowledge to the development of teaching expertise is illustrated well in Kerrie's struggle to teach writing more effectively. After all, had she never encountered Atwell's program, she might have continued to tinker with her curriculum and never been fully satisfied with it. She encountered Atwell's work as a result of attending a conference, an opportunity that came because of her university master's degree program. One might conclude that the writing and the English methods courses she took for teacher certification let her down, left her without knowing some of the better options available for teaching writing. Fortunately, her master's degree did not. Three of her classes were tied to teaching reading and writing and provided arenas within which to reconsider her methods in light of current developments in the field. In addition, her growing personal knowledge of common student problems, born of classroom experience, allowed her to adjust the program, to personalize it, by including mini-lessons that helped resolve these problems quickly and efficiently. Personalization of public knowledge is central to teaching expertise (see Eraut, 1994), one of the reasons for engaging in narrative reasoning of the kind described in Chapter 4.

Other issues emerge. Context is important. During Kerrie's last year at Rocky Mountain, her writing program was running smoothly and well. Initial parental concerns gave way to praise even enthusiasm. Indeed, because of her success, she was invited to present her work at a district-sponsored conference. Other teachers sought her advice. While her desire to emphasize writing remained after she'd moved to Clarke, she found it impossible to teach as she wanted, and drawing on her personal knowledge, she often fell back on earlier instructional practices, ones that required less energy and promised greater control of students, now a serious concern. A change in context during her second year at Clarke — getting her own room, in particular — encouraged a reconsideration of the curriculum and a reinvestment of energy in the problem of how better to teach writing, this despite the make-up of the class. What is noteworthy is that just as with the first change that led to her adoption and adaptation of Writing Workshop, this implementation was internally prompted; no one urged her to make the change. In fact, at Rocky Mountain there were a good many reasons *not* to adopt Writing Workshop, as already noted. Similarly, she was not compelled to alter her curriculum at Clarke to place a greater emphasis on writing. In this respect, neither context encouraged change.

In some respects, we touch lightly on what Bereiter and Scardamalia dub the heroic dimensions of expertise here (1993). Kerrie's commitment to teaching writing was deep and abiding, grounded in her fundamental belief in the value of service, as previously discussed, and needing to serve young people to the best of her ability.

If you are going to be a teacher, you really owe it to the kids to do a good job. You know . . . the reason why I'm teaching junior high is that there has to be someone who is willing to put up with the kind of stuff they do and get them through it. I've said this before, [you've got to] love them along and hang in there with them.

While not unhappy with her approach to writing at Rocky Mountain Junior, Kerrie was not fully satisfied with it. The students were not performing as she thought they could, and it nagged at her. Immediately recognizing the promise of Atwell's program, she jumped at it, even though it would require a dramatic stretching of the boundaries of her expertise, something she welcomed. Kerrie transcended the demands of the context. The changes she made at Clarke required less boundary stretching, although this judgment is tempered by considering the make-up of the class. Nevertheless, this change required additional energy, which was in short supply, given the other demands on her time. Most teacher-initiated changes are probably of this kind, where expertise is bumped along incrementally and unevenly. Had a greater amount of energy been required to make the change, it is possible, perhaps even likely, given Kerrie's self-regulatory knowledge—knowledge of how far she could stretch—that she would not have made it. As already mentioned, Kerrie discovered during her last year of teaching that she had pushed herself further than was wise.

Contextual differences are crucial to developing teaching expertise. Differences in physical plant, formal curriculum, school and teacher culture, and philosophy are all important. To press personal competence boundaries in some contexts undoubtedly requires almost superhuman efforts. Neither school fits this category, however. Rocky Mountain may not have supported Kerrie's efforts to teach writing, but nearly as important, it was not hostile to them. Nor was Clarke hostile. In fact, the existence of the computer lab provided a new way for addressing an old problem, and with it came an opportunity for Kerrie to extend her ability, to work at the edge of her competence, as a teacher of writing. Considering this issue brings to light an ability of Kerrie's that may be related to the development of expertise. Although sensitive to contextual pressures, Kerrie had a knack for finding resources needed to achieve her aims, an expression, perhaps, of educated common sense.

Planning AAP

A lot of [planning] is in my head, but in AAP it's all written down on a master sheet that the four of us [on the team] have. . . . [Planning] has been a problem for me because here they are brainstorming and [the other new team member] and I are just sort of listening and saying, "Okay, I'll do that, I'll do that part." "Okay, be sure and tell me how to do that." Then it's written down and it's in someone else's notes and you've got written down what you think you're supposed to do. But later on, when it's the day before you're supposed to do it, I'm running down the hall to [one of the experienced teachers, the one] who understands everything with perfect knowledge. I talk with her and say, "Now, how am I supposed to do this?" . . . Now, I need more lead time to think about it. . . . In the next planning meeting on Monday I'm going to be saying, "Whoa, slow down, I need to flesh this out and I need to write it down so I remember it." . . . I don't really care what [the other teachers think]. I need to know. I can't be deciding ten minutes before class what it is I'm supposed to be doing. I can't do that. It's when I have knowledge that I don't need a lesson plan—right now, I'm on the edge.

Working in AAP presented a range of problems to Kerrie, not the least among them problems arising from the lack of the "mental representation" expert teachers possess that serves as a "guide to move [lessons] forward" and that "allows the teacher to adapt the plan to students' needs as the lesson progresses" (Westerman, 1991, p. 293). Until she gained this knowledge, a "personal knowledge base" (Eraut, 1994, p. 17), she would remain emotionally "on the edge."

Related problems arose because of the difficulty of balancing the extensive demands of teaching AAP with other professional and personal responsibilities. New to the program, Kerrie was unfamiliar with the experienced teachers' ways of planning and working together; she needed to establish her place within the team. She wanted the other teachers' respect. She feared being "[talked] down to" by the experienced team members and wanted to become a full partner. Yet these teachers, intellectually powerful, articulate women, created the curriculum, and they expected it to be taught and taught well. As a novice AAP teacher, Kerrie found herself scrambling to know what to teach, and sometimes feeling uncertain about how to teach it; full partnership would take time. In short, she lacked that aspect of pedagogical content knowledge associated with knowledge of curriculum and curricular materials (see Grossman, 1990).

By comparison, Kerrie's other experiences teaming required only modest stretching and relatively limited investments of time and energy: "[What we have to do for AAP] is mind boggling, just for one subject of two classes. It's partly because we're teaming. It's much easier to plan when you can shut the door and do your own thing." She found herself in a new situation—lacking situational knowledge—uncertain, heavily dependent on the two experienced teachers, and struggling to keep up her part of the team's work. Planning sessions took place at lunch nearly every day and twice a week after school for a few hours. The time demands were extraordinary and sometimes frustrating.

In AAP we plan big units and these are not turn the page and read the next page and answer the questions [type units]. These are things where the teacher has to do research and then present things all the time. We plan twice a week, like on Monday we're going to go and plan probably through dinner [time]. . . . That's only the planning. That's not getting ready to teach.

The curriculum was fluid, plans often changed, and the work was seemingly never ending despite the large investment of time.

Kerrie was not the only one having difficulty keeping up, however. At one point early in the year, one of the experienced teachers burst into tears in a meeting and left in frustration. Despite her knowledge of the curriculum, she, too, had difficulty coping and keeping up, given her other personal and professional commitments: "Planning was really traumatic at the beginning of the year. There just wasn't enough time." The other novice team member also struggled. Kerrie's and the other new team member's dependence on the experienced AAP team members for ideas and ways of working was evident from the analyses of the planning meeting tapes. At the same time (and in contrast to the efforts of the other new member), Kerrie's efforts to be a team player, to hold up her part of the work, and to become increasingly effective within the team and program were quite apparent. For example, audiotapes coded for amount of team member talk revealed, not surprisingly, that the two experienced teachers dominated the conversation. In the tapes recorded in late winter and early spring, they spoke 79% and 81% of the time, respectively. In a planning session following Christmas, 43 questions were coded. Only five of these were posed by an experienced AAP teacher, and the purpose of three of these questions was to challenge another's point of view. Kerrie posed 12 questions that were coded. Six sought "clarification," one "confirmation" of an idea (e.g., "They need to have an end task in mind, do you think, when they start?"), and two, "how" to do something (e.g., "How would we bring in literature?"). The other new AAP teacher asked 17 "clarification" questions (e.g., "Do they write their answers?") and five "how" questions. This pattern changed somewhat, depending on whether both experienced AAP teachers attended a meeting.

In a subsequent planning meeting 65 questions were coded. The pattern of the new AAP teachers asking "clarification" and "how" questions persisted. Experienced teachers asked primarily "challenge" and "confirmation" questions, underscoring their possession of a large store of knowledge about students, the curriculum, and potential problems. This pattern was still evident in the spring meeting noted above, with both beginning AAP teachers' interaction dominated by the need for clarification. Yet Kerrie's colleague participated in no other way in any of the coded meetings. In contrast, Kerrie amplified some ideas and clarified others, indicating that she sought to shape the program that would eventually emerge, as well as learn how to perform her responsibilities better. The other new AAP teacher seemed content to have others tell her what and how to teach. This difference is important.

These roles—somewhat like the relationship of an apprentice to a mentor or master—were generally confirmed through discourse analysis. The experienced teachers, who had created the curriculum and taught it previously, offered and explained their ideas in detail to their new, less experienced colleagues, including thoughts about how best to accomplish a desired outcome. They also sometimes defended their ideas or justified them, even though they were rarely challenged.

What they have to do is write a four-page paper. . . . They have to write in the character's voice, a response to certain questions, like what do you think the nation should do about the slavery question. . . . They have to answer as the character. Only one person in [each class] can be [any one character]. . . .

Unlike the other new AAP teacher, Kerrie presented and explained ideas, although not often. In one winter meeting, for example, the curriculum was altered to include a newspaper unit that drew heavily on her work in the past. This time, she did the explaining: "[We tell the students], you're going to write up a newspaper — you've going to have things like two editorials, two advertisements . . . ." In response to her explanation, the other teachers, including the two experienced AAP teachers, sought clarification and amplified Kerrie's ideas: "So, basically we have three days to do this . . . ." "How much is the newspaper worth?" "I think there should be individual grades and group grades . . . ." Although brief, this exchange mirrored those of the sessions when the experienced AAP teachers presented ideas.

This exchange, and others like it, are helpful for understanding the development of teaching expertise. The data suggest that both beginning AAP teachers were working at the edge of their competence and knowledge. But unlike her colleague, Kerrie was pushing the boundaries of her understanding and ability here and there by seeking greater involvement in planning, including putting forth her own ideas for consideration (and perhaps rejection) by the team, even while she was gaining situational knowledge by learning about the curriculum and how to teach it from the experienced teachers, her mentors, whose vision of the program she began to grasp. Coming to share this vision was important to Kerrie's development as an AAP teacher. The vision represented yet another aspect of pedagogical content knowledge that needed to be developed, one associated with knowing "what it means to teach a particular subject [and which serves] as a 'conceptual map' for instructional decision making" (Borko & Putnam, 1995, p. 47). In short, coming to share the other teachers' vision meant that Kerrie understood the rules for instructional decision making within the team even as she sought to influence those rules. To be sure, by merely listening to the experienced teachers plan the curriculum, Kerrie could learn much and grasp their vision, but when there is no risk taking, no boundary pushing, there is no possibility of developing expertise.

The form or approach to planning AAP added an additional layer of complexity to the general problem of learning how to work with the team and plan an appropriate program for high-ability students. The approach had evolved and represented a modification of the model proposed by Kaplan (1986). The curriculum was organized thematically, and projects were developed that integrated the disciplines and emphasized "productive, complex, abstract and/or higher-level thinking skills" and "self-appraisal" and "criterion referenced" evaluation (Kaplan, 1986, p. 183). To assure development of higher-level thinking skills, the team sought activities at the upper end of Bloom's Taxonomy of Educational Objectives (Bloom, 1956). Activities moved from the simple to the more complex; they were "scaffolded" in an effort eventually to engage students in synthesizing and evaluating knowledge. Kerrie valued this approach to planning but initially felt she and the other new teacher were "just really feeling our way along . . . ." She thought with time it would "be much, much easier," that she would master this skill.

Kerrie's work in AAP illustrates some of the complexity of teacher problems, which come in interrelated clusters. Some are persistent and require constant attention, while others, once solved, remained solved. Learning how to plan using the Kaplan model is an illustration of the latter. Once Kerrie became comfortable with the model, she had little trouble using it and her energy was freed for other concerns. This is an example of progressive problem solving. While learning how to work with the team was initially a problem, learning how to work together facilitated progressive problem solving. Teams can become "second-order environments," as Bereiter and Scardamalia characterize contexts supportive of the development of expertise. This happens only if experienced teachers are willing to give their expertise away. The openness with which the experienced teachers shared ideas with the teachers new to AAP suggests they were willing to give their expertise away. In doing so, ultimately, their own burdens would be lightened and their development enhanced (see Bereiter & Scardamalia, 1993, p. 24).

Expertise is often viewed as an individual possession, but there is also group expertise; "teamwork *is* expertise . . . " (Bereiter & Scardamalia, 1993, p. 21). For expertise of this kind to emerge would require not only that the experienced teachers give their expertise away, but that they also make room for the new AAP teachers to express and test their own ideas. At some point, in so doing, the established teachers demonstrated a willingness to depart from routine teaching patterns, a necessary condition for enhancing their own development, and to engage the new teachers' perspectives. Inclusion of Kerrie's newspaper unit stood as proof of this willingness. Engagement required generosity, patience, trust, and a willingness to test what was believed to be true.

Kerrie sought opportunities throughout the year to participate more fully in team decisions, indicating a desire to increase her expertise and to improve the team: "[I discovered] I needed to be more assertive [in meetings]. . . . Then I discovered . . . the more I asserted myself, the more I got out of [teaching the curriculum]." In particular, she stated that she wanted to learn how to develop a more fully integrated curriculum, which "I love. I think it's great." This love encouraged her to continue to engage other team members, to learn from them, while further developing and testing her own ideas and skills within the team and in the classroom with students.

In contrast to Kerrie, the other novice AAP teacher showed few signs of pushing the boundaries of her expertise. Contextual demands and personal desire to develop, as mentioned in Chapter 5, obviously interact. Opportunities provided by a demanding and rich environment may be rejected, and personal striving may be met by hostility. Generally speaking, Kerrie found in the team a supportive environment that consistently presented new and interesting professional challenges; her colleague apparently did not.

There were limits to how many of these challenges Kerrie could accept, however. Boundary pushing is most likely to occur when there is a balance between ability and challenge; otherwise, frustration and disappointment may set in (Bereiter & Scardamalia, 1993, p. 102). Difficulties related to her roles as wife and mother lessened the energy she had available to grapple with new challenges, and balance was lost. During the winter, for example, Kerrie took a day off because she was physically and emotionally exhausted.

Things have not been the smoothest between my husband and me for, like, a year. [These problems] take my mind out of what I'm doing. [I have difficulty concentrating]. Things pop into my mind—I think—I've got to get that out of my mind so I can give my effort [to teaching].

During this time, and as a means for coping, Kerrie planned activities outside of school to alleviate stress and revitalize her energy, while cutting back slightly on some work-related demands. Such activities, as Pajak and Blase (1989) argue, are important because "personal life factors must be satisfying and rewarding in order to have a positive influence on the professional role" (p. 307). These outside activities required additional time but were deemed necessary, an expression of her self-regulatory knowledge, which is highly individualistic knowledge of how one works best, of how to manage oneself. Kerrie said she learned how to cope from growing up with a sickly mother. In an interview, Kerrie reconstructed this pattern of thought, a pattern she said she followed when confronted with very stressful situations:

I thought, what would have helped my mom? Exercise. Therefore, aerobics. And therefore, the play [I have a part in next month]. I've chosen to take steps to force me to do things; I've said yes to [requests] that I could just as easily [have refused]. I said yes. People think it adds to my stress, but really it allevi- ates stress. . . .

Kerrie needed time away from work and away from family.

Teaching Geography

Kerrie's assignment to teach three periods of a semester-long seventh-grade geography class came despite her not having an academic major or minor in the area, although she had taken a few geography courses in college. In fact, she had not taken any geography classes as a public school student; she had moved around the country frequently with her military family. Once again we encounter the problem of limited pedagogical content knowledge exacerbated by limited subject matter knowledge.

State history filled the second semester. The principal, Kerrie re- ported, "needed someone to teach [geography]," and she was it. Ironi- cally, this assignment came just as the community of professional geogra- phers, responding to the inclusion of competency in geography as one of the goals of AMERICA 2000 (see National Education Goals Panel, 1995) and geography as a core subject, was becoming increasingly concerned about the quality of instruction offered in the area, and the quality of the education of those teaching it: "Standards adoption and use could be hampered because so few teachers are well schooled in geography" (de Souza & Munroe, 1994, p. 47). The hope of the geography community was to take advantage of "the most significant opportunity in the history of this country for geography to move into the first rank of subjects in America's schools" and thereby assure and ensure geography's position in the curriculum (Wilbanks, 1994, p. 43). But to achieve this aim requires a massive effort including teacher education reform. The problem, as Boehm and his colleagues defined it (1994), was that "Students cannot be held accountable for that which they have not been taught; and teachers cannot teach that which they themselves have never learned" (p. 23).

Geography illiteracy is "attributed to the fact that most teachers asked to teach geography were unprepared for the assignment" (Boehm & Petersen, 1994, p. 211). The problem is not an uncommon one.

The national winds of change were blowing strong in geography, as in mathematics and science teaching, but they barely brushed Kerrie's classroom or the walls of Clarke Intermediate School. Despite efforts to develop materials and textbooks around five themes — location, place, human-environmental relations, movement, and regions — identified by the Joint Committee on Geographic Education and presented in *Guidelines for Geographic Education*, such materials found only a small place in the curriculum at Clarke (see Boehm & Petersen, 1994; de Souza & Munroe, 1994). No current textbook was available, although there were numerous maps and some workbook materials that included mention of the themes, and there was a geography facts test handed to Kerrie by the department chair that she understood represented the content that needed to be covered during the year. These, along with materials designed by the National Geographic Society to prepare students for the "Geography Bee" competition, which served as one of the driving program aims, were given to Kerrie, who found herself scrambling to establish a program.

Although she was speaking of prospective teachers, Grossman and her colleagues (1989) provide a useful way for thinking about Kerrie's problem: attention needs to be given to her "content knowledge, substantive knowledge, syntactic knowledge, and beliefs about the subject matter" (p. 27). Content knowledge refers to the "stuff of a discipline: factual information, organizing principles, central concepts" (p. 27). "The substantive structures of a discipline include the explanatory frameworks or paradigms that are used both to guide inquiry in the field and to make sense of data" (p. 29). The five themes fit in this area. Syntactic knowledge "includes knowledge of the ways in which new knowledge is brought into the field" (p. 29). Knowledge of these three kinds is, as Shulman (1987) and others have argued, a "prerequisite for the development of pedagogical content knowledge and instructional expertise" (Rich, 1993, p. 143). Knowledge of this kind allows teachers to make connections among topics and expansions which otherwise are impossible (see Gess-Newsome & Lederman, 1995). Finally, the focus on teacher beliefs underscores a basic and increasingly important understanding that how teachers understand teaching, learning, subject matter, and students has a profound effect on what they do in the classroom. Indeed, these beliefs form the ideological foundation of the relatively stable styles that come to characterize teacher practice (see Zahorik, 1990).

Kerrie approached the problem of developing a curriculum in geography while lacking content knowledge and depth-substantive and syntactic knowledge of the discipline. The nature of geography and geography teaching exacerbated this already worrisome weakness:

> First, the subject is extraordinarily eclectic and integrative. Teachers must be skilled not only in geography, but also in history, science, art, math, the social studies, and all of the technologies required to teach these subjects. . . . They must be good at gathering, displaying, analyzing, and interpreting data. They must understand technologies like GIS, remote sensing, CD-ROM, and the hardware and software necessary to manipulate such systems. And finally, the geography teacher must be sensitive and humane, aware of the need for multiple perspectives, aware that geography has no single meaning, and aware that students must be guided through learning, not forced to absorb. (Boehm et al., 1994, p. 23)

While Kerrie knew comparatively little about geography as a discipline and was unfamiliar with the available technology, she did have an otherwise broad academic background upon which to draw. Facing similar situations, other teachers would typically rely on textbooks for help: Kerrie had no up-to-date textbook, although she was given a good deal of material from two Clarke teachers. What Kerrie knew and understood best were maps and mapmaking. This was her orientation to the discipline, her belief about what it was important to know; and teacher orientations profoundly influence not only what gets taught, but how it is taught (see Grossman et al., 1989). A focus on maps and mapmaking connects to the first two themes of geography teaching — location and place — and potentially might connect to the other three, depending on the instructional approach taken. Kerrie realized that like beginning teachers in other areas, she would have to learn the content and how to teach it — pedagogical content knowledge — as she taught it, and like some of the experienced teachers in Rich's study of teaching expertise (1993), for a time she would be a novice, though with luck only a "temporary novice" (Mevarech, 1995, p. 154). She understood that her lack of subject matter knowledge would necessarily have a profound effect on what was chosen for inclusion in the curriculum; teachers cannot teach what they do not know (see Carter, 1990). In short, she knew that her knowledge of geography was superficial, dated, and based primarily upon her limited academic experience.

In a review of the research on the development of subject matter knowledge among teachers, Ball and McDiarmid (1990) conclude by posing a set of important questions related to the development of teaching expertise:

> According to common belief, graduating teacher candidates lack adequate subject matter preparation, but they will develop deeper knowledge as a

result of having to explain it to others. In fact, we have little evidence to support this assumption. *Does* this happen? If so, how and under what circumstances? How do teachers' understandings of their subjects change as they teach? . . . Do certain approaches to or conditions of teaching foster teachers' subject matter learning more than others? (p. 446)

Turning to the observation notes: from the beginning of the first year Kerrie taught geography at Clarke Intermediate, she established a routine. When the bell rang, an overhead was already on. It projected a set of geographical facts ("What city is the capital of the United States?"), concepts (e.g., longitude and latitude), and definitions, mostly taken from the National Geographic Society program but consistent with departmental priorities. Students quickly went to the class file box, retrieved personal folders, and wrote in their own words what was on the screen for later study and use. The routine was quickly set; students knew that some kind of activity would follow as soon as they were finished writing in their journals. Drawing on observation notes taken the second week of the school year from first-period class, which included Enrique, a blind child:

> (9:17). K. turns on the overhead. #17: "Describe a fjord." (A deep narrow inlet of the sea between high, steep, cliffs). As soon as she turns on the projector, the students are at the box, getting their folders. She points to the world "fjord" and says, "This word is fjord. The J sounds like a Y." Students are working. (9:23). The students are finishing and putting their folders away. They are excited about a school contest — the winner gets a ride in a limo. "Okay, the minute you get finished, get out your flashcards and atlas. . . . " "Anyone else with maps of their bedrooms to be graded?" . . . Students are making flashcards of geography terms (like those on the overhead). . . . Definitions on the back; the word on the front, from the atlas. . . .

A week later the five themes of geography were introduced by having the students draw the symbols for them which were hanging from the ceiling.

A month later, as students entered the classroom, the overhead read: "107. Which one of the earth's four oceans separates the continents of North American and Africa? (Atlantic). 108. The Arctic Circle passes through which U.S. state? (Alaska)." After the students completed their writing, they began working all over the floor, drawing maps on large blue sheets of paper. Kerrie's map hung in the front of the room. Throughout the period students engaged Kerrie and asked for suggestions for improvement. At one point she left the room and the students did not seem to notice; they kept working.

This pattern continued, including Kerrie's modeling and teaching the standards of good mapmaking and having the students practice map reading skills. From observation notes:

> Discusses and labels oceans. "That only leaves us what ocean? Nathan?" "Pacific Ocean." "The Pacific Ocean." K. circulates. "It looks like the biggest problem here is labeling. Even though I'm not a great artist, I can write clearly. . . . "
>
> To help them memorize concepts, games were frequently played, sometimes using flashcards, sometimes team competitions: "The hardest thing on my list, the Ganges River." The first [team member] goes to the map and points to Africa. The kids see he's missed it, and go crazy. The next kid gets it. "I am the greatest," she exclaims.

In the winter the students engaged in a variety of activities that included group projects requiring application of virtually all they had learned about mapmaking and the use of appropriate symbols and of scale to create a "Desk-Top Country" of their own. For some students the task proved difficult and discouraging, and numerous mistakes were made:

> "Everyone sit down and listen. . . . Yesterday, all of a sudden in second period I realized you guys have made a grave error. Partially it is my fault." She explains they have used a symbol for a ship but have used it on land. "So you may need to put in a honking (huge) bay or adjust your coastline. . . . Remember, everything has to have a name. Cities, an isthmus, everything."

References on the videotapes and in the observations to the themes of geography, other than the first two, location and place, are virtually nonexistent after their initial introduction. Yet in the second semester, when the topic is state history, other geography themes occasionally appeared. For example, in March, a unit on pioneers involved putting together an imaginary wagon train that included a "roster, [an] expansion map (had to decide where precisely to settle), a [description of] a day on the trail, a character sketch, [a] wagon drawing, and setting descriptions." Students had to decide where to settle and defend their decisions, as well as anticipate and prepare for potential difficulties both on the trail and in building a settlement. An activity of this kind involved studying not only human-environmental relations, the third theme, but also reasons behind the movement of people and the development of regions. Some connections were made, ones that would be supported by the Committee on Geographic Education, but they were exceptional.

The pattern set that year in geography was repeated in the subsequent year, but Kerrie introduced the themes on the third day of class; they'd been presented during the third week the year before. She began with location:

> "Who knows what longitude and latitude are?" Hands go up. "Can you tell me, Bill?"
>
> "Four squares that divide up the entire world."
>
> "Good. What's the name of the most important longitude line?"
>
> "The Equator."
>
> "Right. And latitude line?"
>
> "The Prime Meridian."
>
> "Yes. . . . Under 'location,' write 'latitude' and 'longitude.'" She spells the words as they write. "The way I remember which is which, I think of 'longitude' beginning with 'long,' and I think of long hair hanging down. Place: what is this place like?"

A week later the students were taught about regions — "How is this place like other places and how is it different?" — and started a worksheet on the five themes which the entire class finished together under Kerrie's guidance:

> "Chris, can you think of another way (in addition to Bingham Canyon Mine) that we interact with our environment?" The boy talks about building levies in Willard Bay. "What's a levy?"
>
> "A dirt wall."
>
> "Yes!"

Observations and five videotapes made of classes over the next month revealed a consistent emphasis on location and place, which were also emphasized on the district geography test, while the other themes disappeared, apparently forgotten. The instructional pattern was identical to the previous year's. Students drew maps, made flashcards (which were used to play a form of bingo, but with geography facts), and in other ways learned about location and place. Facts, concepts, and mapmaking and interpreting skills, knowledge associated with doing well on the Geography Bee and on the departmental geography test, were what the curriculum was intended to develop, little else. Kerrie hit a plateau; her development in this area of teaching was arrested.

A partial answer to the questions Ball and McDiarmid (1990) pose emerges from our data. A deeper knowledge of subject matter content may or may not come from "having to explain it to others." Experience is not necessarily the best teacher; to learn from experience requires reflection on it, deliberation. While Kerrie's knowledge of the content of geography undoubtedly increased — particularly her knowledge of facts, concepts, and definitions — there is no evidence that her substantive or syntactic knowledge increased or that her beliefs about the subject matter changed as a result of her having taught it. Teaching a subject is probably a necessary but not sufficient condition for developing depth understanding of the subject area. Other conditions are likely needed, including time spent reflecting on experience, perhaps deliberating with others about it.

If the major reason for Kerrie's curriculum's failing to achieve the hoped-for aims of the wider geography community was a lack of subject matter knowledge, coupled with a shortage of materials, the solution seems simple: in-service classes in geography and geography teaching. More content knowledge, and a deeper understanding of the substantive structures and ways of generating geographical knowledge, would undoubtedly have helped Kerrie improve the curriculum and move beyond her relatively narrow understanding of geography as a field primarily concerned with location and place. Yet the solution is not so simple. It needs to be considered in relationship to the other personal and professional demands Kerrie was facing, some of which were of a much higher priority, and in relationship to departmental priorities. After all, Kerrie did teach what was on the test, what the department expected her to teach.

Problems come to teachers in clusters and no one can address them all at once; compromises and trade-offs are inevitable. Like hungry men milling about in front of a soup kitchen, some teaching problems are more pushy and more demanding than others that patiently await their turn; still, all must be fed. Necessarily teachers engage in ongoing triage, deciding, perhaps mostly intuitively, on a shifting field what problems will get attention, what kind they will get, and for how long they will hold it. For geography to gain attention, and for Kerrie to have felt compelled to invest in it and to confront the limits of her expertise more fully and more aggressively, would have required something more than a national outcry by the geography community — a cry unlikely to be heard in noisy and crowded classrooms. The work context would have needed to be changed — a district-wide and funded geography initiative might have been helpful, one that had sufficient power to challenge departmental views of geography. Resources would have needed to be invested in freeing up time so Kerrie could have engaged in the study, if she could have been convinced to set aside other compelling and engaging problems. Materials would have needed to be purchased. Kerrie and her colleagues would have needed help to see new and inviting possibilities for teaching geography and had opportunity to deliberate about them. This last point is especially important and speaks to the place of beliefs in the development of expertise: as in life, so in the development of expertise, "being follows imagination" (Moore, 1992). Imagination needs stimulation, which can come in many ways, including from seeing other teachers teach in ways that challenge accepted views, something which happens rarely, and sharing stories of the sort told during AAP planning periods, for example.

SECOND-ORDER ENVIRONMENTS

As we have argued, schools need to be thought of "not only as places for teachers to work, but also as places for teachers to learn" (Smylie, 1995, p. 92; see Sarason, 1990). "Second-order" environments are such places. Smylie (pp. 104–107) offers insight into seven general qualities of such schools:

1. Teachers collaborate. Such schools "provide teachers opportunities to work and learn together" around "flexible agendas." "This environment would encourage teachers to jointly identify and solve problems and develop new programs and practices" and promote analysis of "current ideas, practices, and taken-for-granted beliefs and assumptions" (pp. 104–105).

2. Power and authority is shared. Teachers share leadership and participate in decision making in authentic ways and "across decision domains."

3. Egalitarianism is practiced among teachers. Status distinctions are "reduced by reciprocity in working and learning relationships. Individual talents and expertise [are] identified and organized so everyone with expertise, regardless of position or status, at some time or another serves as a model for others" (p. 105).

4. Teachers' work is varied and challenging and includes opportunities to exercise choice. "An optimal environment would provide variation and challenge in teachers' work through the types of collaborative working and learning relationships and opportunities for participation . . . " (p. 105). In addition, teachers would have opportunities to engage in interesting work outside of the classroom.

5. There are clear goals and systems for providing feedback that "give work, learning, and innovation direction and meaning" (p. 106). Such goals should be developed jointly and include provision for ongoing and critical feedback.

6. Work and learning are integrated. Learning is understood as part of a teacher's job.

7. "Access is provided to multiple sources of information for learning

and external references to best assess their performance and accomplishments" (p. 106).

These are important qualities, although they say little about the interaction of person and place that leads to development. Persons vary dramatically in how they engage and make their worlds meaningful (see Ornstein, 1993), as Kerrie and the other teacher new to AAP demonstrate. The range extends from the teacher-loner who relishes solitude on one end to the chatty, aggressive, unofficial faculty party organizer on the other; and from the contemplative thinker to the seemingly mindless doer. To be sure, diversity of this kind, that speaks to the teacher particularity discussed in Chapter 2, complicates efforts to encourage teacher development—no program, certainly, will fit all teachers or suit their dispositions—but it is also an important resource. It is a source of engaging problems, a factor that contributes to making schoolwork interesting and challenging. And it is a repository of imagination of amazing scope and depth containing ideas and insights needed to frame and successfully address problems in ways that will enrich and enliven the work lives of teachers and the educational experience of young people. Thus,

> Rather than trying to find the one best way to "develop teachers," we need to consider how to find ways of helping teachers to identify their own support needs and preferences and then to provide a wide variety of opportunities and strategies for them to take control of their own professional development. Just as there is no one way to educate every student, neither is there one way to provide the necessary assistance and support for new [or, we would add, established] teachers. (Cole, 1992, p. 378)

In all this, the role of principal leadership is central. The place of in-service leaders and teacher educators is less clear, although for teachers involved in professional development schools (PDSs), teacher educators have an important part to play establishing conditions supportive of teacher learning (Robinson & Darling-Hammond, 1994; Bullough et al., 1997). They can help teachers to lift their sights and imagine things not as they are but as they could be. They can help generate resources needed for imagination to become reality—to honor expressions of imagination and talent. With teachers they share the responsibility of creating second-order environments, places that invite teachers—indeed, all those who live and work within schools—to press the boundaries of their expertise ever outward and support them in their ongoing quest to improve their practice. The aim is to achieve a "harmony between institutional imperatives [to reform] and individual prerogatives, [and] between the conditions necessary to attempt systematic change and the conditions that engage individual teachers in their work" (Little, 1993, p. 141).

A SUMMATION

The unevenness of Kerrie's development in general, and of teacher expertise in particular, is striking, although not wholly surprising (see Levin & Ammon, 1992). Often expertise is thought of as a state of being, when it is more a matter of becoming, of pushing back boundaries here and there, and as energy is made available for identifying and confronting new and more complicated problems. Moreover, expert "thinking often proceeds not step by step but in leaps" (Hunt, 1993, p. 549) and involves projections of imagination into the unknown. Striving for expertise in teaching is complicated by the nature of education-related problems that are especially messy, overlap, and come in clusters rather than rows. As an experienced teacher, Kerrie brought teaching skill and personalized knowledge with her to Clarke from Rocky Mountain, but there were no guarantees that this knowledge would serve her or her students well at Clarke. She needed situational knowledge. Having once shown expertise in teaching does not guarantee that one will continue to demonstrate expertise, especially in a new setting, and settings are always changing: a new class and a new group of students; a change in content area or level; a shift in district policy toward inclusion or integrated curriculum; faculty turnover; and changing teacher skill and understanding, which themselves alter the context.

Getting to know students quite different from those she had taught at Rocky Mountain was not the only challenge Clarke presented to Kerrie, although it was undoubtedly the most educationally important and personally intimidating, as we shall see in Chapter 7. Planning AAP presented a new set of challenges for Kerrie, ones that held the promise of calling forth greater expertise, but ones that also brought the possibility of public failure. In the context of the planning team, she could not function as she had in the past, by planning only in her head, which other experienced teachers commonly do. This option was not available; neither the team nor Kerrie would allow it: "I'm forced to go and plan AAP, I'm forced to go and plan," she stated in an interview. She relished the challenge of teaching gifted and talented students, and, despite the huge time investment, enjoyed the planning meetings, even though much of the time her role was limited to an evolving apprenticeship. In these meetings she learned a great deal about curriculum and teaching, and with time, as she continued to press for more involvement in team decisions, boundaries were pushed back and Kerrie's knowledge and commitment grew. Working with the two experienced AAP teachers helped her see new educational possibilities, ones formerly not imagined, and beliefs changed. In an interview, for example, Kerrie remarked that formerly she thought her work at Rocky Mountain had been "rigorous," but "[I now realize it] was barely rigorous at all." Her beliefs about what young people were capable of doing had changed, fundamentally and positively. She expected more. Expertise in teaching does not come easily or quickly.

In contrast to these challenges, establishing the Writing Workshop at Clarke involved only a modest boundary stretching. She could and did draw heavily on her prior experience and knowledge gained from the program at Rocky Mountain Junior High School, but her teaching skills changed and broadened nonetheless. Among other new skills, she developed the ability to run a computer lab and to give pointed and effective feedback on student writing at a computer screen.

Kerrie's shifting and parceling out of energy from one problem to another seemed to take place intuitively. She did not formally prioritize problems in either school, although there might be an advantage to doing so. She would probably have needed help to do this. Rather, she seemed to respond to an internal vision of what a productive class was supposed to be and look like and made decisions about how much energy she could give to each class, minimally. This is important at a general and theoretical level because developing expertise may be related to teachers' possessing a deep and very basic understanding of educational purposes, of what schools are supposed to accomplish (see Copeland et al., 1994). At a more specific level, it may depend upon recognizing the educational purposes and envisioning the educational possibilities inherent in specific subject areas and learning contexts, a point to which we will return in Chapter 8.

In geography, Kerrie had no such vision, or at least, her vision was quite narrow; but she did have one in each of the other subject areas she taught, and for which she'd had more than adequate preparation — once again we confront the importance of knowledge of various kinds to the development of expertise. When Kerrie possessed such visions, as when teaching writing, diversions from them called forth an increased investment of time and energy, provided such time and energy were available. Sometimes they were not. Occasionally Kerrie was almost overwhelmed by the demands of teaching, and backed off from a problem for a time. (We will see examples of this in the next chapter.) Certainly a fair amount of a teacher's time is spent dealing with problems that are enervating and ultimately uninteresting from the perspective of professional growth, but nevertheless grimly insistent.

Kerrie had a knack for locating opportunities for development within the school. Since her first year of teaching, involvement in the wider school community was a central part of her conception of professionalism (see Bullough, 1989, chapter 6), a point we will return to later. In an interview I asked Kerrie why she wanted to teach in AAP even while she knew it would be very demanding of her time and energy. She responded:

I always volunteer. I had a hard year last year, but I also had it really easy academically. I was ready to do something else; it was a challenge, [although it's been] a lot of work.

Furthermore, she thought that professionals need to be "at the leading edge, working so that you're pushing the edge. . . . Why not be the best, and be experimenting and pushing, so that you're preparing kids better for what they're going to see in the future?" This attitude, which was much in evidence at Rocky Mountain, transferred to Clarke Intermediate and well represents the qualities of teachers who keep learning.

Her actions were consistent with her words. As noted, since her certification, she had taken more than three dozen courses, served on a variety of committees, and in other ways sought to be engaged in the profession, expand her teaching knowledge, and improve her practice. "Professionals," she said, "are always growing." Not surprisingly, Kerrie's principal characterized her as a "progressive teacher," one who "stays on top of her profession." This said, AAP proved to be "a killer," and she expressed the need to back off from some of her other school commitments as a result: "[You] bite off a little and your mouth gets full really fast."

The quest for expertise in teaching plays out in the complicated interaction of person and place and can be understood only in relationship to a broad range of knowledge, diverse beliefs, personal commitments, and shifting professional demands. Expertise, as Kerrie's story illustrates, is context dependent and highly idiosyncratic in nature. Some contexts— second-order environments—are more friendly to its development than others; and some persons are more likely to manifest expertise than are others. Moreover, expertise is fluid and uneven, as Kerrie's work on the AAP planning team suggests, and may involve dramatic leaps in understanding and skill as well as small, almost imperceptible increases. And sometimes a plateau is reached. Undoubtedly, all teachers have gaps in their knowledge and in how to utilize it effectively. Settled and secure, some teachers are comfortable living within receding boundaries. For others, like Kerrie, the discovery of such gaps is an opportunity to push boundaries a little here and there.

If this is true, then, one wonders whether or not the disposition to engage in progressive problem solving is a learned trait, an expression of a general orientation toward life and temperament, or both, as this chapter in some ways suggests. A context may be rich in possibilities, but individual teachers must choose to act upon them if professional growth is to result. Conversely, a teacher excited about the possibilities of developing new approaches to teaching and pushing out the boundaries of expertise can be worn down over time by an oppressive work context, an inappropriate teaching assignment, or serious and persistent problems at home. Part of Kerrie's story is a gradual wearing down.

Questions for Consideration

1. What is an expert teacher? Do you see signs of expertise in your own teaching? Do you engage in "progressive problem solving?" If so, how commonly do you work at the upper edge of your competence?

2. Do you find that you often pull back from risks and back away from boundaries, rather than push them outward? Are you pleased with your pattern?

3. Have you ever abandoned a program as Kerrie did when she embraced Atwell's approach to teaching writing? If so, what prompted the change? Was it internally or externally motivated (or both)? If you have, what was the result of your efforts? Did you find your expertise growing?

4. How supportive is your work context of the efforts of teachers to improve their practice, to become more expert? What, specifically, is done to support such efforts or to impede them? What would you change if you could? Are the resources available to enhance teacher learning adequate? What additional resources would be helpful? Where might you go to gain these resources? Who could you go to for assistance if you wanted it?

5. How heavily are you invested in improving your practice, in becoming more expert?

6. What types of knowledge would be most helpful in nurturing your development in valued directions? Kerrie struggled in geography. Is your content area knowledge adequate? What are you doing to improve your knowledge base?

7. Was there a time when you lacked situational knowledge? If so, how did you go about gaining the knowledge you needed?

8. Does your self-regulative knowledge serve as an adequate guide for directing your development? Do you know how you learn, and are you effective in directing your learning about teaching?

9. When you have expertise, do you willingly give it away to others? If you teach in a team, how do team members support one another's development?

7

Inclusion and the
Context of Teaching

Contexts dramatically influence not only the opportunities made available for teacher development, but also the direction in which development takes place. Among the most dramatic recent changes in schools pushed along by the postmodern celebration of diversity is the national move toward inclusion. Initially spurred on by federal legislation contained in the Individuals with Disabilities Education Act (1975), ever-increasing numbers of students formerly served in self-contained special education classrooms are in regular education classes. Teachers face the daunting challenge of providing an adequate education for them while not losing sight of their obligations to serve other students. The opportunity to develop new teaching skills and insights are immense in such contexts, but the complexity of the problem and the difficulty of meeting expectations can be overwhelming, if not debilitating.

A good deal of legal uncertainty surrounds mainstreaming (see Huefner, 1994), but regardless, there appears to be a strong movement toward full inclusion. The federal requirement that placement decisions be made on an individual basis maximizes parental influence over student placement and encourages the trend toward full inclusion. Examples abound. In a case involving an elementary-age child born with Down's syndrome, for instance, the federal court for New Jersey supported the child's parents' wishes for inclusion and "viewed integration as 'a right, not a privilege of a select few'" (Zirkel & Gluckman, 1993, p. 99). Paralleling this movement, and driven by a commitment to detrack students, there is a growing body of evidence demonstrating that with early intervention and appropriate and ongoing support, including teacher education and curriculum revision, most students who formerly would have been candidates for pull-out programs or separate special education can succeed in the regular classroom. The key is prevention, not remediation (see Madden et al., 1993). Despite the growing strength of the movement, both inside and outside of special education the debate over inclusion

rages, particularly the inclusion in regular education classrooms of severely disabled students (see Fuchs & Fuchs, 1994). Parents themselves are
divided (see Huefner, 1994).

Meanwhile, regular education teachers find themselves increasingly
facing classrooms sprinkled, sometimes packed, with students who formerly would have been taught elsewhere by specially trained teachers.
Like other Clarke teachers, Kerrie taught such classes. In some respects
this part of her story is not a pretty tale, but it bears telling for the
questions it raises about the contradictory nature of teaching and teacher
development and the negative impact some administrative decisions can
have on that development. The story we tell here underscores the importance of attending carefully to the contexts within which teachers work to
make certain they maximally support teacher learning.

DIVERSITY AND MAINSTREAMING

When making the transition from Rocky Mountain to Clarke Intermediate
School, Kerrie's most serious problem, she said, was "getting to know the
[student] population." Without this situational knowledge, what Grimmett and MacKinnon call "pedagogical learner knowledge" (1992, p. 387),
and an essential component of general pedagogical knowledge, she initially found it difficult to "troubleshoot," to anticipate difficulties within
the classroom and prevent them. As noted, the Clarke student body was
much more diverse than the population Kerrie had known at Rocky Mountain Junior High School, and generally much more challenging.

I think it was [a] bigger [problem] than I thought it would be. I'm still adjusting
to it. . . . I'm unsure . . . of where [some students] are coming from. . . . But I
[am] learning how to connect with different groups of people. . . . The kids
are less well behaved [than they were at Rocky Mountain]. . . . [Excluding the
AAP kids], they don't do homework, they don't buy that this is important. . . .
[Students are more likely] to come from a single-parent family, [to] be blue
collar—or no collar.

Having made good progress learning about her students, during her
second year at Clarke, Kerrie seemed to have no difficulty troubleshooting: "Now I can troubleshoot things that I couldn't troubleshoot [during
my first year at Clarke], because I didn't know [the students well
enough]." Her aim was a personalized curriculum where ethnic diversity,
in particular, could easily find positive expression, and students could mix
across groups and cross boundaries. She had the students do projects in

groups, for example, and students of different backgrounds generally worked together productively and well.

Mainstreamed students made the student population even more diverse. Extending the middle school philosophy at Clarke, the principal and many of the teachers were committed to mainstreaming students, to inclusion. As the principal stated in an interview: "It's good in terms of the diversity issue; this world is made up of all different types of people, and they need to all be respected and valued." Unfortunately, this commitment did not necessarily bring with it either a reduction in class size or additional instructional support for teachers who worked with mainstreamed students. This meant that during her second year at Clarke, Kerrie had at least nine or ten resource students in her first four class periods, including Enrique, a blind child, and Ashton, one of a small group of students in the school born with Down's syndrome. Generally speaking, these students were placed in classrooms by counselors without consulting teachers, but regardless Kerrie would have accepted them, given her teaching principles.

Facing increasingly diverse classes, Kerrie nevertheless sought to avoid categorizing students by ethnic background, resource status, or handicapping condition. Consistent with the research on teacher expectations noted in Chapter 5, her focus was on the individual student and helping that student, as needed, to connect appropriately to the curriculum; she recognized some adjustments would be necessary, but the curriculum was designed to allow a range of student responses. In practice, Kerrie even tended to forget which students were labeled "resource" and focused on responding to their needs, as she could and as she understood them: "I don't like to keep reminding myself that they are kind of deficit; I like to give help to whoever needs it." Drawing on her previous experience, she had "learned that every child takes on a different character in every classroom, and educational records . . . cannot be trusted" (Berliner, 1990, p. 8). Such students were fully integrated into class activities and treated as nearly as possible like other students. Classroom observations failed to identify who was and who was not a resource student. Enrique and Ashton were the exceptions.

Enrique

A child of Spanish-speaking immigrant parents from South America, Enrique was placed in first-period geography, a class described in the previous chapter. He was a quiet boy, independent and usually undemanding. An aide was assigned to Enrique by the school district. While the aide did not attend class with Enrique, she was available when he or one of his teachers requested help. For example, when Kerrie needed to send notes home to Enrique's parents, the aide and Enrique helped her to put the note into Spanish and then write it in Braille. This was a cumbersome and time-consuming task, but important for making certain Enrique received the assistance he needed.

Kerrie received no special training to learn how to teach Enrique effectively, nor was there direct instructional assistance available, despite the difficulty of creating a parallel curriculum for him. Nor was help forthcoming for the other students designated "resource." As noted in the previous chapter, in geography, Kerrie emphasized learning geographical facts, locations, and concepts, primarily through mapmaking, including creating colorful and fanciful maps of imagined countries. Maps were frequently peer evaluated, as an additional means for teaching concepts and assuring quality work, and produced by ever-changing student groups. To make memorization fun, team competitions, followed by rewards of snacks to the winners, were occasionally organized. The room was literally covered with brightly colored maps and pictures of various geographical features. But for Enrique, this did not matter; he could see none of it.

Enrique could participate in some of the regular classroom activities, like the competitions, but not others. Instead, he worked with a textbook and a related collection of Braille maps made available by the school district. When he could not participate in class activities, he either quietly read his textbook at his desk, which he did without complaint, or worked at a table Kerrie had set up in a corner that offered enough room for him to read maps and keep a Perkins Brailler for writing. Despite class size (30 students), Kerrie was well aware of Enrique, as notes from several class observations indicate.

> September 24: (8:34). While other students are working, Kerrie comes to the table and sets things up for Enrique. . . . "Can you tell me (looking at the Braille text) what pages you are on so I can make certain you are on the right map? I want you first to feel the map and get familiar with it, where the water is and what the continents are like." She gets him started. (8:36). Kerrie turns to the rest of the class. "All right, are you ready? . . . First of all I want you to tell me all the names of the projections." "Don't talk." (They put up their hands and do not respond until she calls on them.) "Polar." "Yup." As they give the answers, she writes them on the board. "Okay, on your paper tell me what these are." She has nine maps on the back wall numbered 1 to 9. The task is to properly label the maps: "Mollweide, Interrupted, Polar. . . . " (8:40). Students are quiet and working. Enrique is nois-

ily typing with his Braille machine in the back. (8:42). Kerrie asks,
"Who needs more time?" Lots of hands [go up]. (8:44). "Who still
needs more time? Okay, you have about one minute." (8:45). "Pass
your papers to the right. . . . " [Class corrects the work.] (8:54). [Ker-
rie, returning a map assignment]: "I want to show you the best and
the worst work — why this [map] got an A and this one a D. . . . "
She compares and contrasts two maps — the identity of the person
who drew the bad example is hidden, she says: "he's from another
class." "This [good one] is Brian's. He did a good job." Enrique is quietly reading. (8:56). "I want you to turn your [maps] over and write
one thing you could have done better. Even Brian could find one
thing he could have done better. This is a chance to do even better on
your next map." She passes out paper while they write — this is routinized. The kids pass the paper along down the rows. . . . She passes
out rulers and steps out of class and into the hallway [to check on
something] for a few seconds. Immediately a heavy-set boy swats a
couple of girls with his ruler, [and] a couple [of kids] sword-fight. She
returns . . . and expresses displeasure. (9:00). Pointing (to a series of
brightly colored and labeled posters on which she has colored symbols
for each concept), "These have been on the wall since the beginning
of the school year. They are ways of studying geography (locations, re-
gion, movement — people, goods, ideas — place, human — environment, interaction). [We're going to work with these concepts]. "I
want everyone to hold these [rulers] still. Just listen." And they do.
"Okay, what I'm going to ask you to do" — Enrique walks to her, inter-
rupts, makes a request, then gets a Kleenex (his nose and eyes run),
blows his nose (walks to the garbage can and deposits the used tissue),
and returns to the table as Kerrie finishes her directions. . . . [The students begin working and Kerrie] comes to Enrique. (9:11). She has
him read. "Do you know what scale is?" "Measuring." "Yes." Then
she explains [the concept to make certain he understands]. She has
him read to her. A Memo: Really ought to put writing with the
Braille so teachers can tell what the Braille book says. It is very hard
for K. to tell [what Enrique is working on]. Kerrie asks: "Does the
map come before or after the writing?" "Read this, and tell me what
it says." He reads. "Stop, that's not good." (9:14). She gets her copy of
the textbook. He reads, "This says chapter 7, using a grid." "That's
the one I want you to do . . . it's now time for class to end, so [you'll
do this] next week." She leaves and compliments the class. . . . (9:30).
"Put your colored pencils away. You'll have another day to work on
this . . . put all your rulers away, please." The students stand up to
leave. Kerrie: "When your bottoms are in their assigned seats, I will

excuse you." Holds them until they're all sitting. "Goodbye, have a nice weekend."

This was a typical day for Enrique in Kerrie's classroom. Whenever possible she involved him in class activities, including group work, and when it was not possible, she kept him working while she monitored the class.

Students were well aware of Enrique in the classroom, and they looked out for him and for opportunities to be helpful. Like Kerrie, they obviously liked him a lot. Those who sat nearby helped with his work, and students walked him to and from class. His presence in the classroom required that Kerrie provide a parallel curriculum, but this demanded only a relatively modest investment of time and energy on her part, although the difficulty of working with the Braille textbook was frustrating and at times confusing, as class observation notes illustrate. In most respects, certainly socially, Enrique was nearly a full class participant whose presence enriched the educational experience of his classmates, just as interaction with them enriched his experience. For the most part, Enrique presents an example of a reasonably successful inclusion effort, although Kerrie certainly should have received greater assistance working with him and the other resource students. Ashton's story offers a stark contrast.

Ashton

Bob became aware of Ashton during his first observation of fourth period during fall term. There was a fire drill, and while Kerrie got the other students, all 29 of them, lined up and ready to march toward the exit, Ashton became hysterical, and holding his hands over his ears, cried out loudly, as though in pain. Kerrie told the class to march out and "line up against the fence" while she tried to comfort Ashton and get him out of the building. He would not move until a male counselor came by and assisted Kerrie by physically moving Ashton along. Bob went with the students to the fence. After the fire drill, Ashton was late returning to class. Kerrie left the room once to find him. He returned, sat at his desk, and began picking at the sole of his tennis shoe. Additional observations follow:

> September 1: (11:36). [Students working]. Kerrie circulates and goes and sits next to Ashton. He pulls out a sheet of paper — she questions him, encourages him with his writing. While working with A. she scans the classroom and tells one student who is very loud to quiet down. (11:42). Still working with A. She looks him straight in the eye as they talk. (11:43). Kerrie leaves A. and begins circulating. A. puts away his paper. (11:44). A. out of his seat. Kerrie engages him, takes

him to the back of the room, and shows him a magazine. He is not interested. (11:45). A. goes and sits on a chair and begins digging at his shoes. He gets up and wanders, looks at the magazine rack, takes a *Sports Illustrated* with him to his seat, and puts it in his backpack.

October 18: Bell. Kerrie reads the roll immediately. Students are quiet. All are in their desks but one boy, who finally sits — noise rises. Kerrie stops: "There is side talking. . . . " Waits. Quiet. Completes the roll. "Please clear your desk so there is nothing on it." She starts reading [to the class from *Cal Cameron by Day, Spider Man by Night*]. While Kerrie reads, Ashton draws on [the sole of] his shoe, with his foot propped on top of the desk. (11:17). "Okay, I'm glad you cleaned your desk. We're going to do an art project." Kerrie passes out paper towels: "Take two of them and put one of them on your desk, put the other on your lap." Passes out paper. "I did this twice before getting it right." "Okay, please only take one straw, and don't bend it." Passes out straws. "We're going to make a design. This is black ink. I'm going to come around and squirt some out. You'll want to put your straw near it and blow it into a shape. Then you're going to fold it this way (demonstrating)." She goes around and squirts ink on the paper. Kids blowing intently — it's thick and hard to blow. . . . Kerrie: "This will make you light-headed, so take your time. . . . " Kerrie does Ashton last. . . . [They make interesting shapes]. . . . "Thanks for giving me your attention. While I walked around I heard you say, 'Mine looks like a . . . ,' and that's what I want you to write five sentences about. . . . It's not what I think but what you think [that matters]." It is hard to get (11:36) them settled and writing. "It's still too noisy. . . . Okay, people who are still messing with your pictures, you are done." Ashton still messes with his. Kerrie looks at him and very quietly says, "Ashton, Ashton," and shakes her head "no." (11:39). Students are settled. 22/27 are writing, but not Ashton. Kerrie goes over to help him. She stops him from tapping on the paper and gets him to unfold it, takes a piece of paper out of his folder, and gives it to him. (11:42). Kerrie explains the assignment to Ashton and works with him to get him writing. . . . (11:45). Ashton sits, blowing his straw and tapping at his paper. (11:46). Still tapping. (11:50). Ashton wanders toward Kerrie. He stands by her and asks if he can go wash his hands. He leaves.

November 11: [Students are going to present filmstrips that tell the story of a book they've read]. (11:08). Kerrie finished reading to the class. "Okay, how many of you are ready for the Clarke Filmstrip Fes-

tival? Are you ready to do yours, Ashton?" "Yeah." "Okay, Ashton
looks like he has a killer filmstrip." Kerrie helps Ashton get set up.
Kerrie: "Have any of you read this book? It's one of my favorites,
Ralph S. Mouse." Everyone is silent and attentive. On an audiotape
made at home, A. haltingly tells the story of Ralph S. Mouse. Kerrie,
referring to one of the frames, "There's Ralph, in a pocket." Ashton
stands at the projector; there is a noise when he is supposed to change
frames, but he's not able to keep the pictures and the story together.
As the end approaches, he nervously rocks back and forth. The class
sits silently, able to understand only small parts of the tape. A. finishes. Kerrie: "What do you say, guys?" Applause. A boy yells out
across the room: "Just think, Tatter (his nickname), you're better than
half the kids in the class!" Kerrie: "Who can top that? Who's next?"
. . . A. asks to go to the bathroom. He's gone ten minutes. . . .
(11:36). Students are getting a bit restless. A. sits picking his nose and
rolling boogers, which he sticks on the bottom of his desk, and then
roots for more. This goes on for 10 minutes without interruption.

January 18: (11:10). Bell. Kerrie reads the roll. Ashton drawing on
his shoes, foot on top of the desk — he's flexible! . . . Kerrie reads to
the class from a novel, *Missing May*. A. draws on his shoe. [She has increased the amount of writing they're doing, and students are working on a variety of writing assignments in the computer lab. She calls
out student names and they tell her what they are working on; she
writes it down.] Jack: "I'm still doing a letter to my cousin." Terry:
"A report on handguns." Kerrie: "Ashton, do you remember what you
are working on?" A: "A comic." Kerrie: "That's right." . . . (11:20).
Kerrie helps Ashton get his folder out. He has a few cartoons. "Ashton, write what I'll write on the board in your journal and take it
home to your mom. You sit there (pointing to his desk), and you write
it." She writes on the board: "Ashton needs a simple biography to
read. He needs to pretend he's that person. January 31st he will tell
about his life. Call if there is a question." "Ashton," Kerrie asks, "can
you copy this message on the board and take it to your mom?" "Sure."
He tries to get organized. [He now has a student tracker who is assigned to help him] and she moves around to his side. (11:25). She
gets Ashton writing after he moves to another seat.

February 9: [Students are working on a map]. (11:12). Kerrie: "I
want you to draw a map of your neighborhood." She shows the map
she drew [and explains it]. (11:15). Students move around and get to
work. . . . Ashton is busily working; although his tracker is absent,

he seems to understand what he needs to do. . . . (11:19). A. goes to Kerrie and asks for the pass to go to the bathroom. After a brief chat, he leaves. . . . (11:27). Ashton returns, sits down and starts working. Kerrie is circulating, helping students. . . . (11:32). Ashton goes to Kerrie, who is circulating, holds up his map, and begins talking, "Ms. Baughman, Ms. Baughman," but she's busy with other students. He waves his map. When she finishes [with the other students] she turns to him. He asks her a question; she responds and gives some suggestions. He returns to his seat. A minute later she works her way to his desk and gives some specific advice.

In an interview Kerrie was asked if prior to having Ashton in her class she'd had any experience working with Down's syndrome children: "No, only going to the Special Olympics and being a hugger," she said. She admitted to being surprised that he was not "able to learn more":

He comes across as pretty bright, in a way. He has a way of looking like he's understanding what you are saying. . . . He's manipulative. When he doesn't want to do something, he stops. I didn't know he was going to be so stubborn and manipulative.

Lacking experience with and formal knowledge about such children, she simply did not know how to work with him and seemed deeply frustrated at times: "he was definitely different."

Not knowing what else to do, instead of beginning with a separate curriculum for him, she began the year by letting him try what she had planned for the other students, to see "what he was going to be able to do." Then, early in the school year, she participated in two four-hour meetings to set learning goals for Ashton. Having threatened a lawsuit, Ashton's mother brought a lawyer with her to each meeting. In response, lawyers representing the school district attended, along with the principal, vice-principal, counselor, other teachers, and three district resource specialists. Kerrie felt under tremendous pressure to respond to Ashton's learning needs; but she did not fully know how to respond and at times felt anger at being in such a position. In the meetings she helped set specific learning objectives for him and was determined to help him produce work that would indicate progress toward those goals, even while her doubts about his ability grew, along with her recognition of her own limitations. The idea was that his work would accumulate in a portfolio and stand as evidence for his parents that he was taught.

His mother also helped set the goals. One objective was to teach him how "to write a friendly letter or note, a thank-you note." Kerrie appreciated these suggestions, hoping that they would provide the direction she needed to finally get him engaged in class. She also was expected to keep "an anecdotal record of him . . . I was supposed to do a check sheet [on his behavior] but (laughter) you can't check a kid who's not doing anything!" At the same time, she was supposed to be keeping a similar record for Jake, another boy in the class, whose behavior was extremely disruptive.

As Kerrie learned more about Ashton's abilities and limitations, she adjusted the curriculum, seeking ways for him to engage in activities roughly similar to what the other students would be doing, thinking this would help him feel a part of the class, one of the aims of inclusion. He was different, all right, but he did not want to be too different; he wanted to do what the other students were doing. She began writing "real concrete things in [her] plan book every week to do with [Ashton]." She did this, in part, just to "remember to service him." She thought of him often.

This morning I was thinking, I'm going to do a newspaper unit, which I've done before. I was picturing the things Ashton was going to be able to do with it. I thought about the things his tracker will be able to help him do. I was mentally reviewing the different activities. He'd be able to trace the Lincoln head, but will he be able to come up with words that fit Lincoln? Some, if he knows who Lincoln is.

As time passed, Kerrie became increasingly discouraged, yet she did not know where to turn for help, nor did she believe she could find the time or energy to do what would probably be necessary. She was a new AAP teacher, the department chair, and a member of two important school committees at that time. Nothing she had come up with was fully successful with Ashton, but she kept searching, mostly on her own. Kerrie was told by Ashton's mother that they wanted "him to be able to deal with the media." When pondering how to accomplish this aim, Kerrie asked his mother if he read the comics. She claimed he did:

I was trying to get an idea of what interested him. . . . I'm going to take the funnies every week and have him choose one, cut it out, put it on a piece of paper, and write what it's about. A sentence.

This assignment is mentioned in the previously quoted observation notes for January 18. Her efforts fell flat: "He really can't do it without you practically placing the words in his mouth." She explored other possibilities with comics, but with no better results. What she discovered was that his mother did much of his homework and her suggestions were often off the mark, more wishful than real. To make matters worse, his mother was unable to become involved in the classroom, and Kerrie needed the mother's help: "His mother can kick his butt; he does what she asks." What Ashton did best was to copy writing from the board, also mentioned in the January 18 observation notes. Occasionally, the student tracker who'd been assigned to him three months into the school year was able to get him to work and not merely to cease his disturbing behavior. In retrospect, Kerrie realized that "someone should have counseled me to get a primer basal and to start him in it immediately. [The special education teachers] knew where he was developmentally the previous year, and I could have started there. [What happened] doesn't make any sense!" Other teachers had knowledge essential to Kerrie but for some reason withheld it. Later Kerrie commented, "I was amazed at how little help I was offered." She was amazed, angered, frustrated.

What complicated her efforts, aside from the extensive demands of planning the AAP classes and her involvement on school committees and as department chair, was the make-up of the class. Ashton was not the only student struggling, nor was he the only mainstreamed child there. Throughout the year, Kerrie had a steady flow of troubled boys, starting with Jake, who she had as a student in the seventh grade. Deeply disturbed emotionally, Jake was combative, mouthy, and constantly demanding of attention. Kerrie did her best to keep him on task, which consumed a good deal of energy. Classroom management was a constant concern here, but in no other class. Jake was eventually transferred into an alternative program, but without consulting Kerrie, the counselor replaced him with Jerome, a boy who had been in four different junior high schools in as many months. Jerome refused to work, was disruptive, and spent his days happily chatting with others in the class, seemingly oblivious to their desire to work. Jerome left before Kerrie could have any impact on him, and he was replaced by Lenny. When the counselor inadvertently learned that she had placed Lenny in the same classroom as Ashton, she was sickened, but she made no change.

A large, heavy-set, menacing man-child, Lenny missed much of the school year because he had been physically beaten by other students. Teachers suspected an additional reason, that he had been under arrest, but this was only an unconfirmed rumor (though it rang of truth). Unlike other students in the class, Lenny teased Ashton, but Ashton was not alone. Lenny was a bully. Students seemed tense and uneasy around him: "Everyone is afraid of him," Kerrie remarked. "He is so physical, it wouldn't surprise me that someone kills him or he kills someone, sometime." Cowed, one boy even accepted blame for a problem that Kerrie was certain Lenny had caused. Fearful of Lenny, another boy, physically large himself and otherwise quite aggressive, one day waited outside of class for 15 minutes before cautiously entering. With Lenny in the room, Kerrie could not possibly continue to spend as much time as she once had attending to Ashton. Recognizing potential danger, she had to monitor Lenny constantly and closely. In fact, Kerrie did not dare turn her back on him for any but the briefest moments. When she did, things had a way of happening, suddenly, swiftly, but not unexpectedly. When Lenny was present the air was heavy, charged with the expectation of something bad happening. Additional observation notes from the February 9 class quoted previously follow. It was a good day for Kerrie with Lenny:

> (11:16). Lenny goes and sits in Kerrie's chair and starts looking at the papers on her desk. She talks with him, he moves and picks up a yard-stick and wanders over to his desk, where he disrupts the three people nearest him. (11:19). Ashton goes to Kerrie and asks for the pass to go to the bathroom. Lenny is working! His neighbor bothers him. (11:23). Kerrie circulates, drifts over to Lenny's desk, and takes the yardstick with her and puts it away. (11:25). Lenny gets up and with a menacing but seemingly playful attitude [lunges] toward a girl sit-ting behind him and to his right — she squeals. Kerrie, who is sitting on her desk, looks up, he looks at her, she shakes her head, and he sits back down. . . . (11:42). Lenny and a girl talk seriously about their maps while standing in front of Kerrie's desk. He talks with Kerrie and she tells him where to turn in his map. He walks across the room, two rulers in hand, and excitedly talks with one of the boys, telling him a story of some kind about a fight or a wrestling match, judging from his actions and the sound effects.

Several days after this observation, in an interview we talked about the situation in fourth period.

> I've definitely backed off on Ashton. . . . It's like [I'm] waiting for something to be the right answer, [for the right answer] to come . . . and it's not. . . . You know, if I sat down and took my time, I proba-bly could figure out what to do with him, but he's not in the right place. For one thing, that class! . . . There's no extra energy, espe-cially for [helping] a passive child [like Ashton].

In frustration and exhaustion, she concluded: "He's going to just sit there and draw on his shoe until he dies, or has to go to the bathroom!"

In mid-April, the situation changed dramatically. Lenny was re-moved from school, and Kerrie again shifted her energy to Ashton and began seeking ways of engaging him in class. The difference in the classroom and in Kerrie once Lenny was gone was astonishing and almost immediate. Class seemed more like it had been before his unwelcome arrival — lighter, happier, as is indicated in observation notes made after his departure.

The bell rang signaling the start of fourth period and I wrote a memo in my notes asking, "[Where is Lenny?]."

> The class is very quiet as Kerrie reads — only an occasional muffled brief bit of chatting [between two students] breaks the silence. . . . Kerrie stops reading. . . . (11:15). Quick transition. Kerrie reads two "I used to be" poems written by students. "Those two are good," she says. . . . Quick transition. "As I give you [your midterm report grades], you may leave for the computer lab." . . . Kerrie: "Ashton, what are you doing?" He says nothing. "I have a note for your mom. Can you take it to her?" He grunts and puts his head down. He gets up. "Mrs. Baughman, I'm going to the [school] activity." "Good. Did you pay your dollar?" "Yes." "Good." "I'm going swimming." "Great!" Kerrie writes the note. "Ashton, you wrote a haiku poem. Why don't you go type it at the computer?" Ashton: "No." Kerrie: "Yes." Ashton: "No." Kerrie: "Why don't you type it up and you will get a VISA" (a card that recognizes students for good work). Now whispering playfully to Ashton: "Do you want a VISA? Do you want a VISA?" "Yes." "Okay, when you get to the lab, you type it up. Here's the note for your mother that tells how you need to do your book report. Put it in your pack. [Your tracker] will help you type it or I will. Should we go upstairs [to the lab]?"

Kerrie was relaxed. Class was pleasant and productive, and the edge was gone. Ashton seemed to re-emerge.

Yet the year ended and Kerrie was still engaging in trial and error, seeking means for engaging Ashton. Had Lenny never been enrolled in the class, she might have made significant progress toward providing an adequate program for Ashton, as she did for the eighth-graders generally. We will never know. It is certain, however, that the class make-up, including the line of troubled boys running through it, worked against Ashton's receiving the attention he so desperately needed. But then, was it ever reasonable to expect Kerrie to provide an appropriate education for Ashton and his 29 other classmates? Some contexts bring with them more insistent problems than others, and teachers must make judgments about how to invest their energy. Ashton was passive, Lenny aggressive, dangerous, demanding, and fully capable of preventing everyone else from learning. Kerrie put a large portion of her emotional energy into containing

Lenny and in trying to make certain the class remained a productive place for most of the other students. Is it reasonable to expect more of any teacher?

As mentioned, Kerrie never moved beyond a trial-and-error approach to working with Ashton. She lacked the "case knowledge" to effectively solve problems related to teaching Ashton (see Doyle, 1990). Ironically, the only coursework she had done related to teaching so-called "special" students was tied to completing an endorsement in gifted and talented education. No help there! Moreover, she received no help from the special educators working within the building, although in late spring, district administrators assigned a speech therapist to work with Ashton who also helped him with classwork. Class size was not reduced, either. No effort was made to create a mixture of students which would have increased the likelihood that Ashton would have had a good social experience in Kerrie's classroom. If teacher development was an aim of either the administrators or the counselors, and it should have been, then Kerrie ought to have received some instruction (assuming she could have found time for it) and a good deal of help within the classroom. The context should have been shaped to be more supportive of Kerrie and of Ashton. It was not.

Having both Ashton and Lenny in the same class nicely illustrates how problems interact and compound one another, and further, how contextual events and wider cultural trends can conspire to constrain teacher development and student and teacher learning. To encourage teacher development, careful attention must be given to making certain the contexts within which teachers work "provide support for the process of expertise" (Bereiter & Scardamalia, 1993, p. 102), as noted in the preceding chapter. Such environments present conditions in which "progress or growth is a continuing requirement of adaptation to the environment" (Bereiter & Scardamalia, 1993, p. 244), but they do not overwhelm participants; instead, they invite them to work at the edge of their competence and move beyond. This class, at least when Lenny and Ashton were both there, was nearly overwhelming, even for an experienced teacher like Kerrie.

DIVERSITY AND MAINSTREAMING RECONSIDERED

For Enrique, inclusion offered not only the promise that he would learn, but that he would feel part of the wider society despite his blindness. He was physically, socially, and instructionally included in the classroom, although with greater assistance, the program provided for him could no doubt have been a good deal better. Distinguishing among these types of inclusion is important and helpful for thinking about and designing individual student educational programs, including Ashton's (Huefner, 1994). Ashton certainly was physically included in the classroom. Indeed, he was hard to ignore; so was Enrique. The case for social integration is based in part on the assumption that the "best language, social, dress, and behavior models are in regular education classrooms" and that it is a good thing for both disabled and nondisabled students to interact (Brown et al., 1991, p. 40). Ashton's interaction with his classmates was minimal, however, despite Kerrie's efforts to involve him. Most interaction took place between Ashton, Kerrie, and his student trackers, who tried to get him to work and to behave in appropriate ways. Otherwise, most of the time, he seemed to be in a different world altogether as he picked at or scribbled on the soles of the tennis shoes and pestered Kerrie to let him go to the bathroom. He was not instructionally included in the classroom; the curriculum was clearly inappropriate for him.

Ashton presented a new challenge to Kerrie. Under different conditions, he might have presented an interesting opportunity to learn. Kerrie set out to gain knowledge of how to work with Ashton by observing his interaction with the established curriculum and noting abilities and limitations. She also sought insight and help from his mother, who was invited to come to class, but who did not. Instead, they communicated through frequent notes and through phone calls. Kerrie made some adjustments in her instructional program and began seeking means to engage him within the general activity structure she had created in the classroom. But she had little knowledge of how to work effectively with special-needs children like Ashton. And special educators in the school were of virtually no help whatsoever. This was a sore point. The push toward inclusion within the school seemed to leave special educators uncertain of their roles and responsibilities and hesitant to reach out to regular educators to offer assistance. It was only very late in the school year that Kerrie became aware that a speech therapist had been assigned to work with Ashton and that he was available to assist teachers. No one had told her.

This is not an uncommon situation, however, as Stoler concluded from his survey of regular education teachers: "Comments from the respondents indicated that they currently have at least one or more learning disabled student in their classrooms and are receiving little or no support from the special education department or school administration" (1992, p. 62). Moreover, given the threat of lawsuits on one hand, and the complicated due process procedures involved in making a change in student placement contrary to parental wishes on the other (see Idstein, 1993), it is not surprising that initial placements persist despite teacher frustrations or lack of knowledge and success. Impact on teachers is the last issue addressed when administrators and counselors make placement decisions. Kerrie was stuck, and so were Ashton, Enrique, and the others.

CONCLUSION

Inclusion concerns teachers. It is little wonder that after repeated complaints from its membership the American Federation of Teachers has urged that the rush to inclusion be slowed down, maybe halted:

> Citing reports from their members that students with disabilities were monopolizing an inordinate amount of time and resources and, in some cases, creating violent classroom environments, the union urged that inclusion initiatives be halted until policies are developed to deal with such problems. (Sklaroff, 1994, p. 7)

In addressing the issue, AFT president Albert Shanker aptly captured Kerrie's situation with Ashton: "Suppose along with the thirty other youngsters on your class list, you found at the beginning of the school year you'd been assigned a Down's Syndrome child—without any preparation and without any extra help . . . how would you meet the extraordinary demands of this child without robbing the rest of your students?" (1994, p. 5). And then, add to that class Lenny and his confederates, who were also entitled to an education somewhere. Ashton was placed in Kerrie's classroom not because she knew anything about teaching children born with Down's syndrome, but because she was recognized as a caring and able teacher, one who would make the best of the situation and who would accept difficult students into her classes without complaining. Both Lenny and Enrique were placed in her classes for the same reasons. In retrospect, Kerrie concluded: "The better you are [at teaching], the less help you get, even if it's in an area new to you." Able teachers are often taken advantage of. Their ongoing development is often of little concern to busy administrators and counselors.

The issue is not only that Kerrie lacked the training needed to work effectively with Ashton, or that the supplemental services ostensibly required by law were missing—both of which are egregious errors—but that thoughts of Kerrie and her development are noticeably absent here, as are thoughts of how these placements would affect her other students. All that mattered was that she do her best for Lenny, Ashton, Enrique, Jerome, and the rest. No one seems to have questioned whether what was being asked of Kerrie was reasonable or educationally and ethically responsible. By not complaining, she may have been her own worse enemy. This class severely tested Kerrie's sixth principle, "not to write anyone off."

What can reasonably be expected of public school teachers? Answering this question has profound implications for teacher development, yet answering it is excruciatingly difficult: "The profession is unclear as to the authority, responsibility, and freedom teachers have when they teach, while the system is unclear as to what authority, responsibility, and freedom society has given it" (Provenzo et al., 1989, p. 569). Minimally, all teachers ought to be able to expect that the contexts within which they work will provide them a reasonably good chance at success, and that attention has been given to assuring that the challenges they face will fall generally within their abilities and, if not, within what Vygotsky (1978) dubbed the "zone of proximal development" (p. 86), a concept normally attached to children's learning and development. This is the "distance between the actual developmental level as determined by independent problem solving and the level of potential development as determined through problem solving under adult guidance or in collaboration with more capable peers" (p. 86). Shifting the concept to adults and using it metaphorically is helpful for thinking about the contextual problem of enabling teacher development and of how to assist teachers to stretch their boundaries without overwhelming them. To be sure, students like Lenny and Ashton need to be educated. Teachers must teach them, even if they are robustly reluctant learners. In deciding who should teach them, administrative convenience must give way to careful consideration of individual teacher's ability and level of development, including the kinds of problems most likely to lead to development. Attention must also be given to the range of resources available to help teachers to respond appropriately and well to the problems before them — potential and actual — with an eye toward maximizing the likelihood of students learning and teachers developing in ways that do not routinely require heroism and that are sustainable. Development requires both challenge and support (Oja, 1989). This last point is an especially serious one. The question is not only whether a teacher can or cannot "handle" a Lenny, but whether or not encountering a Lenny or an Ashton will, under attainable work conditions, encourage a teacher's development — that Lenny falls within the zone of proximal development and not outside it. Too rarely are such questions entertained, questions that recognize and respect teacher difference and particularity.

There is an additional issue. With or without help, Kerrie had no additional energy to give to Ashton's class. Her teaching responsibilities were already excessive, and she had underestimated their impact. That a problem seems to fit nicely within a teacher's zone of proximal development does not mean that she can or will address it. Lack of time and energy can prevent engagement, but so can personal and emotional considerations unknown to others. To make them known, teachers must participate in the decisions that shape the contexts within which they work, which includes openly discussing schoolwide concerns, as well as such seemingly mundane issues as student placement, with administrators, counselors, and other teachers.

The positive postmodern values that honor the particularity of each teacher come to mind. The counselor who had created the unfortunate mix of students in the class never spoke with Kerrie about it — but then, Kerrie never sought her out to explain the situation, either. She should have, not to complain, but to seek greater involvement in the decisions affecting her. Her own interests and those of both Ashton and Lenny would have been better served had she made such an effort. But like other teachers, Kerrie did not want to be seen as a whiner, and by temperament she is not one who complains. Getting involved in decision making of this kind is an important key to increased teacher job satisfaction, provided teachers have actual influence over the decisions made (Rice & Schneider, 1994). It is also central to teacher development, simultaneously a condition for development and a means for identifying and realizing other desirable conditions.

On the face of it, Shanker's call for a halt to inclusion until appropriate policies are worked out may seem reasonable, but it may miss the larger, more fundamental question. Discussion of policies that assure needed support services for disabled children (supposedly legally mandated) and that protect the rights of nonhandicapped children to learn and teachers to teach needs to take place within a wider consideration of teachers' roles and responsibilities and what teachers need to maximize job satisfaction and development. Such discussions are essential to the development of teacher professionals (see Chapter 8). Recall our point of view that school reform *is* teacher development. Endless and externally imposed role expansion and the resulting intensification of teachers' labor (Apple, 1986) bring with them the possibility that increasingly larger numbers of able teachers will be driven from teaching, a possibility that serves no one's interests. This is a serious issue, particularly when viewed in light of Kerrie's decision to leave teaching. Sadly, her decision was met with understanding and even envy by most of her colleagues, who shared her work context and frustrations.

Questions for Consideration

1. Is your school and faculty committed to mainstreaming, to inclusion? Is there a specific philosophy used to guide teacher, counselor, and administrator action? If there is such a philosophy, how widely is it supported? Who supports it?

2. How does mainstreaming impact your classroom, your teaching? Do you teach differently than you might otherwise because of the presence of mainstreamed students?

3. Is the presence of mainstreamed students positive for the other students? For you? For them?

4. What role do special educators play in supporting your instructional program? Is their involvement adequate? Are there changes you would like to see implemented?

5. What is your view of mainstreaming?

6. How has mainstreaming impacted your life and learning as a teacher?

8

Professionalism Is Citizenship

"Professional" is a word that usually accompanies the phrase "teacher development." Mostly we have avoided using it. It brings with it much unwelcome baggage, even as it is a word that has great appeal for educators, although not the general public (Menand, 1995), as a means for both resisting unwelcomed legislated reforms limiting teacher autonomy here and abroad (Avis, 1994) and for directing attempts at school reform (Ogawa, 1994). For teachers, professionalism seems to be generally a taken-for-granted virtue.

In this chapter, we explore Kerrie's development in relationship to professionalism, a theme first explored by us in chapter 6 of *First-Year Teacher*. Our analysis illustrates how professionalism, as it is typically understood, is deeply contradictory and in some respects a shaky foundation upon which to anchor personal teacher development efforts. Drawing on the data, we conclude the chapter by proposing an alternative vision to that commonly held of "teacher professionalism," a view we believe is consistent with the ambition and desires of teachers and with the positive elements of postmodernism, the ideas of difference, particularity, and irregularity. Professionalism, we argue, is best understood as a form of ethical citizenship within a specific educational community.

PROFESSIONALISM

Whether or not teaching is a profession has been the subject of endless uninspiring debates. The argument usually begins with an essentialist view of professionalism, that professionals evidence certain specific qualities and abilities that are precious, rare, and deserving of recognition, respect, and reward.

> Primary among the conditions that distinguish a "profession" from other occupations are a specialized knowledge base and shared standards of practice, a strong service ethic, or commitment to meeting clients' needs, strong personal

identity with, and commitment to, the occupation, and collegial versus bureaucratic control over entry, performance evaluations, and retention in the profession. (Talbert & McLaughlin, 1994, p. 126)

Depressing conclusions follow. Working from definitions of this kind, teaching and teachers are found lacking; teaching fails the professionalism test. Reflecting the difficulty of articulating a distinctive knowledge base, handbooks proliferate. Doubt persists about the power of the knowledge base of teaching; after all, novices appear to hold as much formal knowledge as do experts (Eraut, 1994). The public has grave doubts about the commitment of teachers to students, of the claims of professionals of all kinds to "disinterestedness" (Menand, 1995), and politicians gleefully exploit these doubts in perennial attacks on teacher unions and purported teacher selfishness, a direct and painful blow to teachers' service ethic. School systems remain fundamentally bureaucratic, and professional judgment plays a relatively modest role in teacher evaluation and retention decisions. Given conclusions like these, the reform issue, when viewed from inside the wider educational community, is how to elevate teaching from its "quasi-professional status" (Darling-Hammond, 1994, p. 3). How can teachers be made into professionals? How can teaching be made into a high-status profession like law and medicine?

While these questions remain at the forefront of many discussions of educational reform, from the back seats behind those driving reform one increasingly hears questions about the wisdom of tying reform to professionalism. The concerns are many. Sarason (1996) sees in professionalism a conservative impulse assuring that schools will not change: "The truth is that the *professional preparation* of educators is a socializing process that virtually ensures that the culture of the school will [stay as it is]" (p. 379). Soder (1991) challenges the quest to become like the presumably high-status professions of medicine and law, pointing out the ignored irony that while education is seeking to follow their lead to the promised land, the status of both professions is steadily dropping. Medicine, he argues, makes a poor model. Schools cannot be anything like teaching hospitals; the knowledge bases are dissimilar; and the work is fundamentally different. Professionalism, he asserts, is a vague term that has rhetorical value for policymakers but falls flat because the arguments to emulate medicine and law

refuse to define, to name, the central core of teacher. And that central core must deal . . . with some sort of affirmation, some sort of choice. . . . It is to be found in the very nature of teaching, in the moral relationship between the teacher and the student, in the relationship, at least in the K-12 system, between the teacher, the student, the parent, and the state. (pp. 298, 300)

Put succinctly, "if one wishes to talk about teaching as a profession (whatever that might mean), then the ethical base had best be acknowledged and attended to . . . " (1991, p. 295). Usually, it is not. Labaree (1992) argues that the "path to professionalism for teachers . . . is filled with craters and quicksand" (p. 126). His list of concerns is a long one. He poses a troubling question, connected to the ethical obligations of teaching: "How will the public benefit?" This question needs to be at the forefront of all discussions about professionalism. In pursuit of a science of education — high-status, formal knowledge — teachers can expect greater rationalization and standardization of their work, even as professionalism aims at reducing bureaucratization, and the quality of students' education likely will suffer.

National Board certification is currently touted for its presumed professionalizing potential. As a strategy borrowed from medicine, this approach to professionalization also has serious problems. Labaree warns: "board certification of teachers promises to promote higher standards for public education by means of individual initiative and unfettered competition" (1992, p. 131). Thus board certification may have dire consequences for collaboration and teacher collegiality, two essential features of schools that support teacher learning, and shatter the confidence of very able teachers who pay the $2,000 fee and attempt but fail to achieve certification. This is high-stakes testing, and failure is very public and demeaning. Again, increased rationalization and standardization may follow (Labaree, 1992); and since numerical scores are reported, training models of teacher development will be strengthened (see Little, 1993) and will perhaps supplant educational models.

Labaree's lament seems justified. Evaluation and assessment for the National Board for Professional Teaching Standards have been taken over by testing experts and psychometricians and teachers have been shoved aside, out of the conversation that supports and extends "professional" judgment. Rather than serving as a tool for teacher development, as was initially intended, "an occasion for teachers to explain and reflect on their teaching in the company of their colleagues," it has become, according to one of those who designed the program, "simply another test," like those used to evaluate student essays (Petrosky, 1994, p. 36). Ratings replace thoughtful discourse, yet another indicator that Sarason's conclusion that professionalization is inherently conservative is likely correct — hardly a means for teacher empowerment. Lastly, Zeichner (1991) makes a telling point, that in the quest for expert status and authority grounded in a highly specialized knowledge base, teachers may distance themselves from students and the communities they serve and thus undermine efforts to democratize the discourse about schooling by ignoring or silencing legitimate interests. Rather than viewing students and their parents as partners in education, they are reduced to "clients," or worse, adversaries. Hargreaves (1995) dubs this "incestuous professionalism," when parents are excluded from efforts to improve education (p. 18).

These are a few of the dangers and potential problems with professionalization — not all of them, but enough to make the point: professionalism must not be taken uncritically as the aim of teacher development. It is a vague yet seductive term to some policymakers and educators, a term that promotes the illusion of general agreement on the diagnosis of what ails education and how to fix it. But imitating the presumably high-status occupations presents teachers with a Faustian bargain. They may gain professionalism, but the professionalism they gain, as Soder suggests, may come at the cost of their souls, what they most value about teaching.

PROFESSIONAL ARENAS

Talbert and McLaughlin (1994) argue that "communities of teachers — based in collegial networks, departments, whole schools, or districts — constitute the meaningful unit and potential for teacher professionalism in U.S. education" (p. 130). Each level provides opportunities for teachers to "acquire new knowledge, to reflect on practice, and to share successes and failures with colleagues" which are needed to "develop a sense of professional control and responsibility" (p. 130). The levels interact such that a weak community at one level might be compensated for by a strong community at another level. Yet each plays a role in building a wider sense of community, a culture of shared values, visions, and commitment. Talbert and McLaughlin (1994) offer a warning, however: the cultures that are created, particularly the "technical culture — shared standards for curriculum, subject instruction, relations with students, and school goals" (p. 134), may actually be inimical to the interests of students, when, for example, teachers hold to traditional academic standards "in the face of widespread student failure" (p. 140). At such times appeals for change are most likely embedded in the service ethic many teachers hold that reminds them of their obligations to serve all students, not just a favored few. Teachers' service ethic, then, may clash with the cultures of teachers' work.

These levels were helpful to us analytically as we sought to make sense of Kerrie's evolving views of professionalism and her shifting pattern of activity. The contexts within which teachers work, how teacher citizenship is defined, profoundly affect what teachers do and how they understand and justify their doing: "Norms of teaching practice are socially

negotiated within the everyday contexts of schooling" (Talbert & McLaughlin, 1994, p. 141). The levels also proved helpful as a means for better
pinpointing sources of satisfaction and disappointment in teaching.

KERRIE'S EARLY VIEWS OF PROFESSIONALISM

As a first-year teacher and a child of a hardworking and committed
teacher, Kerrie found images of professionalism inspiring. In *First Year
Teacher* we concluded that for Kerrie "the central criterion of professionalism was involvement in the larger educational community in order to
strengthen it" (1989, p. 103). Involvement was the key. This view is a
common one, supported by school restructuring efforts of the past 15
years. The "widely known" program Taylor and Bogotch (1994) studied,
for example, "aimed to professionalize teaching by substantially increasing
teachers' participation in decision making . . . " (p. 306). Further, Kerrie
asserted that teachers should understand research, and central to this was
subscribing to professional journals, as she did in both English and social
studies. There was more: Teachers "should help other teachers out" and
take classes, "like the classes I'm taking. They help me so much. That's
part of my professionalism . . . engaging in those so I can do better or just
expand myself — do what's right for the kids." Teachers also engage in
evaluations of one another. She described the characteristics of a professional teacher within the classroom in this way: "Someone who does a
good job, who does [her] best job, and who is always changing to make it
better. Someone who is fair to the kids. And, in [her] own way, loving.
You can see teachers who are really strict, [for example,] but underneath
that you see love" (Bullough, 1989, p. 103).

This was Kerrie's conception of professionalism during her first year
of teaching: professionals are heavily engaged in trying to make schools
better places for children to learn, and they evidence a lively service ethic,
read pertinent research, help other teachers improve their teaching, and
consistently seek to improve their practice. Her views expanded somewhat
during her second year, when she served as union building representative,
when she argued that professional teachers are members of the association.
Hers was not a view fully consistent with those of the more exclusive
professions where expertise separates the community into narrow special-
izations representing differing status locations. Recall Chapter 6: The aim
in teaching is to give one's expertise away, to share it fully with others so
that all might benefit.

Kerrie placed the majority of the burden for developing professionalism squarely on the individual teacher; institutional arrangements were

taken for granted. The culture of Rocky Mountain Junior High School encouraged this view in a variety of subtle ways. Teacher development was a problem for the individual teacher and not of systemic importance. Individualism was much in evidence; isolation masqueraded as autonomy, both features long recognized as common to schooling (Lortie, 1975). Evidence supporting this conclusion is overwhelming, and only a small portion of it was presented in *First Year Teacher*. When Kerrie was hired, she was assigned to a three-person team of teachers responsible for the core (seventh-grade English, reading, and social studies). The team leader participated in the hiring interview but then showed remarkably little interest in Kerrie or in her development:

> [the team leader] knew I was coming last spring. I had to call her in the summer to come and meet me [at the school]. She acted like, "This is my summer vacation, but okay." That was hard! I mean, here I am going into a new situation, odd person out, and taking someone's place [and she doesn't want to meet with me]. (Bullough, 1989, p. 11)

No one *chose* or *was assigned* to explain to Kerrie even basic information about how the school operated. She discovered, for example, from hearing a list of student names read over the intercom that a VIP program was in place — good student behavior was recognized and publicly rewarded. She described her situation near Thanksgiving of her first year of teaching by saying that she had dropped into the school and "started swimming."

Teaming was a disappointment. The team met infrequently, and when it did meet, scheduling was more often than not the topic discussed. The team leader had the advanced core, another teacher the middle group, and Kerrie, the new teacher, the low-ability group. The curriculum was supposed to be roughly the same for all three groups, excluding reading, where Kerrie was "strictly on [her] own." At first the curriculum was the team leader's, who would respond to Kerrie's questions and requests for help, but not offer assistance or advice. The team leader had done her planning, and it appeared to Kerrie that she saw no reason for team meetings, which became increasingly more rare as the year progressed. During Kerrie's second year, the team virtually dissolved. Kerrie felt unable to call meetings, even though she thought they would be helpful. Ironically, the team leader was assigned and paid under a new program to assist beginning teachers to be Kerrie's mentor the second year. Because of scheduling problems — both teachers had the same consultation period — the team leader could not formally evaluate Kerrie's teaching to give feedback. Kerrie concluded that the entire situation was a farce: "Isn't that comical?" "[It's] stupid."

In January of the first year, Kerrie broke with the team and planned her own "Explorers" unit in social studies. Three weeks later she taught a newspaper unit that others in the team did not want to do: "No one seemed interested in doing it, which was fine. I like to do things by myself. There's no competition with other team members . . . but it's kind of scary." Breaking with the team was important, as Kerrie increasingly took ownership of and responsibility for the curriculum. Her break signaled her growing independence, but it also solidified her isolation.

Kerrie felt no collegiality. What "strokes" she received, for instance, came from students, not from other teachers. When asked in the spring if she could remember receiving any positive feedback from other teachers, she recalled two instances. One was the result of teachers noticing that students were carrying around newspapers during the newspaper unit, and a second came when a teacher walked by Kerrie's classroom, looked in, saw something of interest, and entered to chat. Formally, the team leader was only peripherally involved in Kerrie's development as a teacher and gave no feedback either positive or negative. Kerrie did, however, learn a great deal from her by observing her teach across the open area separating their classrooms. Yet given the close proximity of their two rooms, the paucity of interaction was surprising. An occasional positive remark would have been much appreciated: "I think I stroked her more than she strokes me." Support by colleagues who share a work environment is crucial to teacher feelings of self-esteem, even of greater value than administrator support (Byrne, 1994).

The principal's formal evaluations, representing positive but vague and unhelpful feedback, were seen as worthless. Kerrie was not even aware she was being evaluated the first time. Apparently, data for the first evaluation came from the principal "walking through" her classroom, but Kerrie was not even certain of that. The principal based his second formal evaluation on "about three five-minute" observations. Lortie observed that teachers need "authoritative reassurance" but get precious little of it (Lortie, 1975, p. 149). Kerrie was typical, then.

Kerrie wanted to observe other teachers teaching but said that she was "too chicken to go and ask them. . . . " More accurately, reflecting the strong privacy norms of teaching (Little, 1990), it seems as though such things were simply not done at Rocky Mountain Junior High School. Teachers are often loath to invade one another's space. Regretfully, Kerrie concluded that feedback from the "kids . . . and [what you think of] yourself [is what counts]. That's pretty sad, it really is." She began to look beyond the team for opportunities to develop as a teacher.

Within the wider school faculty, Kerrie began to notice that some teachers behaved in ways that were troubling — "unprofessional," in her judgment. In late winter she observed teachers "fighting" over teaching assignments, for example. She observed a teacher across the hallway roughhousing with boys in ways that concerned her: "He has hurt them before." After considering her options, she marched into the principal's office and lodged a complaint. As a teacher she thought this her ethical duty. Later she discovered that this same teacher was on probation, and she knew why: he did little teaching.

Although Kerrie considered most of the teachers she worked with professional, and some, positively sparkling, there was a sufficient number of unprofessional teachers, teachers like the one across the hallway, to justify in her mind the principal's practice of carefully monitoring teacher behavior. Despite her professionalism, she concluded that bureaucratic control of teachers was an unhappy necessity. We touched on this issue in *First Year Teacher* (Bullough, 1989):

> It was [the principal's] job to watch over teachers, as teachers watch over students: "He keeps tabs on us very well," she asserted. "I think it is his job. It's like me walking up and down the aisles." But she did not like it; it was a necessary evil: "Now, this isn't saying it doesn't bother me, but it tends to keep you on your toes, I think." While she did not believe she needed watching, she suspected that other teachers did. (p. 12)

The principal behaved as he did, she thought, because some teachers behaved as they did. As a beginning teacher, she saw no alternatives. Teachers did not police themselves. Yet she reacted angrily when, suddenly, on a Friday near the end of the first term of her second year of teaching, the principal, apparently under order from district administrators, had a sheet containing a long list of specific objectives passed out to teachers along with directions to fill in the date each objective was met. As she sought to know how serious the order was, she began making plans to fill out the sheet while minimizing its impact on her curriculum. She would comply, but only minimally. Only later would she discover that the principal had no intention of following through on the implicit threat; he did not have sufficient time to monitor teachers this way even if he had the inclination. There was no reason to worry. Believing herself to be a professional teacher, she thought such bureaucratic intrusions into the classroom were neither justified nor appropriate. Certainly they revealed a good deal about administrators' views of teachers as unprofessional and not worthy of trust.

Kerrie listened in "disgust" and dismay as teachers, attending with her an in-service class on stress management, recounted the horrors of teaching. Based on her view of professionalism, she reacted to these teachers unsympathetically:

The [workshop leader] said, you identify your problems. . . . These women were so disillusioned; they're just sick of all this and that. I'm not [where they are]; I hope I'm never there. This one woman was complaining because some child in her classroom was taken out and taken to Disneyland for a week. That was her beef! She was pissed. She was really mad. Someone else was angry because when she takes her kids out for PE, this was elementary school, the parents write excuses saying, "Johnny can't kick the ball today. He hurt his ankle." That type of thing. It's those little things that are getting these people down. I just don't see those as problems. There are bigger problems to worry about than that . . . some of them were classroom management problems. I thought, "Well, you just solve it or you ignore it." Teachers get together and they just say such crappy things . . . that really pisses me off. . . . I don't even want to listen to this bad attitude business. How can you help to have a good attitude if all you ever do is complain when you get together? Everyone was scowling . . . I wanted to say, "Is anyone here happy? . . . I'm just not a bitcher. It just disturbs me that everyone is always tearing down our profession.

Kerrie felt professionals did not talk like this. Professionals took charge of their lives, worked through their problems, and sought to strengthen the profession and improve their practice. Whining only made matters worse, she thought.

Despite her disappointment with the teachers attending this in-service class, it was in the wider teacher network of in-service courses that she began to feel camaraderie and a sense of community; here she felt she belonged and was valued. Here she encountered teachers who were professional, who met her standard. Classes were selected carefully, with an eye toward substance as well as utility. But this was not all she sought; she wanted genuine collegial interaction, which was sorely lacking at Rocky Mountain:

I get more strokes going to . . . in-service [classes], with people I don't even know. I am adding to me, that's really the main reason for going to them. *You talk and share?* Yes. I would say that I have a couple of people I'm closer to at those classes [than people here at Rocky]. One of them is not even a teacher, he's a counselor.

And two weeks later: "[This] builds me up. . . . I'm learning lots of really neat things to make my [social studies] curriculum better. . . . We're talking about architecture . . . mining [economics] . . . [clothing], manners, things like that . . . things that really interest the kids. . . . "

Kerrie's consistent and extensive involvement in in-service courses during her first two years of teaching was in some ways surprising. Temperamentally, she is a private person and "very individualistic, a loner," as she said. Teaching provided a means for coming out of her "shell," a "life goal for the last three years," and an outcome she knew was important to her success as a teacher. Her conception of professionalism, grounded in her service ethic, not only justified this move, but gave it urgency. Kerrie forced herself to become increasingly engaged with other teachers, not only through in-service courses, but also at Rocky Mountain Junior High School, despite the strength of that context's culture of individualism. While others shunned committee work, Kerrie accepted it. This willingness was noticed by other teachers and the principal, and near the end of her first year of teaching, when no respected veteran teacher would accept the nomination, she agree to stand for election as building union representative. She won. The victory (though other teachers did not call it that) fundamentally changed her position within the school and opened up new avenues for service and for development, avenues often vacated by other, more experienced teachers.

Involvement in the wider education community has two benefits: "opportunity and capacity." Little (1990) puts it this way:

> Acknowledged leadership positions afford teachers the opportunity to use their accumulated expertise in arenas outside the classroom, thus yielding benefit to the larger institution. Teachers' professional capacity is enlarged by the discretionary resources that must accompany leadership responsibilities, and by the ability to influence institutional goals and directions. (p. 214)

As building union representative, Kerrie assumed responsibility for organizing "American Education Week for the district." As a second-year teacher, she felt nearly overwhelmed by the responsibility but quickly began to see the benefits of wider involvement, of being professional as she defined it: "I honestly can't complain because I'm doing a lot of things I didn't expect. I know more about [teacher] issues." In addition, she spoke periodically in faculty meetings, which made her better known within the building and helped her overcome her tendency to withdraw into the classroom. As a member of the communications committee, she wrote an article for an issue of the union newsletter about American Education Week activities. New friendships were built and a few enemies were made, non-union colleagues who received the benefit of the union's efforts to improve salaries and working conditions but contributed nothing to the cause: "It pisses me off! . . . It makes me really mad [that they do this]." Such people, she concluded, were unprofessional. Some friendships grew out of her involvement with specific faculty problems: "It's funny, because even though I cannot solve anything myself—lasting solutions—people from the whole school come up and talk to me about things. It's like you're a sounding board . . . they want to talk." The interaction was satisfying. As union representative she also participated on various school committees, which was a means to influence policies and to gain the principal's ear. Yet as an untenured teacher she was cautious about what she said. She knew, ultimately, that the principal's evaluations would determine whether or not she received tenure.

In the midst of her union involvement, Kerrie was asked what she found most satisfying about teaching. Her growing sense of connection to the school faculty, the district, and union teacher communities came through clearly: "Camaraderie. Working with other teachers. Getting to know more teachers. Having more friendships and more of a working relationship [with teachers]." She felt she was on the inside of the school, knowledgeable about what was transpiring, and interpersonally connected: "It's like I know all the latest of what's going on [in the building]. [Whereas the woman I commute with] is clueless." Kerrie felt respected and was very happy with her work:

Teaching isn't just being in the classroom teaching kids. Teaching is all those other things, too. Being on committees. [Helping make this] a better place, a more quality place to work. . . . Some people are happy [when they] are uninvolved. I guess I'm not.

Through union involvement, Kerrie began to understand how power resides in teachers working together to address common concerns. The union was the largest and most active lobbying group within the state, and although it often failed to achieve its aims, it was widely recognized as having considerable political clout. Because of this, anti-teacher union letters to local newspaper editors were relatively commonplace, as were market-oriented conservative politicians' complaints and attacks, particularly following the defeat of candidates judged hostile to the interests of public education and of teachers. Copies of proposed bills and occasionally articles on political events within and without the state were given to Kerrie, and conversation followed. As building representative she expressed to union leaders the wishes of the faculty, and as a member of the communication committee she participated in efforts to educate the public and other teachers about the value of union activities. By her own standards, Kerrie was an engaged and active professional. The key was Kerrie's personal willingness to get involved.

PROFESSIONALISM FROM INSIDE THE SCHOOL COMMUNITY

When we renewed our work together at the beginning of Kerrie's fifth year of teaching at Rocky Mountain Junior High School, involvement was still at the center of her conception of professionalism. The context had changed little, although the student body and faculty had grown larger. Individualism remained the cultural norm, although it had softened somewhat. With the team leader's resignation to assume a new job in the airline industry, the principal reconstituted the team. It appears that this decision was made without consideration of how the three individuals would work together, because Kerrie quickly found herself unable to plan with the other two members. Differences were deep. As mentioned in Chapter 5, one of Kerrie's principles was "love them [students] along." To do this, she thought she needed to have the same group of students for multiple periods and throughout an entire school year. In this way she not only could build strong interpersonal relationships with students but maximize her influence on their development. The new team members insisted on switching students every quarter, which Kerrie found unacceptable. She would not compromise this fundamental belief, which was central to her conception of how best to serve students: "I said, you guys do what you want; I won't do it." Rather than creating an opportunity to re-invigorate teaming, formation of the new "team" sounded its death knell. Kerrie's service ethic clashed with the culture (Talbert & McLaughlin, 1994).

Having completed her term in office, Kerrie was no longer union representative. However, partly because of her work with the union, the principal selected her to serve as "teacher specialist." This position was created by district administrators and involved releasing one teacher in each school for half the day. Responsibilities were varied, including work that, with the exception of conducting peer reviews of teaching, otherwise would have been done by school secretaries, counselors, or administrators. Kerrie did book inventories (a secretarial responsibility), organized district mandated standardized testing (a counselor responsibility), and represented the school on numerous district committees and on the local PTA, serving as vice president (administrator responsibilities).

Kerrie was surprised to have been selected. She was pleased to find out, however, that in making his decision the principal had "checked around with other people" within the school. Only one teacher, a department chair, was obviously opposed to her selection; Kerrie had not been a teacher long enough to have earned the position, according to this teacher. Kerrie wondered about this issue herself. Nevertheless, this teacher's behavior was puzzling: "She was furious that I was [chosen]; she snubbed me repeatedly, which was really stupid."

Once comfortable in the position, Kerrie began to redefine and expand it. It not only presented new opportunities for personal growth, but also a chance to be of service to other teachers and aid them in their development. There were seven first-year teachers in the school. One day she was in her office when one of the male first-year teachers came in and stood "sniffling . . . he wasn't crying, [but] he kind of had watery eyes." He began asking her questions and for advice about what to do when certain situations arose. He was stressed and was "having a hard time." The same day she was leaving school, she saw another first-year teacher, the music teacher, "sobbing." "I mean, we are talking about having a breakdown in the hall."

I thought, if these two are doing this, the others [other first year teachers] probably are feeling those same feelings on some level. I can help these people. I thought about it all the way home. . . . [The next day] I went to the acting principal [the principal was in the hospital], explained the situation, and said, "We are going to lose these people. They are in trouble. . . . " I called them together and talked to them and [offered] to work with them [to] see what we could do. . . . [We met weekly, and the meetings] worked miracles.

Through this effort the school became a bit more collegial and a bit more friendly, at least for a few teachers.

Instead of continuing to take in-service courses, Kerrie enrolled in a master's degree program at the university and became more actively involved in national teacher organizations. These were two new arenas within which to develop and express her professionalism. Given the declining interest of teachers in university coursework, her actions were somewhat unusual (Little, 1990). Recall, it was because of membership in IRA (International Reading Association) that Kerrie had attended a convention where she'd purchased Nancie Atwell's book, which, in turn, had led to the revision of her writing curriculum. The revision was supported by her university classes, which led to additional opportunities to share what she was doing with other teachers similarly enrolled in graduate school. The next summer she participated in the State Writing Project, a spin-off from the Bay Area Writing Project, which gave her an opportunity to explore further how to teach English through writing and refine her program. As word of her program spread, opportunities to share her work with teachers in the district soon followed. Kerrie's professional community expanded significantly.

Many of the teachers Kerrie met at the university and at association meetings were professionals, as she understood that term — engaged, involved, and dedicated people earnestly seeking to improve their practice. In addition, she recognized and increasingly appreciated the work of a few teachers within Rocky Mountain, teachers who shared her values and who supported her efforts and were themselves exceptional professionals. Isolation within the building had initially prevented her from knowing these teachers. Knowing them softened the disappointment that had grown during her first year of teaching when she realized that for many teachers, teaching was just a job, nothing more. She delighted in the accomplishments of these few extraordinary teachers—a man who brilliantly taught grammar, the "daring" woman who Kerrie described as a "standard against which to measure myself," and another man who did wonders with social studies—"I just love him." With these teachers she felt a special and deep bond, one born of Kerrie's having traveled similar pathways and confronted and overcome similar challenges. Leaving these teachers behind when she moved to Clarke was extremely difficult. But at Clarke, she found even more extraordinary teachers.

ROCKY MOUNTAIN JUNIOR HIGH SCHOOL AS A LEARNING ENVIRONMENT

Rosenholtz (1989a) offers a helpful way for thinking about schools as learning contexts for teachers. She suggests three categories that nicely capture and group the qualities of good learning environments offered by Smylie (1995) and presented in Chapter 6: learning-enriched schools, a category that parallels the "second-order" environments discussed by Bereiter and Scardamalia (1993); moderately impoverished schools; and learning-impoverished schools. Although Rosenholtz studied elementary schools, the categories make sense. Four "organizational factors" combined to account for 79% of the variance she found in teachers' learning opportunities:

1. School goal setting. "To the extent that principals and teachers establish, talk about, and institutionalize the same instructional goals, teachers know which way to aim their improvement efforts. Goal-setting may also be a time for stock-taking—for reviewing the growth and accomplishments of the school and of individuals within it . . . " (Rosenholtz, 1989a, p. 77).

2. Teacher evaluation. "To the extent that principals embed their evaluation system in teachers' own improvement goals, set and use objective, clear guidelines . . . to monitor student and teacher progress, regu-

larly observe the actual classroom performance of teachers, and spend considerable time in classrooms doing so, they are better able to supply situation-specific feedback and assistance." Conversely, "when principals view evaluation of teachers as a discretionary activity and choose to either perform it perfunctorily or entirely forgo it, the results clearly impeded individual and school renewal" (p. 77).

3. Sharing goals. "The extent to which teachers share instructional goals . . . contributes . . . to their opportunities to learn. . . . Shared goals about teaching render legitimacy, value, and support, or, if need be, collective pressure to conform to school norms" (pp. 78–79).

4. Teacher collaboration. "Learning may be the direct outcome of collaboration, as teachers request from and offer colleagues, new ideas, strategies, and techniques" (p. 79).

Rocky Mountain Junior High School had no clearly articulated goals, nor were goals often discussed, except when standardized test score results were reported. At such times teachers and administrators discussed how the scores might be raised in specific areas, like spelling, that might otherwise call negative attention to the school. When goals are seldom discussed, it is difficult for them to be shared in any meaningful sense, although they might be taken for granted. The list of objectives passed out for the principal on that fateful Friday was eventually ignored, even by the principal. Teacher evaluation, as we have seen, was capricious and unhelpful, yet mandated. Finally, there was surprisingly little collaboration. Teaming, for example, had only modest positive influences on Kerrie's development.

Using these categories, and building on our earlier discussion on the development of expertise, we conclude that during Kerrie's first year of teaching, Rocky Mountain was organizationally a learning-impoverished school. Yet Kerrie grew tremendously within it, in part by getting outside of it and its culture by seeking a different community, as Talbert and McLaughlin (1994) suggest. Her efforts at self-development not only had a positive effect on her, however. The evidence suggests that through her efforts and those of a few other teachers, the context improved and became somewhat more collaborative and collegial. Formally, the organization had not changed, which was one of the weaknesses of Kerrie's view of professionalism, yet the school did become a better learning environment for teachers and perhaps moved up a level to become a "moderately impoverished" learning context, one that, as mentioned in Chapter 6, was not hostile to teacher development, but not especially supportive of it, either.

ACTING PROFESSIONALLY IN CLARKE

In many respects, organizationally, Clarke came close to being a "learning-enriched" environment for teachers, although we would not characterize it as a "second-order environment" wherein teacher learning was a primary goal. Our judgment is restrained by the events reported in Chapter 7 surrounding Ashton and Lenny's class. Still, learning-enriched environments are not consistently or always fully supportive of teacher development, although this remains the aim. Moreover, as noted above (see "Professional Arenas"), the wider education community is layered, and while a school may not be supportive of teacher development, a department, or, in Kerrie's case within AAP, a team might be. This team "established norms of continuous improvement and experimentation" that are central to teacher development (Guskey, 1995, p. 121).

As previously noted, the principal at Clarke came to the school the same year Kerrie arrived. The difference in the influence of the two principals and the roles they played in shaping the school-learning culture for teachers are stark and instructive. The Clarke principal brought with her a strong middle school philosophy and a commitment to inclusion. The principal reported that she was explicitly hired because of this vision:

> This age level has traditionally been a holding tank—these kids were
> not capable of learning, [their] hormones took over and it was just a
> matter of getting them through that. So when I came here I told them
> that I was very supportive of the middle school philosophy and I
> would . . . pursue that direction [a move begun by the previous principal].

Once she understood it, Kerrie shared the vision, which was quite consistent with her own views (see Chapter 5) and sought to implement aspects of it in her classroom. Several other faculty members did not, and the principal had to, as she said in interview, "reduce the divisions . . . and [break] that old traditional culture down." Nevertheless, this vision, centering on the belief that adolescence represents a unique human developmental period that requires a special kind of supportive environment to maximize learning, gave teachers a sense of direction for their own development efforts. Having previously gotten support from parents and teachers on the School Improvement Council and the School Community Council before implementing her ideas, the principal moved aggressively, but thoughtfully, ahead with her plans.

Teaming teachers was central to the principal's vision both as a means for integrating content and for easing the transition from elementary to secondary school. In her first year she moved the faculty into teams while trying to be responsive to the personal and interpersonal problems that flowed from that decision. Disruption followed, but commitment to the change among the faculty, including Kerrie, grew.

Teacher evaluation was mostly informal, done by the principal as she sought to get to know faculty strengths and weaknesses, information essential to the success of her plans. Often she chatted with teachers, dropped into classrooms, and participated in planning meetings. While these interactions were informal, Kerrie understood that the principal was making judgments about the kind of person and teacher she was and that based on these judgments, opportunities for further development would or would not be forthcoming: "I wanted to look good to her. I'm like all those Do-Bees, I want to look good to my boss." The accuracy of this interpretation was proved when Kerrie was chosen over a more senior teacher for the AAP program, and as part of that program, was given the opportunity at district expense to pursue an endorsement in gifted and talented education along with other team members. She also served as social studies department chair.

Through teaming, primarily, and through participation on a variety of school committees, Clarke teachers had an abundance of opportunities to collaborate. Recall that during her second year at Clarke, Kerrie was part of two instructional teams. The seventh-grade team shared a planning period and met twice weekly during the fall. As mentioned in Chapter 6, to plan for AAP, that team met daily during lunch and then twice a week after school, sometimes over dinner, and for several hours. Consistent with an expanding view of her professional responsibilities to other teachers, Kerrie worked especially hard with one member of the seventh-grade team who had been on remediation and was struggling as a teacher: "I'm trying to be very kind to him, to help him out and not make him feel like he's the lost child." These were both functioning teams. But not all teachers took full advantage of the opportunities. As a result of the organization of the school, the opportunities for teacher development within Clarke were abundant—so abundant, in fact, that Kerrie found it no longer necessary to reach outside of the school for professional interaction, as she had at Rocky Mountain. Indeed, she pulled back dramatically from the wider educator communities. She continued, however, as she had at Rocky Mountain, to reach out to parents by phone and by sending home positive notes about student progress.

Involvement continued to be the centerpiece of Kerrie's thinking about professionalism in both schools, yet facing nearly unlimited opportunities in Clarke, she began to back away from this view somewhat. Too many long hours spent team planning and too much committee work had exhausted her. Both she and one of her teammates who also served on both teams thought they were being pulled too far from their central classroom concerns: "Neither of us will be department chair next year, or anything. I'm the social studies department chair. I'm not going to do that. We're going to devote all our time to the classroom. We're just overwhelmed. There's so much to do. I'm not going to take on anything extra [next year]." These proved to be prophetic words.

Kerrie served on the School Improvement Council (SIC), a committee that met "endlessly," trying to put together a "strategic plan" that would result in a grant from the governor's office and bring much-needed money to the school. Award requirements were specific, and under shared governance rules, the faculty had to come to consensus on the plan — thus the "endless meetings." In frustration, Kerrie remarked: "I couldn't care less about the strategic plan. I want someone else to do it, and then tell me what it is! I'm a teacher, let me do my job!" Zeichner warns that "involvement of teachers in school decision making about programs, budget, and staffing will make excessive demands on their time, energy, and expertise, diverting their attention from their core tasks with students" (1991, p. 366). This is exactly what happened to Kerrie. The contradiction is a deep one: "workload creates pressures for development by giving teachers a reason to learn, but simultaneously places limitations on available time and energy" (Little, 1990, p. 211). There are limits to involvement as a central defining principle of professionalism: "[At Rocky, teachers] weren't automatically involved in so much stuff. Here, [because of shared governance,] you're just automatically involved in [everything] and [I] almost feel like I need to back off a tiny bit just in order to accomplish what I need to in my classroom."

The pressures of shared governance were genuine. As chair of the social studies department, Kerrie served on both the SIC and the School Community Council (SCC). Within guidelines set by the Board of Education, these committees had both policy making and problem solving responsibilities. The SIC had the additional responsibility of reviewing the school budget and expenditures. These were large committees, with a minimum of 23 members on the SIC; and all SIC members were also SCC members, as were some parents. The importance of the SCC is indicated by how often the SCC was supposed to meet. The opening sentence of the section of the teacher's contract, "A Continuing Written Agreement Based on the Principles of Shared Governance," states: "The council shall meet weekly, or more frequently, if business dictates." These were busy committees.

INVOLVEMENT IN DECISION MAKING

Expanded teacher participation in decision making has been a central component of many school restructuring plans. Moreover, increasing teacher involvement has been widely assumed to be an essential element of school reform and a means for enhancing teacher job satisfaction and professional status, particularly for high academic ability teachers and able teachers, who face higher "opportunity costs" for staying in teaching than do others (Hart, 1994, p. 461). Stated negatively, when teachers are excluded from decisions that effect the quality of their work lives, the results are declining self-esteem and "ultimately perceptions of diminished personal accomplishment" (Byrne, 1994, p. 665). Certainly teachers are more involved in decision making than ever before (Sweeney, 1993), yet levels of job satisfaction apparently have not increased, nor have perceptions of influence (Rice & Schneider, 1994).

Studies of teacher participation have usually treated it as a general construct (Taylor & Bogotch, 1994). However, as we have seen, some aspects of teacher involvement may prove to be more important to teacher development and school improvement than others. For example, when Kerrie served as teacher specialist, she assumed a variety of secretarial and administrative responsibilities that involved her in decision making of various kinds, but the results provided few educational benefits to her, to other teachers, or to students. Some decisions, some forms of school involvement, matter much more than others — particularly those that enhance student learning — and some actually have negative consequences.

Administrators are often charged with unwillingness to share power with teachers, thereby impeding reform. But the sword cuts two ways: some teachers may be unwilling to pay the full price of participation, which is to alter practices and perhaps priorities; it can be a high price. As was suggested in Chapter 5, in the discussion of how resistant some beliefs are to change, and in Chapter 6, change comes slowly:

> While evidence of the benefits of increased teacher influence is fragmentary, reformers are assuming that there is a causal relationship between staff influence and school effectiveness. Some studies of school-based improvement programs emphasizing staff participation in decision making, however, have found that the staff were willing to initiate noninstructional changes but tended to avoid issues dealing with instruction or teacher responsibilities. . . . These data suggest that increasing teacher influence may enhance staff satisfaction without necessarily altering the technical core of the school or the educational outcomes; moreover, it may not be a sufficient intervention to ensure school improvement. (Corcoran, 1990, p. 142)

As we have seen, the price of participation can be high, not only in time and energy expended, but emotionally as well. We humans invest heavily in our beliefs and in the practices that support and sustain them. Surprisingly little attention has been given to the emotional life of teachers. Yet as we have also noted, the costs of disengaging are higher still: arrested development and loss of job satisfaction. We suspect few teachers find that withdrawing into their classrooms behind shut doors makes teaching fully satisfying. Indeed, Taylor and Bogotch (1994) found in their study

> that teachers' involvement in matters outside the classroom . . . in the managerial dimension [budgeting, spending, hiring, assigning teachers to school, designing facilities, scheduling students for special instruction] . . . is more strongly related to their satisfaction with present work than is their involvement with pedagogical decisions. (p. 313)

Moreover, the perception that "decision involvement is influential" helps convince teachers of the value of participating in wider decision making; if it is not influential, and shared governance often involves teachers in what they perceive as only trivial matters, both involvement and job satisfaction suffer (Rice & Schneider, 1994). The question is, what kind of participation is most beneficial? Even teamwork is not necessarily virtuous, because teams like those established at Rocky Mountain Junior High School can block innovation as well as stimulate it, as was the case at Clarke Intermediate (see Guskey, 1995).

Teacher participation on decisions that effect school programs and student learning is an important component of professionalism, but it is not a sufficient condition. Not all forms of participation are equally valuable; and the aims and quality of participation are also of concern.

ISSUES OF STATUS AND RESPECT

The move to professionalize teaching seeks to increase teachers' status and respect, both issues that especially "matter for high-quality teachers with other options" (Hart, 1994, p. 468). Yet imitating the slipping but still presumably high-status professions of medicine and law is not likely to result in greater respect or status for teachers. It probably will do much harm. Respect, we believe, comes only from living and working with others who recognize the complexity of teaching and value and honor those who do it well and work to help others do it better — or to do something else if they cannot. Teachers desire the respect of their students, their students' parents, their colleagues, and administrators, first and foremost.

Respect "is necessary to begin school restructuring [and] an outcome of such processes as well" (Louis et al., 1996, p. 763). Respect comes from getting deeper into a community and sharing expertise, not from increasing distance among community members through claims (however convincing) to special expert standing. Self-respect comes from making a positive difference in the lives of others. Finger-pointing, self-righteous politicians hurt teachers with their constant and usually uninformed attacks, sometimes inspired by the desire to undermine American public education for their own gain (Berliner & Biddle, 1995). But teachers know better and usually can parry the blows. It is when the attacks come from within a teacher's own community, those close to where she works, that the blows and the ignorance of those doing the attacking really hurt and do the most emotional damage. Yet it is important to note that Americans are generally pleased with their local schools and teachers, those with which they are most familiar. It is some abstract, distantly removed, and often caricature school system they are unhappy with, the one moralizing politicians constantly berate (Elam & Rose, 1995).

The respect Kerrie gained by working both at Rocky Mountain Junior High School and at Clarke Intermediate School suggests to us a different model of professionalism, one that resonates with the nature of teaching and with what teachers most care about: ethical citizenship within a specific educational community. Teachers, administrators, parents, and students make up this community, and teachers necessarily must choose if and how they will be involved in it and at what levels. To choose wisely, they need abundant and diverse opportunities for genuine involvement in decision making that matters supported by a clear set of values and by a reward structure that is flexible and resonates with teacher commitments. Kerrie choose to be involved deeply, but by working in contexts characterized by uncertain and, especially at Clarke, expanding role definitions and conflicting expectations, she paid a very high price: the cost of maintaining her definition of professionalism was less involvement with her family, and ultimately, increasing stress and signs of emotional exhaustion.

Within both schools a lively and ongoing discussion of roles and relationships was needed, one that would define the nature of ethical citizenship for teachers, students, administrators, and parents. Similar discussions should have taken place within the union, but too often, union contracts ignore teacher development and shackle teacher initiative rather than liberate it. Unions must get at the forefront of efforts to help members become better teachers (Ponessa, 1996). A good place to begin such discussions is with those within a specific educational context who are seen by others within it as citizen-exemplars. The two experienced AAP teachers with whom Kerrie team taught and the "daring" and inspiring colleague at Rocky Mountain who helped Kerrie "see where [she] could go" are examples of such individuals. By the way they conducted themselves, these teachers inspired others to higher levels of performance and commitment. They both supported and challenged others. We suspect that all schools have teachers whom others seek to emulate, who are found inspiring, and whose professional lives challenge their colleagues to become better than they are. Because of the culture of individualism, we also suspect that some of these models are unknown to all but a few within their work contexts, but they are there, as we have seen even at Rocky Mountain Junior High School. Another place to look is toward "exemplary members of the wider professional community, some of whom, like the 'distant teachers' mentioned by John-Steiner (1985, p. 36), are no longer living" (Bullough, Knowles, & Crow, 1992, p. 192). These are the great historic figures of teaching whose lives also inspire emulation.

Rather than looking to law and medicine for professional guidance, teachers, administrators, and parents, in addition to looking inward, can gain insight into ethical citizenship from other ethically oriented service professions — in particular, the ministry, which continues to enjoy relatively high status and respect primarily because ministers understand the importance of being deeply involved in the communities they serve. If teachers have the respect of those they serve, they have allies who will support them when misguided and politically inspired attacks on public education come. At the same time, as teachers get more deeply into the communities they serve and strive to serve them better, as Kerrie did, they will develop the political skills needed to do a better job of educating others about the complexity and difficulty of teaching. Familiarity, we believe, will breed respect. As Hargreaves (1995, p. 18) argues: "being a more politically aware and developed teacher means empowering and assisting others to reach higher levels of competence and commitment." This includes all members of the educational community, including parents. To be a professional teacher is to be an ethically engaged citizen, one who works to improve not only oneself, but the wider educational community, and through this service assures that the young are cared for. This is service within boundaries, however, boundaries that can be defined only by knowledgeable and understanding educational communities.

Questions for Consideration

1. What is your definition of professionalism? Compare and contrast your definition with that presented by the authors. What distinguishes a professional teacher from an unprofessional teacher?

2. Has your definition of professionalism changed over the years? If so, how and why? What prompted change?

3. Are there individuals within your faculty who inspire you professionally? What is it about these individuals that you most admire? What is it that they do that inspires you? How are you like these people? In what ways are you different?

4. What place do published research and professional journals play in your professional life? Do you read journals? Do you belong to associations? How are you involved in the communities within which you serve? What benefits and costs flow from involvement? Have you ever overextended yourself and become too involved?

5. What professional ideal is supported implicitly or explicitly by your work context? Do you find this institutionally supported teacher role consistent with your own beliefs about professionalism? Are there differences? If so, what are they, and what can be done to reconcile them?

6. Drawing on the four characteristics discussed in the text, would you judge your school a learning-enriched, moderately impoverished, or learning-impoverished work context? What is the basis of your assessment? What part do you play in making the context the way it is? What opportunities exist to make the context more supportive of teacher learning?

7. What educational and social values does your educational community embody? How committed are you to this community?

8. What citizenship ideal do you represent to your students, parents, and other faculty members?

9

Journey's End...
A Small Tragedy

Kerrie left teaching. Following completion of the book she wrote for her brother-in-law, she went to work for him in his dietary products business. She likes her new job, which includes counseling adults who have serious weight and other health problems. She is doing well financially and gains a great deal of emotional satisfaction from the work. She sees lives changing for the better and feels appreciated and respected. There are lots of "warm fuzzies." The career shift has proved invigorating and life affirming.

When she left teaching, Kerrie did not leave behind her need to serve; service remains central to her conception of who she is. A different kind of service now grips her. It seems the timing of her brother-in-law's offer was propitious because Kerrie did not have to face her changing feelings about teaching and seek ways of rekindling her passion. She was feeling "older," "less tolerant," and increasingly "frustrated," even while she pushed herself to remain engaged. She wrote: "I found my ability to cope with daily occurrences in an accepting, loving manner was dwindling rapidly. I was losing not only my composure but my inner peace." Without commitment and passion, teaching becomes drudgery, the kind of work that produced the complaining and irritating teachers Kerrie encountered in that inservice course on stress management a decade ago.

Ending Kerrie's journey in this way produces sadness, a sadness multiplied each time another able teacher walks away from the classroom, shuts the door, and never returns. Their departure is often a human tragedy — when they are forced to leave because work conditions have deteriorated beyond what is tolerable, or, as with Kerrie, when leaving is made relatively easy because the rewards for staying are insufficient.

WORK CONDITIONS, COPING, AND STRESS

The rewards of teaching in a learning-enriched school were many, but involvement had its price: teaming, AAP, shared governance, SIC, and SCC, along with faculty meetings, grade level meetings, coping with mainstreaming, learning a new curriculum—the list seems endless. Once I really plunged in at Clarke and got involved, I was nearly overcome by the amount of planning and meeting time the school context required.

Then there were the more or less normal challenges of teaching: large class sizes I was required to teach, mainstreamed students, behavioral problems. Apathetic, tired parents, parents who lacked interest in their children's education, did not help the situation. Their standards were not my standards, and it showed up in the language and classroom behavior of their children all too often.

Once I was away from school, I realized that I had made a very difficult break with a minimum of pain. I let go of my teaching materials and handed my precious territory over to someone else for good. That was the hardest part of leaving. I am very territorial. I was fleetingly tempted to return to teaching, but I didn't. Suspecting that I would regret returning to the classroom, I didn't want to go through the experience of starting over again. While the nature of the work certainly did not force me to leave, it did make other forms of work appealing when the opportunity came. And it came. I didn't plan to leave teaching. But I left it.

Teaching is high-stress work (Malik, Mueller, & Meinke, 1991), and it is getting more stressful. Stress is increasing for many reasons. Certainly teaching the urban students at Clarke was much more difficult and demanding than teaching seventh grade at Rocky Mountain. But the deeper and more serious source arises from the shift from a modern age to a postmodern one: the growing uncertainty among teachers about roles and responsibilities and the proliferating of increasingly unreasonable expectations. Within schools, ambiguous goals and uncertain evaluation standards increase teacher uncertainty and insecurity (Rosenholtz, 1989a). It is little wonder, and more than a bit ironic, that researchers, speaking from outside the school walls, are so pleased to have discovered that "teachers' views of their roles may be less narrow than in the past" (Hart, 1994, p. 461), as though the outcome is unquestionably positive and progressive. As we have noted, the pressure is constantly to expand roles and to accept ever greater responsibilities, and this pressure is both external, driven by the social context of teaching, and internal, driven by teachers' service ethic. In any case, a large body of research concludes that role ambiguity and especially role conflict are related to teacher stress and to burnout, that dark feeling of emotional exhaustion, disconnectedness, and hopelessness, that one's work is pointless and there is nothing one can do about it (Byrne, 1994). Indeed, some research has shown that the best predictors of stress are workload ("too much work . . . too much responsibility for pupils, and inadequate rest periods") and student misbehavior ("difficult pupils, lack of class discipline") (Boyle et al., 1995, p. 54). Workload is directly related to teacher role definitions and expectations.

Unfortunately, in Western cultures where there has been a triumph of the therapeutic (Rieff, 1966), the typical and first and last response to teachers' feeling overwhelmed by their work is to suggest stress management classes or "employee assistance programs" (Pajak & Blase, 1989, p. 307): "These need to focus on the development of skills which will facilitate a shift from appraising potential stressors as being factors that are beyond the individual teacher's control to appraisals leading to a more problem-focused coping style" (O'Connor & Clarke, 1990, p. 49). Because "an individual's coping pattern is a key determinant in his or her proneness to burnout" (Byrne, 1994, p. 668), such classes may prove helpful.

We mentioned that Kerrie took an in-service course on burnout. For her, the result was disappointment with other teachers' lack of professionalism; they were complainers, whiners. Not that their complaining was unjustified; it probably was. But given Kerrie's first-year teacher therapeutic view of coping, what troubled her was that the individuals in the course were not resolving their own problems; somehow they were inadequate professionally, even though their feelings may in large part have been produced by frustrations at home interacting with conditions as work (Pajak & Blase, 1989) or by lousy work conditions alone. Recall Lenny. Recall Ashton. The problem, as Kerrie saw it, was one of individual, not systemic, failure. Coping was a matter of individuals managing the problems that came their way on their own, more or less (see Bullough, 1989, chapter 5).

Yet over time and working within the broader educational community, Kerrie reconsidered her views of both professionalism and coping. Troubled by teary-eyed and sobbing first-year teachers at Rocky Mountain Junior High School, for example, she acknowledged, at least implicitly, the limitations of individual coping strategies. She recognized the shared interests and responded to the shared concerns of this group of quietly desperate teachers. A seminar was created. Her participation as building union representative encouraged development of this wider view of professionalism and the responsibilities of professionals, a view nicely captured by Rosenholtz (1989b):

> . . . if teaching is collectively viewed as an inherently difficult undertaking, it is both necessary and legitimate to seek and to offer professional assistance. This is exactly what occurs in instructionally successful schools, where, because of strong administrative or faculty leadership, teaching is considered a collective [enterprise] rather than an individual [one]; requests and offers of assistance among colleagues are frequent; and reasoned intentions, informed

choices, and collective actions set the conditions under which teachers improve instructionally. (p. 430)

In such schools, teachers join together to solve their problems.

This view is mostly consistent with and supportive of the case Smith and Bourke (1992) make for "organizational coping":

> The necessity for the individual to acquire knowledge and skills as a personal defense against stress is heightened by [workload pressures,] but so is the necessity at the school- and system-wide levels for educational managers to realize that they, too, can reduce or increase stress through their activities. . . . [T]here is a need to regulate the demands placed upon teachers through such actions as rationalizing assessment practices, providing adequate teaching resources, clarifying instructional goals and by taking care to allocate timetables carefully to share the workload amongst staff members. . . . [E]ducation systems must provide the support structures which help teachers to make functional reactions to stress. Such support structures include the counseling services which are so often lacking, effective student welfare and discipline policies, collegial support structures, and the essential matter of training teachers to manage their time effectively. . . . Providing adequate rewards and recognition [for teachers], using collaborative methods of decision making, recognizing individual teacher needs, providing an appropriate pace for change, and providing clear job specifications for teachers are essential elements of the required management style. (pp. 45–46)

"Providing clear job specifications for teachers" suggests that someone else defines what teachers will and will not do. This is a serious error and a modernist response. Earlier we noted that at Rocky Mountain Junior High School, goals were never discussed, and neither were roles. Moreover, while Clarke Intermediate School had goals, these were established by the new principal, with remarkably little teacher input. Once again, teacher roles and responsibilities were not discussed, and as we have seen, the boundaries slipped ever outward as Kerrie and her colleagues attempted to respond to their own and others' expectations of them. It seems odd that at Clarke, a shared governance school, teacher roles would not be discussed; and that researchers, as quoted above, would argue for "collaborative decision-making methods" and simultaneously suggest that administrators set "job specifications." Such is the confusion surrounding teaching and teachers' roles; such is the need for greater clarity.

To be sure, a reduction of role ambiguity and conflict would help teachers better cope with stress and avoid burnout. But being excluded from the conversation that produces role definitions may only add to their dissatisfaction and disappointment; as we have said, role definitions are intimately and directly linked to workload considerations. Participation in decision making by teachers must produce results. Obviously, organizational coping must support and sustain individual teacher efforts to make their professional lives more fully meaningful and satisfying; otherwise, it will represent nothing more than a bit of administrator sleight-of-hand and produce more meaningless meetings, complemented by a few therapeutic gripe sessions. At the same time, the aim is not to remove all sources of teacher stress, even if it were possible; a measure of stress may encourage personal development, especially when it originates from respected colleagues. Determining which levels of stress are productive and which are not is a matter of teachers' self-regulatory knowledge. Moreover, stress is linked to teacher militancy, which also has the potential to encourage organizational change (Bacharach & Bamberger, 1990).

Kerrie needed boundaries. She probably needed help setting them. So do other teachers. Recall the experienced AAP teacher breaking into tears in frustration; recall the other new AAP teacher withdrawing and relying on others to carry the program. What these two events suggest is that team members pushed one another and themselves too far, beyond what they could reasonably expect. They did so because of their desire to serve the bright students they taught, but also because of their profound commitment to the team and not wanting to disappoint. Kerrie was a "pleaser," and pleasers do not disappoint. But she was also learning a great deal and felt excited about the work even as it drained her energy. The team provided a rich context for development but created conditions ripe for burnout, of consuming all and more of the energy each member possessed. After all, AAP was only part of her assignment, a small part at that, only two of six class periods.

Kerrie realized she had overextended herself only a few months before taking leave and eventually resigning from Clarke Intermediate. Perhaps her own self-regulatory knowledge was not fully adequate, yet one suspects that she would have adjusted, pulled back from some commitments, and better managed her professional life had her brother-in-law's offer not come. Evidence supporting this conclusion comes from the "pact" she made with another teacher to cut back on her commitments. But the offer came, and exhaustion made it especially appealing. Moreover, perhaps it was an expression of her own self-regulatory knowledge that prompted the other teacher new to AAP to withdraw, recognizing she simply could not meet expectations without seriously negative personal and familial consequences. From this vantage point, it is difficult to be as critical of her as we were in Chapter 5. Role boundaries need to be set publicly, not privately.

TEMPERAMENTAL MATTERS

In *First Year Teacher*, coping and burnout were discussed. Following a discussion of how Kerrie coped with problems as a first-year teacher, Bob wrote:

> While Kerrie felt very good about her progress [over the first year], some fears still hovered in the distance. One was burnout. There are better and worse ways of surviving the first year. Some ways lead to dying professionally. Kerrie wondered, for example, if after a few years she would become like some of the other teachers she observed, who hid behind their desks and were disengaged from students and from teaching. (Bullough, 1989, p. 87)

Kerrie did not become like those other teachers. Very rarely did she complain about students or about teaching. Nor did she hide behind her desk. But quietly she was changing, wearing down.

One thing that I had been searching for and seeking is peace. You don't find [peace] in a classroom full of thirteen-year-olds. Their language is so bad. I was really tired—you know, it would be great if you could just go in the classroom and teach, but you can't. It is crowd control, and really you are just socializing them and teaching them skills. If they pick up any curriculum—[any content]—on the way, that is purely a bonus. It is pretty frustrating.

In his study of being called to serve, Coles (1993) describes how exhausting service can be, even for those most centered in a service ethic. The most stout of heart become discouraged, and the reasons are readily apparent. Problems proliferate; solutions are complex and fragile; successes are forever fleeting; disappointments are devastating and personal. In the quest to become increasingly competent, perhaps expert, and to prompt others to stretch their abilities ever further, it is often forgotten that challenge must be balanced by support. Celebrations are needed — occasions to tell teacher stories of triumph and to mythologize accomplishments, to savor successes. Forever rushing, teachers need time and space for both conversation and communion.

Teacher temperament matters a great deal in how work is experienced and stress is managed. Already we have noted how seldom attention is given to teachers' emotions: "Understanding the emotional life of teachers, their feelings for and in their work, and attending to this emotional life in ways that positively cultivate it and avoid negatively damaging it should be absolutely central to teacher development efforts" (Hargreaves, 1995, p. 21). Kerrie needed "peace"; she needed solitude. Both proved elusive that last year, as elusive as the "warm fuzzies" she cherished. Solitude requires periods of isolation, periods packed with quiet meditation and reflection, time to reorient and recapture one's self, one's particularity. Needing to be alone must not be mistaken for individualism, however. Nor should the need for solitude be confused with the feelings of isolation (often positively experienced as autonomy) that come from shutting the classroom door and locking out other, potentially meddling, adults. After all, when the door is closed, the classroom is usually brimming with chattering children, who only rarely can see beyond themselves. There is no solitude here, no healing power.

BACK TO CONTEXT

We have come full circle, back to context and the interaction of person and place. From the perspective of our inquiry, the most successful efforts to encourage teacher development are those that pay the greatest attention to creating contexts supportive of that development, where opportunities for teachers to learn and to increase their expertise are incorporated into the regular operation of the school day. Too often, we believe, staff development is a matter of adding programs, not of rethinking teachers' work to provide and support abundant and diverse opportunities for teachers to learn and to make teaching more pleasureful and manageable. Rethinking work in this way produces results: "teacher enthusiasm for professional development is greatest in schools that made both formal and informal learning an integral part of the teachers' work" (Sprinthall, Reiman, & Thies-Sprinthall, 1996, p. 690).

We further believe that successful approaches to teacher development are likely to be those that honor teacher diversity and particularity, that attend to the emotional well-being of teachers while assuring ongoing conversation about community values and goals, including citizenship ideals (see Chapter 8). Such conversations are necessary to community building, to creating the "new constellations" (Bernstein, 1992) needed to sustain standards of civility and standards of professional conduct in an increasingly uncertain age. As a basis for judging and improving teacher and student performance and enhancing the quality of school life, these standards must resonate with teachers' service ethic and honor diversity while also helping establish boundaries of acceptable service so that the sacrifice of service is sustainable and not suicidal. This is extremely important.

Finally, as we argued in Chapter 2, teachers inevitably stand for something; they have a moral orientation to the world. We wish to underscore here the importance for student learning and for teacher development of this orientation being made explicit and of it being brought into conversation with wider professional citizenship ideals. We ask, teacher development to what end? Those who work within schools ought to be able to say just what kind of community they serve, what kind of citizen they are within that community, and how work conditions are composed to support that vision or how they need to be changed to support it better.

A BROADENED VIEW OF DEVELOPMENT

Internationally, interest in teacher development is growing, and there is increasing agreement on guiding principles. Two sets of principles follow, the first from the U.S. Department of Education's "Building Bridges: The Mission and Principles of Professional Development," and the second from the American Federation of Teachers' "Principles for Professional Development." Both are sensible summaries of current thinking and are supportive of many of the arguments we have made. They should be read in light of a fundamentally important conclusion: "the conditions needed for teacher development are essentially the same ones that enable students to learn" (Sprinthall, Reiman, & Thies-Sprinthall, 1996, p. 697).

Professional development:
   Focuses on teachers as central to student learning, yet includes all other members of the school community.
   Focuses on individual, collegial, and organizational improvement.
   Respects and nurtures the intellectual and leadership capacity of teachers, principals, and others in the school community.
   Respects best available research and practice in teaching, learning, and leadership.
   Enables teachers to develop further expertise in subject content, teacher strategies, uses of technologies, and other essential elements in teaching to high standards.
   Promotes continuous inquiry and improvement embedded in the daily life of schools.
   Is planned collaboratively by those who will participate in and facilitate that development.
   Requires substantial time and other resources.
   Is driven by a coherent long-term plan.
   Is evaluated ultimately on the basis of its impact on teacher effectiveness and student learning, and this assessment guides subsequent professional development efforts. (What makes for good staff development, 1996, p. 11)

Professional development should:
   Ensure depth of content knowledge.

Provide a strong foundation in the pedagogy of particular disciplines.

Provide more general knowledge about the teaching and learning processes and about schools as institutions.

Be rooted in and reflect the best available research.

Contribute to measurable improvement in student achievement.

Expect teachers to be intellectually engaged with ideas and resources.

Provide sufficient time, support, and resources to enable teachers to master new content and pedagogy and to integrate these into their practice.

Be designed by representatives of those who participate in it, in cooperation with experts in the field.

Take a variety of forms, including some we have not typically considered. (What makes for good staff development?, 1996, p. 11)

As we have suggested, and as Kerrie's story illustrates, teacher development builds on biography: how it is best understood in relationship to the living of a life, and how life experience and personality interact with context to produce a story that is recognized as both unique and typical. Obviously, who Kerrie is and the nature of the contexts within which she worked are central elements of the story. Yet it is also a story of teaching; the themes are teacher themes; and the problems and issues are shared ones.

The common themes are important. They have policy and practical implications. But the unique story elements are also important, in part because they remind us of the mystery and majesty of human development, which must not be forgotten in a rush to embrace teacher development as the sine qua non of school reform. Goethe captured a portion of this mystery in *Faust* (II:8144), as he told of the quest of Humunculus to be, his metamorphosis. In the quest, advice is sought from various sources. One is the sea-god Nereus, who had little to offer but much to say. As Nereus's daughters approach, he breaks off conversation, gives what advice he can, and poses a question. The question speaks to the mystery of human development.

> On Venus' radiant, pearly chariot drawn,
> Comes Galatea, lovely as the dawn.
> Since Cypris turned from us her face,
> She reigns in Paphos in the goddess' place.
> And so, long since, the gracious one doth own,
> As heiress, templed town and chariot-throne.
> Away! It spoils a father's hour of pleasure,
> Harshness of tongue or hate of heart to treasure.
> Away to Proteus! Ask that wondrous elf:
> How one can come to be and change one's self.

Such is the mystery of teaching and the formation of a teaching identity. It is a story of continuity and change, of resistance and reformation, of being and becoming, of hopefulness and heartbreak. The hope is that in becoming, teachers will more fully be; that being a teacher will enable the fullest expression of the person. Good schools, then, are ones that fully support teachers and teacher development, that are learning-enriched, second-order environments. Teachers feel fully at home and slightly ill at ease in such places, as Nereus might have said.

Questions for Consideration

1. To what extent are teacher roles and responsibilities discussed in your school? At what level are you involved in that discussion?

2. Are there clear role definitions in operation within your school? If so, what is their origin? If not, how does the lack of clear definitions impact your development and the quality of your school life?

3. Do you find teaching stressful? If so, what about teaching is most stressful? What about it is most pleasing? What can you do to increase your pleasure and decrease unproductive stress? Are there changes in context that would help you achieve this aim? If so, what are they?

4. Do you ever find yourself on the edge, unable to cope with the pressures of teaching? If so, who might be able to help you? Do you know other teachers who are struggling, having a difficult time coping? If you do, how might you help them? How might the work context become more supportive of teacher learning while still remaining productively challenging?

5. What coping strategies do you use? Are they effective? What part do family members and other teachers play in how you cope? Do you see possibilities within your school for organizational coping?

6. How nearly does your work context represent the two sets of principles for professional development? Are there possibilities for making your school more consistent with the principles, more friendly to teacher development?

7. How do you feel about Kerrie's decision to leave teaching? How do you feel about your own career and its direction? Do you need to make some changes? Can you see yourself still teaching a year, five years, ten years from now? When you visualize your future as a teacher, how do you feel? Is there cause for celebration?

References

Abbs, P. (1981). Education and the living image: Reflections on imagery, fantasy, and the art of recognition. *Teachers College Record*, 82(3), 475–496.

Apple, M.W. (1979). *Ideology and curriculum*. London: Routledge & Kegan Paul.

Apple, M.W. (1982). *Education and power*. Boston: Routledge & Kegan Paul.

Apple, M.W. (1986). *Teachers and texts: A political economy of class and gender relations in education*. New York: Routledge & Kegan Paul.

Arendt, H. (1958). *The human condition*. Chicago: University of Chicago Press.

Atwell, N. (1987). *In the middle: Writing, reading, and learning with adolescents*. Upper Montclair, NJ: Boynton/Cook.

Avis, J. (1994). Teacher professionalism: One more time. *Educational Review*, 46(1), 63–72.

Bacharach, S.B., & Bamberger, P. (1990). Exit and voice: Turnover and militancy intentions in elementary and secondary schools. *Educational Administration Quarterly*, 26(4), 316–344.

Ball, D.L., & McDiarmid, G.W. (1990). The subject-matter preparation of teachers. In W.R. Houston (Ed.), *Handbook of research on teacher education* (pp. 437–449). New York: Macmillan.

Barnes, C.P., & Goodhue-McWilliams, K. (1992). *Those who can, teach*. Fullerton, CA: California State University.

Bellah, R.N., Madsen, R., Sullivan, W.M., Swidler, A., & Tipton, S.M. (1985). *Habits of the heart: Individualism and commitment in American life*. Berkeley: University of California Press.

Bellah, R.N., Madsen, R., Sullivan, W.M., Swidler, A., & Tipton, S.M. (1991). *The good society*. New York: Alfred A. Knopf.

Bereiter, C., & Scardamalia, M. (1993). *Surpassing ourselves: An inquiry into the nature and implications of expertise*. Chicago: Open Court.

Berliner, D.C. (1986). In pursuit of the expert pedagogue, *Educational Researcher*, 15(7), 5–13.

Berliner, D.C. (1988). Implications of expertise in pedagogy for teacher education and evaluation. In *New Directions for Teacher Assessment: Proceedings of the 1988 ETS Invitational Conference* (pp. 39–67). Princeton, NJ: Educational Testing Service.

Berliner, D.C. (1990, September). *Characteristics of experts in the pedagogical domain*. Paper presented at the International Symposium on Research on

Effective and Responsible Teaching, University of Fribourg, Fribourg, Switzerland.

Berliner, D.C. (1994). Expertise: The wonder of exemplary performances. In J. Magieri & C. Collins (Eds.), *Creating powerful thinking in teachers and students* (pp. 161–186). Fort Worth, TX: Harcourt Brace.

Berliner, D.C., & Biddle, B.J. (1995). *The manufactured crisis: Myths, fraud, and the attack on America's public schools*. Reading, MA: Addison-Wesley.

Bernstein, R.J. (1992). *The new constellation: The ethical-political horizons of modernity/postmodernity*. Cambridge, MA: The MIT Press.

Bloom, B.S. (Ed.). (1956). *Taxonomy of educational objectives: Handbook I. Cognitive domain*. New York: David McKay.

Bode, B.H. (1928). The place of thinking in education. In B.W. Stillman, *Training children to study: Practical suggestions* (pp. 1–11). Boston: D.C. Heath.

Boehm, R.G., Brierley, J., & Sharma, M. (1994). The bête noir of geographic education: Teacher training programs. *Journal of Geography, 93*(1), 21–25.

Boehm, R.G., & Petersen, J.F. (1994). An elaboration of the fundamental themes in geography. *Social Education, 58*(4), 211–218.

Borko, H., & Putnam, R.T. (1995). Expanding a teacher's knowledge base: A cognitive psychological perspective on professional development. In T.R. Guskey & M. Huberman (Eds.), *Professional development in education: New paradigms and practices* (pp. 35–65). New York: Teachers College Press.

Bowers, C.A. (1987). *The promise of theory: Education and the politics of cultural change*. New York: Teachers College Press.

Boyle, G.J., Borg, M.G., Falzon, J.M., & Baglioni, A.J., Jr. (1995). A structural model of the dimensions of teacher stress. *British Journal of Educational Psychology, 65*, 49–67.

Brewer, R.E., & de Beer, J. (1991). *Education for the ministry, common lessons: Series D*. Sewanee, TN: The University of the South.

Brown, L., Schwartz, P., Udvari-Soldner, A., Kampschroer, E.F., Johnson, K., Jorgensen, J., & Gruenewald, L. (1991). How much time should students with severe intellectual disabilities spend in regular education classrooms and elsewhere? *Journal of the Association for Persons with Severe Handicaps, 16*(1), 39–47.

Bruner, J. (1990). *Acts of meaning*. Cambridge, MA: Harvard University Press.

Bullough, R.V., Jr. (1988). *The forgotten dream of American public education*. Ames: Iowa State University Press.

Bullough, R.V., Jr. (1989). *First year teacher: A case study*. New York: Teachers College Press.

Bullough, R.V., Jr. (1993). Case records as personal teaching texts for study in preservice teacher education. *Teaching & Teacher Education, 9*(4), 385–396.

Bullough, R.V., Jr. (1994). Digging at the roots: Discipline, management, and metaphor. *Action in Teacher Education, 16*(1), 1–10.

Bullough, R.V., Jr. (1996). Becoming a teacher: Self and the social location of teacher education. In B.J. Biddle, T.L. Good, & I.F. Goodson (Eds.), *The international handbook of teachers and teaching* (pp. 87–148). Dordrecht, Netherlands: Kluwer.

Bullough, R.V., Jr. (with Baughman, K.). (1993). Continuity and change in teacher development: First year teacher after five years. *Journal of Teacher Education, 44*(2), 86–95.

Bullough, R.V., Jr., & Gitlin, A. (1995). *Becoming a student of teaching: Methodologies for exploring self and school context.* New York: Garland.

Bullough, R.V., Jr., Goldstein, S., & Holt, L. (1984). *Human interests in the curriculum: Teaching and learning in a technological society.* New York: Teachers College Press.

Bullough, R.V., Jr., Kauchak, D., Crow, N.A., Hobbs, S., & Stokes, D.K. (1997). Professional development schools: Catalysts for teacher and school change. *Teaching & Teacher Education, 13*(2), 153–169.

Bullough, R.V., Jr., & Knowles, J.G. (1990). Becoming a teacher: Struggles of a second-career beginning teacher. *Qualitative Studies in Education, 3*(2), 101–112.

Bullough, R.V., Jr., & Knowles, J.G. (1991). Teaching and nurturing: Changing conceptions of self as teacher in a case study of becoming a teacher. *Qualitative Studies in Education, 4*(2), 121–140.

Bullough, R.V., Jr., Knowles, J.G., & Crow, N.A. (1992). *Emerging as a teacher.* London: Routledge.

Bullough, R.V., Jr. (with Stokes, D.K.). (1994). Analyzing personal teaching metaphors in pre-service teacher education as a means for encouraging professional development. *American Educational Research Journal, 31*(1), 197–224.

Byrne, B.M. (1994). Burnout: Testing for the validity, replication, and invariance of causal structure across elementary, intermediate, and secondary teachers. *American Educational Research Journal, 31*(3), 645–673.

Carlson, R.A. (1975). *The quest for conformity: Americanization through education.* New York: John Wiley.

Carter, K. (1990). Teachers' knowledge and learning to teach. In W.R. Houston (Ed.), *Handbook of research on teacher education* (pp. 329–348). New York: Macmillan.

Casey, K. (1990). Teacher as mother: Curriculum theorizing in the life histories of contemporary women teachers. *Cambridge Journal of Education, 20*(3), 301–320.

Cherryholmes, C.H. (1988). *Power and criticism: Poststructural investigations in education.* New York: Teachers College Press.

Clark, C.M. (1988). Asking the right questions about teacher preparation: Contributions of research on teacher thinking. *Educational Researcher, 17*(2), 5–12.

Cole, A.L. (1988, April). Personal knowing in spontaneous teaching practice. Paper presented at the annual meeting of the American Educational Research Association, New Orleans.

Cole, A.L. (1992). Teacher development in the work place: Rethinking the appropriation of professional relationships. *Teachers College Record, 94*(4), 365–381.

Cole, A.L., & Knowles, J.G. (1993). Teacher development partnership research: A focus on methods and issues. *American Educational Research Journal, 30*(3), 473–495.

Coles, R. (1989). *The call of stories: Teaching and the moral imagination*. Boston: Houghton Mifflin.

Coles, R. (1993). *The call of service: A witness to idealism*. Boston: Houghton Mifflin.

Connelly, F.M., & Clandinin, D.J. (1988). *Teachers as curriculum planners: Narratives of experience*. New York: Teachers College Press.

Connelly, F.M., & Clandinin, D.J. (1990). Stories of experience and narrative inquiry. *Educational Researcher, 19*(5), 2–14.

Copeland, W.D., Birmingham, C., DeMeulle, L., D'Emidio-Caston, M., & Natal, D. (1994). Making meaning in classrooms: An investigation of cognitive processes in aspiring teachers, experienced teachers, and their peers. *American Educational Research Journal, 31*(1), 166–196.

Corcoran, T.B. (1990). Schoolwork: Perspectives on workplace reform in public schools. In M.W. Mclaughlin, J.E. Talbert, & N. Bascia (Eds.), *The contexts of teaching in secondary schools: Teachers' realities* (pp. 142–166). New York: Teachers College Press.

Crow, N.A. (1987). *Socialization within a teacher education program: A case study*. Unpublished doctoral dissertation, University of Utah, Salt Lake City.

Csikszentmihalyi, M. (1993). *The evolving self: A psychology for the third millennium*. New York: HarperCollins.

Darling-Hammond, L. (1994). Professional development schools: Early lessons, change, promise. In L. Darling-Hammond (Ed.), *Professional development schools: Schools for a developing profession* (pp. 1–27). New York: Teachers College Press.

de Souza, A.R., & Munroe, S. (1994). Implementation of geography standards: Potential strategies and initiatives. *Journal of Geography, 93*(1), 46–49.

Dewey, J. (1916). *Democracy and education*. New York: Macmillan.

Dewey, J. (1922). *Human nature and conduct: An introduciton to social psychology*. New York: Henry Holt and Co.

Diegmueller, K. (1996). Despite attention, work on standards is well under way. *Education Week, 15*(25), 1, 22.

Doyle, W. (1990). Classroom knowledge as a foundation for teaching. *Teachers College Record, 91*(3), 347–360.

Ehrenhalt, A. (1995). Learning from the fifties. *The Wilson Quarterly, 29*(3), 8–29.

Elam, S.M., & Rose, L.C. (1995). The 27th annual Phi Delta Kappa/Gallup Poll of the public's attitudes toward the public schools. *Phi Delta Kappan, 77*(1), 41–55.

Elbaz, F. (1991). Research on teacher's knowledge: The evolution of a discourse. *Journal of Curriculum Studies, 23*(1), 1–19.

Elbaz, F. (1992). Hope, attentiveness, and caring for difference: The moral voice in teaching. *Teaching & Teacher Education, 8*(5/6), 421–432.

Elkind, D. (1994). Educational reform: Modern and postmodern. *Holistic Education Review, 7*(4), 5–12.

Elliot, J. (1991). *Action research for educational change*. Milton Keynes, UK: Open University Press.

Elshtain, J.B. (1994). The masculine mystique. *The Wilson Quarterly*, *18*(3), 82–85.

Eraut, M. (1994). *Developing professional knowledge and competence*. London: The Falmer Press.

Erikson, E.H. (1958). *Young man Luther: A study in psychoanalysis and history*. New York: W.W. Norton.

Erikson, E.H. (1968). *Identity, youth and crisis*. New York: W.W. Norton.

Erikson, E.H. (1975). *Life history and the historical moment*. New York: W.W. Norton.

Fay, B. (1987). *Critical social science*. Ithaca, NY: Cornell University Press.

Fenstermacher, G.D. (1978). A philosophical consideration of recent research on teacher effectiveness. In L. Shulman (Ed.), *Review of research in education* (pp. 157–185). Washington, DC: American Educational Research Association.

Fenstermacher, G.D. (1994). The knower and the known: The nature of knowledge in research on teaching. In L. Darling-Hammond (Ed.), *Review of research in education* (pp. 3–56). Washington, DC: American Educational Research Association.

Floden, R.E., & Clark, C.M. (1988). Preparing teachers for uncertainty. *Teachers College Record*, *89*(4), 505–524.

Fuchs, D., & Fuchs, L.S. (1994). Inclusive schools movement and the radicalization of special education reform. *Exceptional Children*, *60*(4), 294–309.

Fullan, M. (1993). *Change forces: Probing the depths of educational reform*. London: The Falmer Press.

Fuller, F.F., & Brown, O.H. (1975). Becoming a teacher. In K. Ryan (Ed.), *Teacher education* (pp. 25–52). Chicago: University of Chicago Press.

Genberg, V. (1992). Patterns and organizing perspectives: A view of expertise. *Teaching & Teacher Education*, *8*(5/6), 485–495.

Gergen, K.J. (1991). *The saturated self: Dilemmas of identity in contemporary life*. New York: Basic Books.

Gess-Newsome, J., & Lederman, N.G. (1995). Biology teachers' perceptions of subject matter structure and its relationship to classroom practice. *Journal of Research in Science Teaching*, *32*(3), 301–325.

Giddens, A. (1994). *Beyond left and right: The future of radical politics*. Stanford, CA: Stanford University Press.

Gillum, G. (1993). *Of all things!: Classic quotations from Hugh Nibley*. Salt Lake City, UT: Deseret Books.

Glass, J.M. (1993). *Shattered selves: Multiple personality in a postmodern world*. Ithaca, NY: Cornell University Press.

Glasser, B.G., & Strauss, A.L. (1967). *The discovery of grounded theory*. Chicago: Aldine.

Goethe, J.W. (1941). *Faust: Parts one and two* (A.M. Priest, Trans.). New York: Alfred A. Knopf.

Good, T.L., & Brophy, J.E. (1994). *Looking in classrooms*. New York: Harper-Collins.

Goodson, I.F. (1994). Studying the teacher's life and work. *Teaching & Teacher Education*, *10*(1), 29–37.

Graham, R.J. (1989). Autobiography and education. *The Journal of Educational Thought*, *23*(2), 94–105.

Graham, R.J. (1993). Voice, archive, practice: The textual construction of professional identity. *The Journal of Educational Thought*, *27*(2), 186–199.

Grant, G.E. (1992). The sources of structural metaphors in teacher knowledge: Three cases. *Teaching & Teacher Education*, *8*(5/6), 433–440.

Green, T.F. (1971). *The activities of teaching*. New York: McGraw-Hill.

Greene, M. (1991). Retrieving the language of compassion: The education professor in search of community. *Teachers College Record*, *92*(4), 541–555.

Griffiths, M. (1993). Educational change and the self. *British Journal of Educational Studies*, *41*(2), 150–163.

Griffiths, M., & Tann, S. (1992). Using reflective practice to link personal and public theories. *Journal of Education for Teaching*, *18*(1), 69–84.

Grimmett, P.P., & MacKinnon, A.M. (1992). Craft knowledge in the education of teachers. In G. Grant (Ed.), *Review of research in education* (pp. 385–456). Washington, DC: American Educational Research Association.

Grossman, P.L. (1990). *The making of a teacher: Teacher knowledge and teacher education*. New York: Teachers College Press.

Grossman, P.L. (1992). Why models matter: An alternative view on professional growth in teaching. *Review of Educational Research*, *62*(2), 171–179.

Grossman, P.L., & Stodolsky, S.S. (1994). Consideration of content and the circumstances of secondary school teaching. In L. Darling-Hammond (Ed.), *Review of research in education* (pp. 179–222). Washington, DC: American Educational Research Association.

Grossman, P.L., Wilson, S.M., & Shulman, L.S. (1989). Teachers of substance: Subject matter knowledge for teaching. In M.C. Reynolds (Ed.), *Knowledge base for the beginning teacher* (pp. 23–36). New York: Pergamon Press.

Grumet, M.R. (1988). *Bitter milk: Women and teaching*. Amherst, MA: University of Massachusetts Press.

Guba, E.G. (1978). *Toward a methodology of naturalistic inquiry in educational evaluation*. Los Angeles: Center for the Study of Evaluation, UCLA Graduate School of Education.

Guidano, V.F. (1991). *The self in process*. New York: The Guilford Press.

Guskey, T.R. (1995). Professional development in education: In search of the optimal mix. In T.R. Guskey & M. Huberman (Eds.), *Professional development in education: New paradigms and practices* (pp. 114–131). New York: Teachers College Press.

Habermas, J. (1979). *Communication and the evolution of society* (T. McCarthy, Trans.). Boston: Beacon Press.

Hamilton, R.F. (1996). *The social misconstruction of reality: Validity and verification in the scholarly community*. New Haven: Yale University Press.

Hargreaves, A. (1994). *Changing teachers, changing times: Teachers' work and culture in the postmodern age*. New York: Teachers College Press.

Hargreaves, A. (1995). Development and desire: A postmodern perspective. In T.R. Guskey & M. Huberman (Eds.), *Professional development in education: New paradigms and practices* (pp. 9–33). New York: Teachers College Press.

Hart, A.W. (1994). Work feature values of today's and tomorrow's teachers: Work redesign as an incentive and school improvement policy. *Educational Evaluation and Policy Analysis, 16*(4), 458–473.

Hart, A.W., & Murphy, M.J. (1990). New teachers react to redesigned teacher work. *American Journal of Education, 98*(3), 224–250.

Hartley, D. (1993). Confusion in teacher education: a postmodern condition? *Journal of Education for Teaching, 19*(4,5), 83–93.

Holmes Group (1986). *Tomorrow's teachers.* East Lansing, Michigan: Author.

Huberman, A.M. (1989). The professional life cycle of teachers. *Teachers College Record, 91*(1), 31–57.

Huberman, M. (with Groundauer, M.M., & Marti, J.). (1993). *The lives of teachers.* New York: Teachers College Press.

Huefner, D.S. (1994). The mainstreaming case: Tensions and trends for school educators. *Educational Administration Quarterly, 30*(1), 27–55.

Hunt, M. (1993). *The story of psychology.* New York: Doubleday.

Idstein, P. (1993). Swimming against the mainstream. *Phi Delta Kappa, 74*(4), 336–340.

Jalongo, M.R., & Isenberg, J.P. (1995). *Teachers' stories: From personal narrative to professional insight.* San Francisco: Jossey-Bass.

John-Steiner, V. (1985). *Notebooks of the mind: Explorations of thinking.* Albuquerque, NM: University of New Mexico Press.

Kagan, D.M. (1993). Contexts for the use of classroom cases. *American Educational Research Journal, 30*(4), 703–723.

Kagan, J. (1994). *Galen's prophecy: Temperament in human nature.* New York: Basic Books.

Kaplan, S.N. (1986). The grid: A model to construct differentiated curriculum for the gifted. In J.S. Rensulli (Ed.), *Systems and models for developing programs for the gifted and talented* (pp. 180–193). Mansfield Center, CT: Creative Learning Press.

Kegan, R. (1982). *The evolving self: Problem and process in human development.* Cambridge, MA: Harvard University Press.

Kelchtermans, G., & Vandenberghe, R. (1994). Teachers' professional development: A biographical perspective. *Journal of Curriculum Studies, 26*(1), 45–62.

King, P.M., & Kitchener, K.S. (1994). *Developing reflective judgment: Understanding and promoting intellectual growth and critical thinking in adolescents and adults.* San Francisco: Jossey-Bass.

Korthagen, F.A.J. (1993). Two modes of reflection. *Teaching & Teacher Education, 9*(3), 317–326.

Labaree, D.F. (1992). Power, knowledge, and the rationalization of teaching: A genealogy of the movement to professionalize teaching. *Harvard Educational Review, 62*(2), 123–154.

Lasch, C. (1978). *The culture of narcissism: American life in an age of diminishing expectations.* New York: W.W. Norton & Company, Inc.

Lasch, C. (1991). *The true and only heaven: Progress and its critics.* New York: W.W. Norton.

Lasch, C. (1995). *The revolt of the elites and the betrayal of democracy*. New York: W.W. Norton.

Lehman, D. (1991). *Signs of the times: Deconstruction and the fall of Paul de Man*. New York: Poseidon Press.

Levin, B.B., & Ammon, P. (1992). The development of beginning teachers' pedagogical thinking: A longitudinal analysis of four case studies. *Teacher Education Quarterly*, *19*(4), 19–37.

Levinas, E. (1969). *Totality and infinity: An essay on exteriority*. Pittsburgh: Duquesne University Press.

Lincoln, Y.S., & Guba, E.G. (1985). *Naturalistic inquiry*. Newbury Park: Sage.

Lippmann, W. (1955). *Essays in the public philosophy*. Boston: Little, Brown.

Little, J.W. (1990). Conditions of professional development in secondary schools. In M.W. McLaughlin, J.E. Talbert, & N. Bascia (Eds.), *The contexts of teaching in secondary schools: Teachers' realities* (pp. 187–223). New York: Teachers College Press.

Little, J.W. (1993). Teachers' professional development in a climate of educational reform. *Educational Evaluation and Policy Analysis*, *15*(2), 129–151.

Lortie, D.C. (1975). *School-teacher: A sociological study*. Chicago: University of Chicago Press.

Louis, K.S., Marks, H.M., & Kruse, S. (1996). Teachers' professional community in restructuring schools. *American Educational Research Journal*, *33*(4), 757–798.

MacDonald, J.B. (1994). *Teaching and parenting: Effects of the dual role*. Lanham, MD: University Press of America.

MacIntyre, A. (1981). *After virture, a study of moral theory*. London: Duckworth.

Madden, N.A., Slavin, R.E., Karweit, N.L., Dolan, L.J., & Wasik, B.A. (1993). Success for all: Longitudinal effects of a restructuring program for inner-city elementary schools. *American Educational Research Journal*, *30*(1), 123–148.

Malik, J.L., Mueller, R.O., & Meinke, D.L. (1991). The effects of teaching experience and grade level taught on teacher stress: A LISREL analysis. *Teaching & Teacher Education*, *7*(1), 57–62.

Mattingly, P.H. (1975). *The classless profession*. New York: New York University Press.

Maxwell, J.A. (1992). Understanding and validity in qualitative research. *Harvard Educational Review*, *62*(3), 279–300.

McCollum, A.B. (1981). The first vision: Re-Visioning historical experience. In N.E. Lambert (Ed.), *Literature of belief* (pp. 177–196). Provo, UT: Brigham Young University Religious Studies Center.

McKeon, R. (Ed.). (1947). *Introduction to Aristotle*. New York: Modern Library.

Menand, L. (1995). The trashing of professionalism. *Academe*, *18*(3), 16–19.

Mevarech, Z.R. (1995). Teachers' paths on the way to and from the professional development forum. In T.R. Guskey & M. Huberman (Eds.), *Professional development in education: New paradigms and practices* (pp. 151–170). New York: Teachers College Press.

Miles, M.B., & Huberman, A.M. (1984). *Qualitative data analysis: A sourcebook of new methods*. Newbury Park, CA: Sage.

Mills, C.W. (1959). *The sociological imagination*. New York: Oxford University Press.

Mooney, R. (1957). The researcher himself. In *Research for curriculum improvement* (1957 Yearbook), (pp. 154–186). Washington, DC: Association for Supervision and Curriculum Improvement.

Moore, T. (1992). *Care of the soul: A guide for cultivating depth and sacredness in everyday life*. New York: HarperCollins.

Morson, G.S. (1986). Preface: Perhaps Bakhtin. In G.S. Morson (Ed.), *Bakhtin: Essays and dialogues on his work* (pp. vii–xiii). Chicago: University of Chicago Press.

Munby, H. (1986). Metaphor in the thinking of teachers: An exploratory study. *Journal of Curriculum Studies, 18*(2), 197–209.

Munby, H., & Russell, T. (1994). The authority of experience in learning to teach: Messages from a physics methods course. *Journal of Teacher Education, 45*(2), 86–95.

Murphy, J.W. (1989). *Postmodern social analysis and criticism*. New York: Greenwood Press.

National Education Goals Panel (1995). *The national education goals report*. Washington, DC: U.S. Government Printing Office.

Nespor, J., & Barylske, J. (1991). Narrative discourse and teacher knowledge. *American Educational Research Journal, 28*(4), 805–823.

Nias, J. (1989). *Primary teachers talking: A study of teaching as work*. London & New York: Routledge.

Noddings, N. (1984). *Caring*. Berkeley, California: University of California Press.

Oakes, J. (1985). *Keeping track: How schools structure inequality*. New Haven, CT: Yale University Press.

O'Connor, P.R., & Clarke, V.A. (1990). Determinants of teacher stress. *Australian Journal of Education, 34*(1), 41–51.

Ogawa, R.T. (1994). The institutional sources of educational reform: The case of school-based management. *American Educational Research Journal, 31*(3), 519–548.

Oja, S.N. (1989). Teachers: Ages and stages of adult development. In M.L. Holly & C.S. McLoughlin (Eds.), *Perspectives on teacher professional development* (pp. 119–154). London: The Falmer Press.

Ornstein, R. (1993). *The roots of the self: Unraveling the mystery of who we are*. San Francisco: Harper Collins.

Pajak, E., & Blase, J.J. (1989). The impact of teachers' personal lives on professional role enactment: A qualitative analysis. *American Educational Research Journal, 26*(2), 283–310.

Pajares, M.F. (1992). Teachers' beliefs and educational research: Cleaning up a messy construct. *Review of Educational Research, 62*(3), 307–322.

Patterson, D. (1991). The eclipse of the highest in higher education. *The Main Scholar: A Journal of Ideas and Public Affairs, 4*, 7–20.

Perry, C.M., & Rog, J.A. (1992). Preservice and inservice teachers' beliefs and the sources of those beliefs. *Teacher Education Quarterly, 19*(2), 49–59.

Petrosky, A.R. (1994). Schizophrenia, the national board for professional teaching standards' policies, and me. *English Journal, 83*(7), 33–41.

Pinnegar, S. (1996, April). Depending on experience. Paper presented at the annual meeting of the American Educational Research Association, New York.

Pogrow, S. (1996). Reforming the wannabe reformers: Why education reforms almost always end up making things worse. *Phi Delta Kappan, 77*(10), 657–663.

Polanyi, M. (1958). *Personal knowledge: Toward a post-critical philosophy*. Chicago: University of Chicago Press.

Polkinghorne, D. (1988). *Narrative knowing and the human sciences*. Albany, NY: SUNY Press.

Ponessa, J. (1996). Union dues. *Education Week, 15*(30), 15–17.

Prawat, R.S. (1991). Conversations with self and settings: A framework for thinking about teacher empowerment. *American Educational Research Journal 28*(4), 737–757.

Prawat, R.S. (1992). Teachers' beliefs about teaching and learning: A constructivist perspective. *American Journal of Education, 100*(3), 354–395.

Provenzo, E.F., Jr., McCloskey, G.N., Kottkamp, R.B., & Cohn, M. (1989). Metaphor and meaning in the language of teachers. *Teachers College Record, 90*(4), 551–573.

Rest, J. (1986). *Moral development: Advances in research and theory*. New York: Praeger.

Rice, E.M., & Schneider, G.T. (1994). A decade of teacher empowerment: An empirical analysis of teacher involvement in decision making, 1980–1991. *Journal of Educational Administration, 32*(1), 43–58.

Rich, Y. (1993). Stability and change in teacher expertise. *Teaching & Teacher Education, 9*(2), 137–146.

Richardson, V. (1996). The role of attitudes and beliefs in learning to teach. In J. Sikula (Ed.), *Handbook of research on teacher education, second edition* (pp. 102–119). New York: Macmillan.

Rieff, P. (1966). *The triumph of the therapeutic: Uses of faith after Freud*. New York: Harper & Row.

Riseborough, G.F. (1985). Pupils, teachers' careers and schooling: An empirical study. In S.J. Ball & I.F. Goodson (Eds.), *Teachers lives and careers* (pp. 202–265). London: The Falmer Press.

Robinson, S.P., & Darling-Hammond, L. (1994). Change for collaboration and collaboration for change: Transforming teaching through school-university partnerships. In L. Darling-Hammond (Ed.), *Professional development schools: Schools for a developing profession* (pp. 203–219). New York: Teachers College Press.

Rosenholtz, S.J. (1989a). *Teachers' workplace: The social organization of schools*. New York: Longman.

Rosenholtz, S.J. (1989b). Workplace conditions that affect teacher quality and commitment: Implications for teacher induction programs. *Elementary School Journal*, 89(4), 421–39.

Ryan, K. (1986). *The induction of new teachers*. Bloomington, IN: Phi Delta Kappa Educational Foundation.

Sandel, M.J. (1996). America's search for a new public philosophy. *The Atlantic Monthly*, 277(3), 57–74.

Sarason, S.B. (1990). *The predictable failure of educational reform: Can we change course before it's too late?* San Francisco: Jossey-Bass.

Sarason, S.B. (1996). *Revisiting "The Culture of the School and the Problem of Change."* New York: Teachers College Press.

Scardamalia, M., & Bereiter, C. (1989). Conceptions of teaching and approaches to core problems. In M.C. Reynolds (Ed.), *Knowledge base for the beginning teacher* (pp. 37–45). New York: Pergamon Press.

Scharff, D.E. (1992). *Refinding the object and reclaiming the self*. Northvale, NJ: Jason Aronson.

Schwarz, B. (1995). The diversity myth: America's leading export. *The Atlantic Monthly*, 275(5), 57–67.

Serow, R.C. (1994). Called to teach: A study of highly motivated preservice teachers. *The Journal of Research and Development in Education*, 27(2), 65–72.

Serow, R.C., Eaker, D.J., & Forest, K.D. (1994). "I want to see some kind of growth out of them": What the service ethic means to teacher-education students. *American Educational Research Journal*, 31(1), 27–48.

Shanker, A. (1994). The rush to inclusion. *American teacher*, 78(4), 5.

Sherman, R.R. (1992). Telling stories. *Educational Studies*, 23(1), 1–17.

Shulman, L. (1987). Knowledge and teaching: Foundations of the new reform. *Harvard Educational Review*, 57(1), 1–21.

Silverman, D. (1993). *Interpreting qualitative data: Methods for analysing talk, text and interaction*. London: Sage.

Sklaroff, S. (1994). AFT urges halt to "full inclusion" movement. *Education Week*, 13(16), 7.

Slater, P.E. (1965). Role differentiation in small groups. In A.P. Hare, E.F. Borgatta, & R.F. Bales (Eds.), *Small groups: Studies in social interaction, revised edition* (pp. 610–627). New York: Alfred A. Knopf.

Smith, M., & Bourke, S. (1992). Teacher stress: Examining a model based on context, workload, and satisfaction. *Teaching & Teacher Education*, 8(1), 31–46.

Smylie, M.A. (1995). Teacher learning in the workplace: Implications for school reform. In T.R. Guskey & M. Huberman (Eds.), *Professional development in education: New paradigms and practices* (pp. 92–113). New York: Teachers College Press.

Soder, R. (1991). The ethics of the rhetoric of teacher professionalization. *Teaching & Teacher Education*, 7(3), 295–302.

Spencer, D.A. (1986). *Contemporary women teachers: Balancing school and home*. New York: Longman.

Sprinthall, N.A., Reiman, A.J., & Thies-Sprinthall, L. (1996). Teacher professional development. In J. Sikula (Ed.), *Handbook of research on teacher education* (2nd ed., pp. 666–703). New York: Macmillan.

Stoler, R.D. (1992). Perceptions of regular education teachers toward inclusion of all handicapped students in their classrooms. *Clearinghouse, 66*(1), 60–62.

Strauss, A., & Corbin, J. (1990). *Basis of qualitative research: Grounded theory procedures and techniques.* Newbury Park, CA: Sage.

Sweeney, J. (1993). Secondary school culture: The effects of decision making participation on teacher satisfaction. *High School Journal, 76*(2), 94–99.

Sykes, G. (1996). Reform of and as professional development. *Phi Delta Kappan, 77*(7), 465–467.

Talbert, J.E., & McLaughlin, M.W. (1994). Teacher professionalism in local school contexts. *American Journal of Education, 102*(2), 123–153.

Taubman, P.M. (1992). Achieving the right distance. In W.F. Pinar & W.M. Reynolds (Eds.), *Understanding curriculum as phenomenological and deconstructed text* (pp. 216–233). New York: Teachers College Press.

Taylor, C. (1989). *Sources of the self.* Cambridge, MA: Harvard University Press.

Taylor, D.L., & Bogotch, I.E. (1994). School-level effects of teachers' participation in decision making. *Educational Evaluation and Policy Analysis, 16*(3), 302–319.

Taylor, W. (1984). Metaphors in educational discourse. In W. Taylor (Ed.), *Metaphors in education* (pp. 4–20). London: Heinemann Educational Books.

Thomas, D. (1993). Treasonable or trustworthy text: Reflections on teacher narratives studies. *Journal of Education for Teaching, 19*(4,5), 231–249.

Tobin, K. (1990). Changing metaphors and beliefs: A master switch for teaching? *Theory into Practice, 29*(2), 122–127.

Van Manen, M. (1994). Pedagogy, virtue, and narrative identity in teaching. *Curriculum Inquiry, 24*(2), 135–170.

Vygotsky, L.S. (1978). *Mind in society: The development of higher psychological processes.* Cambridge, MA: Harvard University Press.

West, P. (1996). Many governors touting technology as a magic bullet. *Education Week, 15*(25), 1, 22.

Westerman, D.A. (1991). Expert and novice teacher decision making. *Journal of Teacher Education, 42*(4), 292–305.

What makes for good staff development? (1996). *Education Week, 15*(30), 11.

Whitehead, J. (1989). Creating a living educational theory from questions of the kind "How do I improve my practice?" *Cambridge Journal of Education, 19*(1), 41–52.

Wilbanks, T.J. (1994). Geography education in national context. *Journal of Geography, 93*(1), 43–45.

Witherell, C. (1991). The self in narrative: A journey into paradox. In C. Witherell & N. Noddings (Eds.), *Stories lives tell: Narrative and dialogue in education* (pp. 83–95). New York: Teachers College Press.

Yee, S.M. (1990). *Careers in the classroom: When teaching is more than a job.* New York: Teachers College Press.

Yin, R.K. (1989). *Case study research: Design and methods.* Newbury Park, CA: Sage.

Zahorik, J.A. (1990). Stability and flexibility in teaching. *Teaching & Teacher Education, 6*(1), 69–80.

Zangwill, I. (1909). *The melting pot.* New York: Macmillan.

Zeichner, K.M. (1991). Contradictions and tensions in the professionalization of teaching and the democratization of schools. *Teachers College Record, 92*(3), 363–379.

Zirkel, P.A., & Gluckman, I.B. (1993). Full inclusion of students with disabilities. NASSP *Bulletin, 77*(553), 96–100.

Index

About the Authors

Robert V. Bullough, Jr. is Professor of Educational Studies, University of Utah, Salt Lake City, Utah. His major areas of interest are teacher education and curriculum studies. His most recent publications include a co-edited volume, *Teachers and mentors: Profiles of distinguished twentieth-century professors of education* (1996) and *Becoming a student of teaching: Methodologies for exploring self and school context* (co-author, 1995). The father of four children, he also enjoys gardening, house and furniture restoration, and collecting old books in education.

Kerrie Baughman taught junior high school for eight years. Currently she is an independent distributor of dietary products. Actively involved in the youth program of her church, Kerrie is the mother of two grown children. Her interests include traveling, reading, writing, and knitting.